How to Reduce Your Property Taxes

How to Reduce Your Property Taxes

by
Frank J. Adler

HarperBusiness
A Division of HarperCollins*Publishers*

Neither the author nor publisher assumes any responsibility for the use or misuse of information and sources contained in this book.

HarperCollins books may be purchased for educational, business, or sales promotional use. For information please write: Special Markets Department, HarperCollins Publishers, Inc., 10 East 53rd Street, New York, NY 10022.

FIRST EDITION

Library of Congress Cataloging-in-Publication Data

Adler, Frank J. (Frank Jack)
    How to reduce your property taxes : a totally legal way to cut your bill by hundreds, even thousands of dollars / Frank J. Adler.
        p. cm.
    Reprint. Originally published: Miami : Genesis Press, © 1995.
    Includes index.
    ISBN 0-88730-820-1
    1. Real property tax—United States. 2. Real property tax—Canada. 3. Real property tax—United States—States. 4. Tax assessment—United States—States. 5. Tax assessment—Canada. 6. Tax protests and appeals —United States—States. 7. Tax protests and appeals—Canada. I. Title
HJ4165.A35 1996
336.22'0973—dc20   96-16321

96 97 98 99 00 RRD 10 9 8 7 6 5 4 3 2 1

Table of Contents

Introduction . . . . *ix*

1   **Property Tax Fundamentals** 1
    The Most Dangerous Tax of All
    Basic Concepts
    The Budget
    What the Tax Assessor Does
    How Property Tax is Determined

2   **Keeping Them Honest** 7
    Understanding Your Tax Bill
    Gathering the Facts

3   **Reasons For Challenging Your Property Tax** 17
    The Assessed Value
        of Your Residential Property is Too High
    Other Reasons for Appealing Your Property Tax
    Factual Errors
    Errors in Land Description
    Illegal Assessments

4   **The Comparative Sales Approach** 25
    Where Can You Find Good Comparables?
    Residential Property Information Sheet
    The Comparable Sales Analysis Report
    Residential Equity Analysis

5   **The Cost Approach Method** 31
    Valuing the Land
    Valuing the Improvements
    How to Determine the Replacement Cost of Your Home
    Researching the Cost Approach Method
    Residential Property Information Sheet
    Replacement Cost Report

6   **The Equity Approach for Residential Property** 39
    Equity Analysis
    Residential Equity Analysis
    Sales to Assessment Ratio
    Using the Sales Ratio Approach
    Sales Ratio Analysis

7   **The Appeal Process** 45

How to Win Your Appeal
Informal Appeal
Things Not to Do
Appealing to the Local Appeal Board
How to Cross-Examine the Assessor
The Ruling From the Local Board

8   **Dealing with Your Bank** 53
    Discounts
9   **Condominiums** 57
10 **Conclusion** 59
11 **Definitions of Terminology**
    Used in the State and Provincial Summaries 61

United States of America

Alabama 67
Alaska 73
Arizona 77
Arkansas 81
California 85
Colorado 89
Connecticut 93
Delaware 101
District Of Columbia 105
Florida 111
Georgia 119
Hawaii 123
Idaho 129
Illinois 133
Indiana 139
Iowa 145
Kansas 153
Kentucky 159
Louisiana 163
Maine 167
Maryland 171
Massachusetts 177
Michigan 183
Minnesota 187
Mississippi 193
Missouri 197
Montana 201
Nebraska 207

Nevada 213
New Hampshire 219
New Jersey 223
New Mexico 229
New York 233
North Carolina 237
North Dakota 241
Ohio 247
Oklahoma 251
Oregon 255
Pennsylvania 259
Rhode Island 263
South Carolina 267
South Dakota 271
Tennessee 275
Texas 279
Utah 283
Vermont 287
Virginia 293
Washington 299
West Virginia 303
Wisconsin 307
Wyoming 313

Canada

Alberta 319
British Columbia 323
Manitoba 329
New Brunswick 335
Newfoundland & Labrador 339
Northwest Territories 343
Nova Scotia 349
Ontario 353
Prince Edward Island 359
Quebec 363
Saskatchewan 367
Yukon 371
Appendix A 375
Appendix B 389
Appendix C 391
Glossary 401
Index 409

Introduction

I never intended to write a book about property taxes. I'm not a lawyer, an accountant, or a tax consultant. I'm just an average Joe, who like millions of other Americans, happens to own a residential property.

At the end of every August for the last fifteen years, I have received a proposed property tax bill from my county government. Each year I would attempt to study this confusing form, noting that my home had risen in value according to the county property assessor and therefore my taxes had increased.

I always thought this was a mixed blessing. Certainly I was glad that the value of my home had increased because the property would yield more dollars when I decided to sell it. The negative side was that my tax bill had more than doubled in a decade! After comparing the prices similar houses were selling for in my neighborhood, I wasn't convinced that my home was worth what the tax assessment said it was. But what could I do about it? So for years I did what most Americans and Canadians do. I shrugged my shoulders and wrote out a check.

Everything changed in August of 1991. When the proposed property tax bill came in I was astounded to discover that again my home's assessment had increased in value. Not only did it go up, but it went up a shocking $35,400.00, a 15% increase. I couldn't believe my eyes. How was it possible that in a year of crippling recession, when people were losing their jobs by the hundreds of thousands and businesses were closing in record numbers, that a home in a middle-class neighborhood like mine was dramatically increasing in value. What made this assessment even more difficult to believe was that homes in my area were selling very slowly, and when they sold, they sold for reduced prices. I concluded that this was some computer glitch that would be relatively easy to straighten out.

At the bottom of my proposed tax notice were printed the following instructions: *"If you feel the assessed value of your property is inaccurate or does not reflect fair market value contact your county property appraiser at (305) 375-4081, 111 NW 1 Street 8th Floor (8:30 AM to 4:30 PM)."*

I really didn't have any idea what the fair market value of my home was. I wasn't in the real estate business. I was busily engaged in a day by day, never ending struggle trying to earn a living. Who had time to go fight city hall? The idea of hiring an accountant, lawyer, or property tax consultant to represent me was economically out of the question considering the hourly rates they charge for their services. So I decided to pursue the matter myself.

After calling the property tax assessor's telephone number for over an hour, I finally got through. A computerized, recorded message informed me that problems concerning assessments required the taxpayer to have an "in person conference with a property appraiser." These meetings were being held for the next two weeks only, from 8:30 AM to 4:30 PM, Monday through Friday, at a county government building located in downtown Miami, on a first come, first served basis. This meant that I would have to sacrifice one workday, but I was adamant about clearing up this obvious and expensive mistake.

The following Monday, after rearranging my appointments, I made time for my trip to the county property assessor's office. Hoping that I could be back at work by noon, I left my home at 6:00 AM. After driving downtown through an hour's worth of crowded stop and go traffic, spending fifteen minutes searching for a parking garage that had daily spaces, and walking three quarters of a mile to the government building, I finally arrived at 7:40 AM.

I knew that the office opened at 8:30 AM, so I anticipated waiting on line for almost an hour. I also expected to be in the front of the line so I could straighten out the problem quickly and return to work. My expectation turned out to be wrong. What I found was a line of at least fifty people ahead of me. They had started assembling at 6:30. The line already stretched from the locked entrance door all the way down the hall, halfway to the elevators. After staring at the line in sheer amazement, I groaned out loud knowing this was going to be a long morning. The elevators came and went, depositing more people behind me. By the time the property appraisers office opened, a few minutes past 8:30, the entire hallway was crowded with irate citizens.

Two hours later I stepped up to the counter and waited for the middle-aged, balding, heavy-set bureaucrat to assign me to an advisor. He looked at his watch, then at me, and said, "The appraisers are going on coffee break for fifteen minutes. Please wait here."

I didn't really know what to say or do. My frustration index was so high I just wanted to reach across the counter and strangle the man. Instead, I just silently stood there not daring to move or speak, fearing that I might do something that would result in my immediate imprisonment or worse.

At five past eleven I was escorted to a small, neat, cubicle in the middle of many other small, neat cubicles that divided up the large room. A man wearing glasses got out of his swivel chair and extended his hand. The black plastic plaque on the desk read "Steven Adams." He smiled and asked, "How may I help you?" I explained my problem, pointing out that I thought a mistake had been made on my assessment. He listened attentively and nodded his head at regular intervals. He asked to see my proposed tax bill and I handed over the neatly folded document. After studying the document for a moment he said he would check into the matter. He got up and walked out of his office. At last I thought I was making some progress.

Mr. Adams left me waiting for about twenty minutes in that cubicle. When he returned he was carrying a cup of coffee, my tax bill, and another form. He explained that he had checked my property on the computer and perhaps a mistake had been made. He told me a number of properties in my subdivision had sold for more money and a few had sold for less. I pointed out that a number of the homes on my island were waterfront properties which were much more expensive, but my house was land-locked and was therefore considerably less valuable. He agreed and said he had pointed this out to his supervisor. The supervisor's reply was that if I wanted a reduction I would have to appeal to the Value Adjustment Board. With that information, Mr. Adams smiled meekly and handed me a petition form for 1991. I refused to take the form. I loudly protested, but Mr. Adams assured me that he had done all he could do in my case. I asked to talk to the supervisor but he informed me that was against the property appraiser's rules. I requested the supervisor's name, but for the sake of security and safety that was against departmental policy. Mr. Adams dangled the form in front of me. He advised me that it was my right to go in front of an impartial administrative judge and present my case, as long as I filed my petition prior to the September 16th deadline and paid a filing fee of fifteen dollars. Knowing I had just collided head first with a bureaucratic stone wall, I accepted my defeat, took the form and left.

I can't ever remember being so angry. I had just wasted the better part of a workday to accomplish absolutely nothing. As far as I was concerned, the entire procedure was an insult to any law-abiding, taxpaying citizen who came to the government with a grievance. To add insult to injury, after walking three-quarters of a mile back to the parking garage,

I was presented with a bill for five hours of parking which totaled fifteen dollars. I drove back to my office so annoyed that I could feel the steam coming out of my ears.

When I arrived home that evening my wife nonchalantly asked me how my appointment went. I grumbled something obscene and she smiled knowingly. "Just pay the darn thing and don't worry about it," was her advice. I didn't answer. I went to our bedroom to change clothes, taking the form out of the inside pocket of my suit jacket and placing it on my dresser.

After dinner, still irritated by the events of the day, I decided to go to the library at the local university not too far from our home. After using their computerized research system for over an hour, I discovered that there were a number of scholarly works dealing with property taxes and there were various real estate and property appraisal books which briefly discussed the theory of property taxes. A practical "how to" book for protesting ones property tax did not seem to exist.

The events of that day started me on a long and fascinating journey into the little known world of property taxes. I decided not to take the easy way out and just pay the tax. The system was abusive and unfair, and I was determined to right a personal wrong. On Tuesday, September 10, 1991, I went to the Clerk of the Value Adjustment Board in the County Courthouse and filed my Petition of Appeal.

Over the course of the next six months I spent a great deal of my leisure time speaking with various real estate professionals. I read all the material on property tax I could find and slowly I began to understand the system and how to work within it. With my newly acquired knowledge I built my appeal, gathering and organizing the necessary facts. On Friday, February 14, 1992, I presented my argument, fully documented, to the Special Master of the Dade County Value Adjustment Board. The evidence I had gathered was compelling and on Wednesday, March 11, 1992, I received a notice in the mail that I had won my case and I would be receiving a refund. On Monday April 27, 1992, I received a refund check from the Dade County Tax Collectors Office for $837.23. Lastly, on August 19, 1992 I received a check for $15.00, the amount of the petition filing fee from the Tax Collectors Office.

You can fight City Hall! That was the sweetest, most satisfying money I've ever earned. It was the vindication of a basic American privilege, the right to challenge your government and win if your cause is just. I could have taken the easy way out and not bothered to protest, but that's not what this democracy is based on. What would have happened if the colonial protestors in Boston Harbor had taken the easy way out and not hosted that all important Tea Party? Would there have been a United States of America?

The following tax year (1992) the county again tried to increase the assessed value on my home. Using the same techniques that had been successful the previous year, I again challenged the system, and again I won.

In 1993, using the same approach, I was able to successfully reduce the assessed value on my home, my parents' home, an investment residential property my parents own, and my commercial building. To date I have challenged the property assessor's opinion as to fair market value of taxable property on six occasions on four separate properties and have been successful every time. (Please refer to Appendix A for documented evidence of this claim.)

I decided to write this book on how to appeal your property taxes because I believe there is a tremendous need for it. I firmly believe that there are tens of thousands of residential property owners who each year pay more tax than they should be paying!

Everyone in the country is affected by property tax. Owners of all types of real property (residential, commercial, industrial, and agricultural) are directly affected because they receive tax bills annually. People who lease real property are also affected because part of their monthly rent is calculated on the amount of property tax the landlord must pay.

The big problem is, how do you know for sure that you're not paying more than your fair share? Suppose you went to the local supermarket and bought $75.00 worth of groceries. At the check-out line you gave the cashier a hundred dollar bill and the cashier gave you back some money. Would you count your change to be certain that you got back the right amount? Of course you would, because that is the prudent and intelligent thing to do. Then why shouldn't you do the same thing on a costly household expense like your annual property tax? Why should you assume that the government is correct and has treated you fairly?

The purpose of this book is to help you learn how to analyze your property tax to be certain that you are not among the thousands of overcharged taxpayers. This book includes a successful step by step explanation on how to appeal your property tax and, most importantly, how to win your appeal. The scope of this book is restricted to residential property with special emphasis on single family homes and condominiums. I hope you enjoy the read and profit annually from the experience.

If you have been successful in reducing your property tax, or you feel that you have been abused by the system and would like to tell your story on national radio or television, please write to me. My mailing address is:

Frank J. Adler
P.O. Box 611802
Miami, Florida 33261

Property Tax   **1**
Fundamentals

The Most Dangerous Tax of All

The stated purpose of this book is twofold:

1. To be able to determine whether or not you are paying more than your fair share of ad valorem real property tax; and,

2. if you are overtaxed, how to appeal successfully and have your taxes reduced. To accomplish this goal it is necessary to have a basic understanding of the property tax system.

In the United States and Canada there are basically three distinct taxing concepts used by government to raise revenue. The one we are most familiar with is the tax based upon the amount of income one earns. If your income decreases for whatever reason, then the amount of income tax that you must pay declines as well. The second is the sales or excise tax, which is a surcharge placed on the items you voluntarily purchase. The government does not force you to pay sales tax until you purchase an item. Third is the ad valorem property tax, which is a levy placed on real and personal property.

What makes property tax such an insidious burden is that its basic premise is different from all the other taxes we are forced to pay. We all need shelter! It doesn't matter if we own a home or rent an apartment. We all require a place to live. But property tax is not levied based on your income, or on what you paid for your property, or on your ability to pay. *The amount of property tax you must pay is determined strictly on the current market value of the property in the subjective opinion of a government official.*

To demonstrate just how treacherous a tax this can be, consider the following two examples:

Let's assume that Mr. and Mrs. John Q. Taxpayer bought their home thirty years ago for $25,000. At that time Mr. Taxpayer was earning $9,500 per year. During the first year they owned the house their property tax was $470.

During the last thirty years the Taxpayers kept the house in good condition with normal maintenance, but didn't make any major structural changes that would significantly add to the value of the property. Today the same home is valued at $175,000 and the last property tax bill was $4,200. The couple's children are fully grown, married, and out of the house, and the couple is nearing retirement age. Knowing that their income will drop dramatically when they are no longer working, they are seriously considering selling their home because they will no longer be able to afford the ever increasing property tax.

Another scenario which is all too familiar in North America today is the young couple, both working, barely able to save up enough money for a small down payment on a first home. The monthly mortgage expenditures are high but manageable as long as nothing goes wrong. Suddenly there is a crisis, such as a natural catastrophe (hurricane, tornado, earthquake, etc.), or the largest factory in town closes and moves to Mexico. Consequently, the municipal government requires more revenue from the citizenry to continue to provide its "basic and necessary" services. They raise the property taxes just high enough so our young couple can no longer afford to make their monthly payments and they consequently lose their home.

These examples, and many others like them, are not far fetched figments of the author's imagination. They are part of the serious threat from a regressive tax which is continually escalating because of the combined factors of ever increasing, reckless, and wasteful government spending, continuous weakening and downsizing of our economic institutions, and the inflated assessments on property made by the ineffective mass appraisal methods employed by the bureaucratic government property tax assessors and their staffs.

Basic Concepts

In the United States and Canada, the authority to collect property tax generally comes from state or provincial statutes. The provisions of the laws vary from state to state and province to province. The tax is generally administered at the local level, usually by counties for themselves and the various cities, school districts, water management districts, and townships that fall within their jurisdictions.

Generally, property tax generates the largest portion of local government revenue for providing essential services such as police and fire protection, schools, local government agencies, county court systems, and libraries.

Property tax is levied on real and personal property. Real property may be defined as the land and all things permanently attached to it. Examples of real property would be a house, a swimming pool, a tree, and a light switch built into the wall of a house. Personal property is defined as property which is not permanently attached to the land and can be moved. Examples of personal property are furniture, a car, a boat, and cattle.

The Budget

Months before the end of the fiscal year the various departments of local government (county, city, school districts, etc.) determine and submit their desired operating budget for the upcoming year. Public meetings are held during which the size and purpose of each department's budget is debated. When the process is complete, an overall proposed budget is submitted to elected commissioners for additional public discussion and debate, and eventually a new budget is approved.

Once a taxing district determines what its next fiscal year's operating budget requirements are, it then determines what income it will derive from grants, licenses, and other miscellaneous income. The difference between the operating budget and the non-property tax income will be the amount of property tax the district will have to levy in order to raise the required revenue. Therefore property tax is used as a budget balancing device as well as a major source of revenue.

BUDGET EXAMPLE

- Total Budget Expense: $20,000,000

- Less: Grants and Miscellaneous Income: $2,000,000

- Balance Needed from Property Tax: $18,000,000

What the Tax Assessor Does

The tax assessor is the government official responsible for valuing all taxable real and personal property. In the United States and Canada he is known by a number of different names, such as the assessment commissioner, property evaluator, or appraiser. He may be elected or appointed, or be a career civil servant.

To effectively begin the valuation or assessment process the assessor must first be able to locate and identify all taxable property. This is done by developing and employing an accurate mapping system which displays every parcel of land in the jurisdiction with its exact dimensions.

Next it is essential to discover the buildings and other improvements permanently attached to the land. This is accomplished by on-site inspections of each parcel of land as well as constant monitoring of new building permits drawn in the area. The frequency of on-site inspections may be specified by the statute governing property tax in your state or province. The discovered property is then classified according to a number of criteria, including its usage, size, construction type, total square footage, location and age.

Having discovered, identified, and classified all the properties in the jurisdiction, the assessor is ready to value or assess each property. To save time and money, mass appraisal techniques are generally employed. By using data from recent sales, the appraiser attempts to accurately value similar properties in each classification. This is called the market or comparable approach and it asks the question, "What have properties similar to this property sold for during the taxable year?"

If sales data is not available, or not appropriate for certain types of property, the assessor will use the cost approach method which asks the question, "How much would it cost to replace this property using similar materials and labor?" The important point is that the property appraiser assesses each property in his jurisdiction giving the properties a dollar amount value based on current fair market conditions.

How Property Tax is Determined

The amount of property tax imposed is determined by two separate factors: **(1)** The assessed value of taxable property, as established by the local assessor, and **(2)** the tax rate.

The tax rate is a percentage determined by dividing the budget amount by the total value of all taxable property in the tax district. For example, if the total budget of a county were one million dollars and the total value of all the properties in the county were one hundred million dollars, then the tax rate would be one percent.

BUDGET DIVIDED BY TOTAL ASSESSMENT VALUE EQUALS TAX RATE

$$\$1,000,000 \div \$100,000,000 = 1\%$$

This one percent can be expressed as one dollar of property tax per hundred dollars of assessed value on the property, or ten dollars of property tax per thousand dollars of assessed value on the property.

The amount of tax levied against a property is determined by multiplying the tax rate by the assessed value of that property. For example, if a property is assessed at $100,000 and the tax rate is 1%, then the property tax would be $1,000. An example: tax rate equals one dollar per hundred dollars; property assessment equals $100,000

$$\$100,000 \div 100 = 1000 \times \$1 = \$1,000 \text{ property tax}$$

In the above example the assessed value of the property is divided by a hundred dollars giving 1,000 units multiplied by the tax rate of one dollar, which yields a property tax charge of $1,000.

An example: Tax rate = $70 per $1,000 and the assessed value of a property is $68,350. $68,350 \div 1000 = 68.35 \times 70 = \$4,784.50$. In the above example, the assessed value of a property is divided by $1,000 yielding 68.35 units, which is multiplied by the tax rate of $70, giving the property tax amount of $4,784.50.

NOTES

Keeping Them Honest   **2**

Understanding Your Tax Bill

All tax bills should include the following information:

- Tax Rate(s)
- Total Value
- Exemptions for which the Taxpayer Qualifies
- Taxable Value
- Name And Address Of Property Owner Of Record
- Legal Description
- Mortgage Service Company (if applicable)
- Total Amount Of Tax Due
- Delinquent Taxes Due (if any)

In Dade County, Florida, the tax collector is accumulating tax revenues for the school districts, cities, townships, the state, special districts (water, sewer, road), and the county. Exhibit A, on page 8 is a sample of a 1993 Metro Dade County "COMBINED TAX BILL." The numbers in the left-hand margin of the following paragraphs correspond to the numbering in the illustration.

1. ***Ad Valorem property tax bill for 1993.***
   Ad valorem tax means that it is a tax based on the current market value of the property.

   The tax rate in this bill is expressed in dollars and cents per one thousand dollars of taxable assessed value of the property. For example, the tax rate under SCH OP (school operating tax) is 9.2830000 per millage (thousand), which simply means that this tax costs $9.283 per thousand dollars of taxable assessed value.

Exhibit A: Understanding Your Tax Bill

1   COMBINED TAX BILL
1993 AD VALOREM TAX BILL 1993

MILL CD 3000   FOLIO   30 2000 000 0000   NAME: JANE DOE

9

SCHOOL AND STATE DISTRICTS

AUTHORITY	RATE	AMOUNT	AUTHORITY	RATE	AMOUNT	AMOUNT DUE IF PAID IN	
SCH OP	9.2830000	524.49			0.00	NOV 4%	1,988.74
SCH DEB	0.6400000	36.16			0.00	DEC 3%	2,009.46
FIND	0.0510000	2.88			0.00	JAN 2%	2,030.17
WM DIST	0.5970000	33.73		SUB TOT	597.26	FEB 1%	2,050.89

2

CITY-TYPE SERVICES PROVIDED BY COUNTY   MAR 0%   2,071.60

MUN SVC	2.3740000	134.13			0.00
					0.00
					0.00
				SUB TOT	134.13

3

10

DADE COUNTY DISTRICTS   PRIOR YEARS

CNTY WD	7.3050000	412.73	MDCC	0.7500000	42.38	**TAXES DUE** **11**
DEBT SVC	0.8300000	46.89			0.00	**VALUATIONS**
LIBRARY	0.3510000	19.83			0.00	TOT VALUE 82,000
FIRE RE	2.3440000	132.44		SUB TOT	654.28	HMSTD EX 25,000

4

12

NON-AD VALOREM ASSESSMENTS

5

SPECIAL ASSESSMENT	DIST	RATE	FT/UNIT	AMOUNT	WID EX 500
WASTE MANAGEMENT	T123	399.00	1.00	399.00	
COLONIAL DRIVE	LO018	0.4520	64.00	28.93	
MIAMI LAKES	M183	0.0212	12170.00	258.00	
				0.00	
				0.00	
				0.00	TAXABLE VALUE
			SUB TOT	685.93	56,500

IMPROVEMENT DIST.	DIST	INT/RATE	YEARS	INTEREST	INSTALLMENT AMOUNT

6

COMMENTS

DETACH HERE

MAIL THIS PORTION
WITH PAYMENT

13

COMBINED TAX BILL
1993 REAL PROPERTY TAXES

VALUATIONS		Mill Code	Folio Number	DISC AMOUNT DUE IF PAID IN	
TOT VALUE	82000	3000	30 2000 000 0000	4% NOV	1,988.74
HMSTD EX	25000	MTG		3% DEC	2,009.46
WID EX	500			2% JAN	2,030.17
				1% FEB	2,050.89
				0% MAR	2,071.60

7

SEQ 000001-000003   PRIOR YEAR TAXES DUE   DELINQUENT AFTER MARCH 31

JEFF ESTATES

14

JANE DOE   PB-66-13

8 1957 METRO LN   LOT 1 BLK 10

MIAMI FL 33016   LOT SIZE SQU   12170

The amount is the total charge for each individual tax. The total amount is the taxable value multiplied by the tax rate (millage).

2. **Taxes levied on your property for Schools and State districts.**
    SCH OP - School Operating Tax

    SCH DEBT - Voter Approved School Debt

    WM DIST - South Florida Water Management District

    FIND - Florida Inland Navigation District

3. **Taxes levied by Municipality shown or City-Type Services provided by Dade county in unincorporated areas.**
    OPER - City Operating Tax

    DBT SVC - Bond Debt Tax

4. **Dade County Districts taxes**
    CNTY WD - County Wide

    DBT SVC - Bond Debt Tax

    LIBRARY - County Library Operating Tax

    FIRE-RE - Fire & Rescue Service Tax

    EEL - Environmental Endangered Land Districts

5. **Non-Ad Valorem Assessments**
    SPECIAL ASSESSMENTS - Assessments for Waste Management, Lighting, Maintenance, Guard, Downtown Metro-Mover Districts, or other government services.

    DIST - District Identification Initial and Number

    RATE - Amount Per Assessed Footage or Units

    FOOTAGE/UNITS - Number of Units or Measurement

    AMOUNT - Rate Multiplied by Footage/Units

G & T - Garbage and Trash Service Provided by Metro Dade County

L - Lighting District

M - Landscape Maintenance

D - Dade County People Mover (mass transit system)

G- Security Guard District

6. ***IMPROVEMENTS DISTRICTS - Assessments for Water, Roads, or Sewer Improvements to Your Property.***
W - Water District

S - Sewer District

R - Road District

INTEREST RATE - Annual interest percentage on assessment

YEARS - Total number of years to pay original assessment

INTEREST - Amount of interest accrued on unpaid balance since last payment

INSTALLMENT - Total assessment divided by number of years to pay

AMOUNT - Current interest and installment amounts due

7. ***Mortgage Servicing Company***
This identifies your mortgage servicing company to the tax collector. Be certain that the appraiser has listed the right company. Verify that your mortgage company has paid your tax bill early enough to take advantage of any discount offered and that you are credited with the discounted amount. Request a receipt from the tax collector which you will need for your Federal Income Tax.

8. *Name and Address*

This is the name and address of the property owner of record. It is necessary to verify that the tax assessor has recorded the rightful owner and that the spelling of your name and your street address are correct.

9. *The Total Amount of Tax Due*

In Metro Dade County, all taxes are due and payable on March 1. Discounts for early payment are offered. On this bill, discounts for early payment range from 4% for payment made in November to 1% for payment made in February.

10. *Subtotals*

Subtotals are indicated for each section of the tax bill. The combined subtotals equal the zero percent discount or March amount due.

11. *Prior Year Taxes Due*

This section indicates whether there are delinquent taxes due from the prior year. If a figure is printed in this section and you have paid all of your taxes, it is extremely important to contact your local tax assessor immediately and reconcile this problem or you might eventually lose your home in a foreclosure tax sale.

12. *Valuations*

The Total Value is the worth the assessor places on the property before any exemptions are deducted. The total value of this property is $82,000.

Exemptions are tax relief allowances that either lower the total value of property or generate a tax rebate. There are many different types of exemptions such as veterans, old-age, low-income, blind, disabled, and renters exemptions, to mention a few. Check the state by state summaries in the second half of this book and speak with your local assessor to determine what tax relief exemptions are available in your state.

On this sample tax bill there are two exemptions which are deducted from the total value of the property. The first is the standard Florida primary resident Homestead Exemption (HMSTD EX) of $25,000.00, and the second is a Widow's Exemption (WID EX) of $500.00. If you subtract the two exemptions from the "Total Value" amount you have the "Taxable Value" of $56,500.00 for this property. *Taxable value is the money amount that is always used to compute taxes due.*

In Florida the assessor uses 100% of full market value in calculating residential total value. Some state statutes allow for only a fraction of the assessed value of the property to be used in determining the amount of property tax. For example, the laws of the state of Missouri allow 19% of the assessed value of residential property to be used. This means that a house with an assessed value of $100,000 would be multiplied by .19 (19%) equalling a total value of $19,000. This number, less any exemptions that would be allowed, would then be multiplied by the tax rate. The in-depth, state-by-state summaries list the latest known percentages used by the tax assessor in each state and province, but it is strongly recommended that each taxpayer verify what percentage of assessed value his or her tax assessor is currently using to determine total value.

To compute the SCH OP tax (number 2) we simply use the following formula: the taxable value of property divided by one thousand yields the number of units to be multiplied by the tax rate equalling the total amount of the tax ($56,500 / 1000 = 56.5 x $9.283 = $524.49).

It's simple once you understand the language. Let's do the next one, which is SCH DEB (school debt). The rate is 0.6400000 which means 64.0 cents per thousand dollars of taxable value. The mathematics would be $56,500.00 / 1000 = 56.5 x 0.6400000 = $36.16. The key is to determine what is the taxable value of the property. Remember to always deduct all the exemptions you are entitled to from the total value. The other important factor is how the tax rate is expressed. Some property tax bills express the tax rate in dollars per hundred dollars total value, or even in cents per dollar of total value. If you're not sure how your tax district expresses the tax rate, call your local assessor for an explanation. It is important to verify the correctness of your tax bill because the county tax collector's office has made mathematical mistakes in the past. Refer to Appendix B for a number of other examples of how to compute your property tax.

13. Folio Number
This is the section were the FOLIO NUMBER (permanent identification number) is recorded. This number is used to identify your property by the county tax assessor as well as the tax collector. It should always be used as a reference when writing or calling about your property.

14. LEGAL DESCRIPTION
A legal description of the taxable property describes precisely where your property is located on the mapping system used by the tax assessor.

Gathering the Facts

The only way to determine whether or not your property tax should be challenged is to investigate the correctness of the data on your tax bill.

The best way to begin the analysis of your data is by going to your tax assessor's office and examining your property record card. This record will be filed by your individual property identification number, so be certain to bring your tax bill with you in order to correctly reference your number.

Your property records and most of the other records at the tax assessor's office are open to public scrutiny as decreed by the public information laws. You are well within your legal rights to examine your file, as well as those of your neighbors, in order to determine the fairness of your tax burden. If the appraiser's office is not cooperative, politely but firmly point out your legal rights and arrange for a mutually satisfactory time for you to be allowed to view the records necessary to conduct your research.

A typical property record card is shown in exhibit (B), page 14. The property assessor is responsible for maintaining accurate records for thousands of parcels of various classifications of property. During all this mass fact gathering and record keeping procedure, errors are bound to occur. Therefore it is important to confirm the information on the property record card for accuracy. The following items are areas that need to be authenticated:

Exhibit B

PROPERTY RECORD CARD

(a) Folio 15-2684-007-4296			(b) PROPR ADDR 1342 93 ST MCD 1300				
** BATCH #0000000 **		(c)LAND S/SQFT:11.76		(d) BLDG S/SQFT: 27.22			
10/14/92 (e) LAST INSP.	06/1988	ZNG0100	CLUC0001	SLUC0100	(f)BLDGYR1953		
(g) NAME AND LEGAL	PREV CHG 03/23/92	VALUE	HISTORY	RES YEAR	1979		
01 MARTIN J. TODD &W SUSAN	YEAR	1989	1991	06/06/92			
02 1342 93 ST	LAND	141000	142655	176400			
03 BAY HARBOR ISLANDS FL	BLDG	92318	92318	84156			
04	TOTAL	233318	234973	260556			
331541901	HEX	25000	25000	25000			
01 26-27-34-35 52 42	WVD						
(h)							
02 BAY HARBOR ISLAND PB 46-5	TOTEX						
03 LOT 13 & W1/2 LOT 14 BLK 32	NOTEX	208318	209973	235556			
04 (c) LOT SIZE 100.000x125	CO NE	208318	209973	235556			
05 OR 10742-1111 0480 4	S/UNIT	S/SF:	84.27				
06 ·····································-PREV SALES			DATE	TYPE			
07 RYAN INC	(m) 136500	(n) 08/1979	1	SALE 1			
08 MARTIN J. TODD							
09 OR 10487-2442 0879 1							
10	MUNICIPAL TAX STATUE:	TAXABLE	DIST 01				
11	STATE EXEMPT:	(i)	(j)	(k)			
12	STRIP	PLATE	XF	BATH	BDR	UNIT	BLDS
13	(l)		2	3	2	1	1
14	AJFT	3092	OWNERS	01	IN-RESIDENCE		01
15	IMPROVEMENT	.TYP	NO.	DATE	TYP		NO. DATE
16		PAAB	17991	1092	RC	0180	
17		MBC:	99999	0692	CO	0180	
18		MLC:	10015	0691	BRC		
19		ERC:	1163	0186	CRC		
20		MISC	79262	0680	LRC		

(a) Your folio or permanent identification number (PIN). Be certain it is your number, or you might be investigating the wrong property.

(b) Street address. Verify that it is correct.

(c) Land value per square foot. Confirm that they have the correct dimensions of the land. An error here will invalidate their assessment figure.

(d) Building value per square foot. Authenticate that they have the correct dimensions of the building. An error will discredit their assessment figure.

(e) Date of last on-site inspection. This is an interesting column because many states have a required revaluation time specified by state statute. If the on-site inspection has not occurred during that time, the assessment is illegal. Furthermore, recent on-site detrimental influences (e.g. flooding basement, insufficient well or septic capacity, sinking foundation, radon, asbestos, acid rain or other pollutants) require a recent on-site evaluation by the assessor in order to adjust the appraisal downward in value.

(f) Year building was constructed. This is an important date because it is used to calculate the depreciation of the building. If the tax assessor has the wrong year their entire cost analysis is incorrect.

(g) Name and address of legal present owners of the property. Make certain this information is correct.

(h) Legal description of the property. This describes where in the mapping system used by the tax assessor your property is located. In this example, plot book (PB) 46, page 5 is the location for the map that shows Lot 13 and half of Lot 14 on Block (BLK) 32 in the BAY HARBOR ISLAND section. It is necessary to use the plot maps in order to substantiate that this is your property, and that the lot size listed is correct.

(i) XF (extra features) are features which add value to the home such as a swimming pool, enclosed porch, multiple car garage, etc.

(j) BATH (bathrooms) reports the number of full baths inside the house. Authenticate the accuracy of the assessor's count because a mistake in your favor is worth an abatement in the assessment.

(k) BDR (bedrooms) describes the number of bedrooms in the house. Validate the correctness of the assessor's information because an error in your favor merits a reduction in the assessment.

(l) AJFT (total adjusted square feet) is the number of square feet of living space that the house is credited in having. It is necessary to measure the house, room by room, to be certain this figure is correct. Once again, an error in your favor is worth a reduction in your property's assessment.

(m) Previous Sales Price.

(n) Date of Previous Sale.

NOTES

Reasons For Challenging Your Property Tax   **3**

The Assessed Value of Your Residential Property is Too High

Since your property tax is based on the fair market value of your property, it is essential that the assessor's valuation of your property accurately indicates the true and fair market value or a fraction thereof as established by the laws of your state or province.

The meaning of market value as defined by the International Association of Assessing Officers is:

> *The highest price in terms of money a property will bring in a competitive and open market under all conditions for a fair sale, the buyer and seller, each acting prudently and knowledgeably, and assuming the price isn't affected by undue stress.*

This definition requires **(a)** the closing of a sale at a specified date, and **(b)** the transfer of title from seller to buyer under circumstances where:

1. Buyer and seller are ordinarily motivated.

2. Both parties are well-informed or well-advised and each is acting in what he/she considers his/her own best interest.

3. A reasonable time is allowed for exposure in the open market.

4. Payment is made in cash or its equivalent.

5. Financing, if any, is on terms generally available in the community at the specified date and typical for the property type in its locale.

6. The price represents a normal consideration for the property sold, unaffected by special financing amounts and/or terms, services, fees, costs or credits incurred in the transaction.

One of the most frequent and significant reasons to appeal your real property taxes is that your property has been overvalued and over-assessed by the tax assessor. It is critical that you analyze your assessment using the same method that the assessor's office uses (comparative sales approach, cost approach, or assessment sales ratio) to be certain that your assessment is not too high, and you are not paying more than your fair share. Ask your tax assessor which method is used to determine property value and base your research on that approach. In addition, I like to use two or three different methods in order to document a very comprehensive argument.

Other Reasons for Appealing Your Property Tax

FACTUAL ERRORS

Due in part to the large number of properties and the volume of data the tax assessor is working with, many tax records contain clerical errors, miscalculations, and omissions that affect your tax bill. Your property record card and other records used to determine your ad valorem property tax valuation must be carefully scrutinized.

Examples of some common errors that occur:

1. *All Computations must be Substantiated.*
   All mathematical functions, like addition and subtraction of cost factors or depreciation deductions, must be re-calculated to check for errors.

2. *The Dimensions of Your Land Have been Erroneously Recorded.*
   The land lot your home is built on is a 100 feet long by a 100 feet wide. The assessor has mistakenly recorded 100 feet length by 200 feet width causing your lot size to be overstated and over-assessed.

3. *The Dimensions of Your Building or Improvements have been Erroneously Recorded.*
   The size of your home or a recent improvement is mistakenly overstated causing you to be over-assessed. To be certain that

the dimensions are correct, measure them carefully using exterior walls as demonstrated in exhibit (C), page 21.

4. **The Description of the Property is Incorrect.**
The property described on the tax bill is not yours. Perhaps the property identification number is wrong, the legal description is incorrect, or the tax bill was sent to the wrong address.

5. **Finished Areas Are Incorrectly Listed.**
Your record card indicates that you have a finished basement when in fact you don't have a basement at all, or it's only half finished.

6. **Your Property is Incorrectly Classified.**
Your residential property has been erroneously classified as industrial.

7. **Vital Information has been Omitted from Your Record Card.**
For example, you are entitled to a homestead exemption and it was not recorded. You are a war veteran who is entitled to an exemption, or part of your property is exempt from taxes because of special usage of the land (it is being used by a religious or non-profit organization). Check your state summary for an up-to-date list of exemptions you are legally entitled to.

8. **Building Components Are Incorrectly Described.**
Carefully examine the description of the building components listed on your property record card for accuracy. Examples of areas that might be incorrectly described are:

- FOUNDATION

- EXTERIOR WALLS

- FLOORS

- ROOF

- INTERIOR FINISH

- FIREPLACE (falsely credited)

- ELECTRICITY (satisfactory or unsatisfactory)

- YEAR YOUR HOME WAS BUILT

- CONSTRUCTION GRADE WRONG (quality of overall construction)

HOW TO MEASURE YOUR HOME
TO DETERMINE ITS TOTAL SQUARE FOOTAGE

1. Measure your home using exterior walls.

2. Draw a diagram similar to the example shown.

3. Separate the home into sections for easier calculations.

4. Be sure to specify how many stories each section has. Multiply the sections by the number of stories.

5. Label garages and unheated/non-air-conditioned areas clearly in your diagram. These areas are not included in total living area square footage.

Refer to diagram on page 21.

Errors in Land Description

The assessed value of your property is determined by two separate elements, the land and your home (improvement to the land). In determining the value of your land the tax assessor either used the comparable sales or cost approach method.

The property record card describes your land and that description must be thoroughly examined for accuracy. Areas where problems of correctness may arise are:

1. **Erroneous Property**
Property described on the assessor's record is not your property.

2. **Erroneous Dimensions**
The size of the land lot is incorrect. This may be determined by checking the survey map attached to your deed or by measuring the land.

3. **Erroneous Description**
The land is described as waterfront property when in fact it is land-locked. The legal description of your property as it relates to the tax map is incorrect.

Exhibit C. Determining Total Square Footage

	30'		30'	
20'	Section A 2 story		Section B 2 story	20'
15'	Section C 1 story		Section D 1 story	15'
25'	Garage		Outdoor Porch	12'

		Ground Area		Living Area
A.	30' x 20'	= 600	x2	= 1,200'
B.	30' x 20'	= 600	x2	= 1,200
C.	15' x 30'	= 450	x1	= 450
D.	15' x 30'	= 450	x1	= 450
	Total Square Feet			**= 3,300**
	Garage	25' x 30'	=	750'
	Porch	12' x 30'	=	360'

4. **Erroneous Classification**
   The land is classified as industrial when in fact it is residential.

5. **Erroneous Tax District**
   Your land has been mistakenly placed in a taxing district which is not yours.

6. **Errors in Influence**
   Your property is given credit for having a pleasing view when in fact it is flat terrain and physically detached from an aesthetic view by an obstruction.

Carefully examine every heading in your property record card as well as all other documents received from the tax assessor's office. Mistakes, omissions, and miscalculations may be sufficient grounds for successful reductions in your property tax.

Illegal Assessments

An illegal assessment is one that either violates a state statute or a recommended guideline established by a supervising state agency. Examples of illegal assessments are:

1. **Property Is Assessed at More Than the Legally Allowable Percentage as Prescribed by State Law**
   In Missouri, for example, residential property may only be assessed at 19% of current market value by law. If residential property were assessed at a higher percentage in that state it would be illegal. Successfully demonstrating that the assessed value is higher than the prescribed legal limit will require the taxable amount to be adjusted downward. To obtain your lawful percentage, check the state-by-state summary section of this book or ask your local tax assessor.

2. **Improper Classification of Property**
   The property is residential but it has been classified as commercial by the tax assessor. This is illegal and probably will result in a higher assessment for the property.

3. **Assessment Higher than State Issued Sales-Assessment Ratio**
   Many states attempt to equalize assessments in the various counties by calculating sales to assessment ratio studies based on market value. If your ratio is significantly above the percent-

age for similar property in your area (15% or higher), then the assessment might be illegal.

4. ***Assessor Used Wrongful Approach to Valuation***
The state manual requires the tax assessor to use the cost approach to obtain property valuation, and the assessor based his opinion on the comparative sales approach.

5. ***No Notice of Increased Assessment was Issued or Received***
State law requires that a taxpayer receive a written notice of proposed assessment increase and the notice was not issued or sent.

6. ***Proper On-site Inspection Procedure Was Not Followed***
State law might require that a property must be inspected every five years or that a property must be inspected prior to an increase in assessment. If this requirement was not followed the assessment is illegal.

7. ***Personal Exemptions***
Each state grants tax-relief exemptions to which you are legally entitled if you qualify. Refusal of any exemption offered by your state after properly applying and qualifying for it is illegal. Some examples of tax-relief exemptions are:

- Veterans of the Armed Forces

- Disabled veterans of the Armed Forces

- Widows of veterans

- Handicapped persons (blind, disabled)

- Low income families

- Property owner 65 years of age and older

- Equipment added to property which prevents air and water pollution, or conserves energy

- Farmers

- Renters

- Certain types of property usage

8. **Valuation Guidelines Established by a State Agency have Not been Properly Followed**

   The guidelines for valuing properties as described in the state and/or county assessors manual have not been followed. The manual instructs the tax assessor to use a depreciation rate on residential property of 3% per year. Any rate lower than 3% would be illegal. Your tax assessor has manuals available in his office that you may use as reference, or you may check with your county library.

9. **The Value of Your Property May Have Decreased**

   Your home may have lost value in the current tax year due to damage caused by a natural disaster such as a hurricane, flood, earthquake, tornado, or a blizzard. Let's assume that a home's roof is destroyed because of a hurricane and it will cost $10,000 to replace. Consequently, the fair market value of that home has decreased by $10,000. If the roof is not replaced in the current tax year then the homeowner should appeal to the property tax assessor to reduce the amount of the assessed value of the home by $10,000. Normally, one or two estimates from a state licensed roofer or contractor should be adequate proof of damage.

   Normal required maintenance and repairs to a home may also cause a loss in value. Let's assume that an older home has a central heating system that required a new boiler that costs $5,000. If the repair is not done in the current tax year the homeowner should request a reproduction in the assessed value of the home. The logic is that if the homeowner attempted to sell the home he/she would likely have to sell the home at a reduced price or be required to replace the faulty boiler.

   An essential major repair such as a new roof, new central heating or air-conditioning system, work on a damaged foundation, etc., decreases the fair market value of that home. Due to the individual nature of such situations it is the homeowner's responsibility to point out the existence of the problem and to prove the cost of repair to the property assessor in order to achieve a reduction in the home's assessed value.

The Comparative Sales Approach 4

The most reliable and accurate method to certify the true market value of your residential property is to use the comparative sales approach. This method compares your property to similar homes that have been sold within the last two years in your area. Do not use comparable sales that are more recent than the tax year for which you plan to appeal.

When looking for comparable sales (called "comps"), it is essential to choose homes which share many of the same features that your home has. Using the information you have found and validated from your property record card, the list of criteria should include the following:

1. **Similar Location:**
   In order to equate apples with apples it is essential that your comparable sales be located as close to your property as possible.

2. **Type of Home:**
   It is basic that we compare similar styles of home. If you own a ranch home we cannot use a split-level home as a comparable.

3. **Basement:**
   It is necessary for the basement area to be similar. It is not a true comparable if your home does not have a basement and the property you are comparing does, the reason being that it is difficult to place a monetary value on a basement. It is possible however to place a value on finished basement as opposed to an unfinished basement.

4. **Size of Lot:**
   The overall square footage of the lot (land) should be as similar to your property as possible. It is possible to establish a per square foot value on the land and adjust the price up or down as is necessary.

5. **Size of Living Area:**
   The approximate sizes of the homes should be fairly close. Cost adjustments can be calculated for differences in size.

6. *Age:*
The ages of the comparables should be approximately the same or it will be necessary to make an adjustment in value for the difference in physical depreciation (the loss in value of the structure caused by normal wear and tear).

7. *Adjustable Features:*
The following is a partial list of adjustable features that should be the same in both properties. If they are not, the cost to add or deduct a feature is calculated (including depreciation) and the value of the property will be adjusted up or down, depending on the circumstances.

- Number of Bedrooms
- Number of Bathrooms
- Number of Fireplaces
- Type of Heating
- Central Air Conditioning
- Size of Garage
- Finished Basement
- Swimming Pool
- Patio Area

Where Can You Find Good Comparables?

The best place to start is in your tax assessor's office. Many modern offices use recent sales information acquired from the county clerk's office to develop and substantiate their mass assessment techniques. Normally the assessor's lists are categorized by legal descriptions or permanent index numbers. After locating the proper list it is necessary to spend time carefully examining and gathering comparables which are favorable.

If the tax assessor's office does not have the recent sales records, or does not choose to allow you to use them, try the county clerk's office. They record all transfers of real property and you may ask to see how they have the recently recorded sales arranged. Normally you will have to locate the deed through the grantee's index (which is a very cumber-

Exhibit D

RESIDENTIAL PROPERTY INFORMATION SHEET (for Comparable Sales Analysis)

Name: _____ Address: _____ Property ID: _____ Desc.: _____

TYPE
- [ ] Single Family
- [ ] Multiple
- [ ] Town House
- [ ] Row House
- [ ] Manufactured
- [ ] Cabin, Dome, etc.

HEAT/COOLING _____

FLOOR AREA
- 1st _____
- 2nd _____
- 3rd _____
- Total _____
- Region _____

Lot size (length x width = square feet): _____ s.f.

- [ ] Pool _____ s.f.

QUALITY
- [ ] Low
- [ ] Fair
- [ ] Average
- [ ] Good
- [ ] Very Good
- [ ] Excellent

PLUMBING
- Fixtures _____
- Rough-in _____

HIGH VALUE
- [ ] Class I
- [ ] Class II
- [ ] Class III
- [ ] Class IV

- [ ] Deck _____ s.f.

STYLE
- [ ] No. Stories _____
- [ ] Bi-level
- [ ] Split level
- [ ] 1-1/2 story-fin.
- [ ] 1-2/2 story-unf.
- [ ] 2-1/2 story-fin.
- [ ] 2-1/2 story-unf.
- [ ] End Row
- [ ] Inside Row

INTERIOR WALL
- Height _____ ft.

MULT. UNITS
- Units _____
- Age _____
- Condition _____

- [ ] Fireplace(s) _____

EXTERIOR WALLS
- [ ] Hardwood/Plywood
- [ ] Stucco
- [ ] Siding or Shingle
- [ ] Masonry Veneer
- [ ] Common Brick
- [ ] Face Brick or Stone
- [ ] Concrete Brick

MANUF. WALLS
- [ ] Alum., Ribbed
- [ ] Lap Siding
- [ ] Hardboard
- [ ] Plywood

Total size of home in square feet (see Figure C , p. 21)

- [ ] Patio _____ s.f.

ROOF COVER
- [ ] Built-up
- [ ] Comp. Shingle
- [ ] Wood Shingle
- [ ] Shake
- [ ] Clay tile
- [ ] Concrete tile
- [ ] Slate
- [ ] Metal _____

BASEMENT AREA
- Unf. _____
- Fin. _____
- Basement Entrance
- [ ] To Outside
- [ ] To Garage

No. of Bedrooms _____

BALCONY AREA _____

PORCH BRZWY _____

GARAGE TYPE
- Cars _____
- [ ] Detached
- [ ] Attached
- [ ] Built-in
- [ ] Subterranean
- [ ] Carport
- [ ] Gable, Shed or Flat

CLIMATE
- [ ] Mild
- [ ] Moderate
- [ ] Extream

No. of Bathrooms _____

some approach), but perhaps they have more convenient cross-references.

Real estate brokers might be another source for finding valid comparables. Many offices have on-line computer hookups to the area's multi-listing service that keep track of sales in the area. These comparables are used by realtors to help establish values on properties that owners wish to sell or buyers wish to purchase.

A professional real estate appraiser or property tax consultant may be hired to conduct a thorough investigation. If an appeal is warranted, they will also assemble the necessary evidentiary material required to support your appeal.

Property Research Analysts is a computerized data research firm with access to most property tax roll records and sales information throughout the United States and Canada. Their address and telephone number are:

650 N.E. 126th Street
North Miami, Florida 33161
(305) 891-0000

To use their services you must complete their comparable specification sheet illustrated in exhibit (D), page 27 and they will search their databases for valid comparables for your property. A report consisting of the three most favorable comparables, if available, will be sent to you either by mail or fax. The present fee for their comparable search service is $100. If they are unable to find three favorable comparisons, your money will be refunded. Figure (E), page 29, is a sample report issued by Property Research Analysts.

THE COMPARABLE SALES ANALYSIS REPORT

Explanation of Figure E

In order to compare similar properties, it was necessary to adjust each of the comparable homes either up or down in value depending upon the individual features of the home. After making the necessary adjustments, the adjusted value per square foot and the adjusted total value represent a true comparable feature for feature. The average adjusted value per square foot is $15.33.

(14.57 + 16.15 + 15.28 ÷ 3 = 15.33)

Figure E

COMPARABLE SALES ANALYSIS REPORT

FEATURE	SUBJECT PROPERTY	COMPARABLE #1	COMPARABLE #2	COMPARABLE #3
Address	1342 93rd St.	1391 100th St.	1351 99th St.	1211 98th St.
Proximity		6 blocks away	5 blocks away	4 blocks away
Av.value/s.f.	$18.57	$15.80	$16.34	$14.27
Selling Price	$232,125 (Assessment)	$197,500	$205,000	$167,000
Construction	Concrete, Brick, Stone	CBS	CBS	CBS
Design	Single level, ranch	s.l. ranch	s.l. ranch	s.l. ranch
Lot Size	100 x 125 (12,500 s.f.)	100x125 (12,500)	98 x 128 (12,544)	90x130 (11,700)
Condition	Good	Good	Good	Average -$7,000‡
Age	19	21	20	23
Total number of Rooms, Bedrooms, Baths	8 rooms, 3 bedrooms, 2 bath	8/3/2	9/3/3 +$13,000‡	8/3/2
Air Conditioning	Central	Central	Central	Central
Garage	Detached	Detached	attached -$18,000‡	semi-attached -$9,000‡
Living-Area s.f.	3,025 s.f.	3,680 s.f. - $10,349‡	3,487 s.f. -$7,549‡	2,128 s.f. +$12,800‡
Basement	no	no	no	no
Extra (i.e.pool..)	1 fireplace, patio	patio - $5,000‡	patio, pool fireplace +$15,000‡	patio, pool, fireplace +$15,000‡
Comparative adj.		more s.f. no fireplace -$15,349‡	more land, garage, room, pool -$2,451‡	cond. & garage, lot size, pool +$11,800‡
Total value adj.	$191,625 (Adj. Assessment)	$182,151	$202,549	$178,800
Adjusted value per sq. ft.	$15.33	$14.57	$16.15	$15.28

‡ = Adjustment +/- $

Comparative Data Compiled by:
Property Research Analysts
650 N.E. 126th Street ,North Miami, Florida 33161
Telephone: (305) 891-0000 • Fax: (305) 891-0000

Therefore the assessment on the subject property should be $191,625 (15.33 x 12,500 s.f. = $191,625). The reduction in assessed value should be $40,500 ($232,125 - $191,625 = $40,500).

Explanation of adjustments made:

a) Comparable #1 Adjustments - living area larger by 655 sq.ft. causing a deduction of $10,349 (655 x 15.80, price per unadjusted sq.ft.). Comparable #1 does not have a fireplace which, for the sake of this example, we arbitrarily valued at $5,000. Therefore we deduct $15,349 from the assessment of $197,500 giving a total adjusted value of $182,151, or adjusted value per square foot of $14.57 ($182,151 ÷ 12,500 sq. ft. = $14.57).

b) For Comparable #2, we add $13,000 for an extra bathroom, and $15,000 for a swimming pool. We add these two amounts because both features are extras which our subject property does not have. We deduct $7,549 because this property has a larger adjusted living area and $18,000 because this property has an attached garage, giving us a total adjusted value of $202,549 or $16.19 adjusted value per square foot ($202,549 ÷ 12,544 sq. ft. = $16.15).

c) For comparable #3 we add $12,800 because this property has a smaller adjusted living area than our subject's home and $15,000 for a pool. We deduct $7,000 because the overall condition of the comparable home is average as compared to good for the subject's home. We deduct $9,000 for the garage, which is semi-attached, as opposed to the fully detached garage of our subject's home. Therefore, we have a total adjusted value of $178,800 divided by a lot size of 11,700 sq. feet, which equals $15.28 of adjusted value per square foot.

The Cost Approach Method

5

Tax assessors also use the cost approach method to determine the value of residential property. There are two components that make up the value of your property, the land and the improvement to the land (things affixed to the land such as buildings, wall-mirrors, swimming-pools, fences, pavement, trees and shrubbery, etc.).

Valuing the Land

The most accurate method of valuing land is by comparing the price that similar, vacant, residentially-zoned land in your area sold for per square foot during the taxing period. The square foot amount would then be multiplied by the total square footage of your land to arrive at an amount.

For example, a parcel of vacant land in your area, zoned residential, measures 100 feet of frontage by 100 feet of length and sold for $20,000. The land portion of your property measures 75 feet of frontage by 100 feet of length. How much is your land worth?

The first step is to determine what the vacant land sale is worth per square foot. To do that we multiply the frontage (width) by the length of the property to derive the number of square feet, and then divide the selling price by the total number of square feet.

100 feet x 100 feet = 10,000 square feet

$20,000 (selling price) / 10,000 sq. ft. = $2.00 per square foot

To determine the value of the land on your property we first determine the total number of square feet by multiplying frontage (width) by length and then multiply the total by $2.00 (the per square foot amount of the vacant land).

75 feet x 100 feet = 7,500 square feet

7,500 square feet x $2.00 per sq. ft. = $15,000 total value

In the absence of vacant land sales in your area, the tax assessor uses comparable sales of residential property in your area for the taxing period to determine the value of your land. Using the cost approach, he values the improvements to the land and deducts that amount from the total sales price to obtain the land value. He then divides the land value by the total square footage to obtain a price per square foot amount. This square foot amount is then multiplied by the total square feet of your land to arrive at a value.

The last method described may be subject to a great deal of manipulation and subjectiveness by the tax assessor. If this method is employed it is necessary to carefully analyze the various cost factors used to determine the value of the improvements and the annual percentage rate of depreciation. This will prevent the tax assessor from using land value as an inflated, unrealistic fudge-factor to unjustifiably increase the amount of assessed value of your property.

Valuing the Improvements

The improvements to the land which are listed on the property record card are evaluated to determine how much it would cost to replace them. A dollar value is assigned to each item. The total cost is then adjusted downward due to physical depreciation (caused by aging) and other unfavorable factors.

The components used to obtain the replacement cost of a home include the following:

- BUILDING TYPE (framing and foundation)
- CONSTRUCTION TYPE (brick, frame, stone,etc.)
- ELECTRICAL WIRING AND FIXTURES (type and grade)
- ROOF (variety, grade, presence or absence of gutters/eaves)
- HEATING AND AIR-CONDITIONING (type and grade)
- COMPONENTS OF FINISH USED IN ROOMS (floors, hall-ways, trim)
- FEATURES USED IN BATHROOM (quality, type, and grade)
- PLUMBING (type and grade)
- EXTERNAL FINISH (type and grade)
- WINDOWS (screen, storm, and quality)

- SQUARE FOOTAGE (total size of the structure)
- ADJUSTED SQUARE FOOTAGE (total amount of indoor living space)
- AGE (the year constructed, the economic life remaining)
- CONDITION OF THE BUILDING (good, ordinary, shoddy)

The cost approach method is an extremely useful tool for the taxpayer if properly employed. By using the same information that the assessor has used (taken from the property record card), it is possible to verify the dollar amounts allocated for each category. In many cases the assessor has used values that are inaccurate, overstated, or prescribed by the state taxing agency. It is possible to prove, by using up-to-date valuation data, that the figures used by the tax assessor are erroneous, obsolete, or contrived.

Another benefit derived from employing the cost method is that it will force the property owner to authenticate the assessor's arithmetic. Due to under-staffing, general errors, and the large volume of parcels the assessor's office processes, it is not unusual for mathematical errors to occur. A careful examination of your property record card may reveal arithmetic miscalculations which negatively influence your property's assessment.

You should also carefully scrutinize each individual feature listed on your property record card for accuracy. In many instances the assessor's description of your property is erroneous and these mistakes may unfavorably affect the assessment of your property. Measurements of square footage, number and type of rooms, number of stories, type of construction, basement type and finish, just to mention a few, should be carefully examined for completeness and exactness.

The cost approach method may be an excellent supplement to further substantiate your appeal for property tax abatement. If you have found and documented examples of actual valid sales (comparables) using the comparable sales approach, and your presentation also includes a favorable cost approach analysis, your case will probably be compelling, and you will achieve the tax reduction you are entitled to.

The cost approach method is also a valid primary argument for assessment reduction in the absence of recent comparable market sales in your area. This method will then be the same method utilized by the tax assessor and it becomes a question of accuracy of property description, reliability of dollar amounts used, and the annual percentage rate used for physical depreciation. The assessor normally uses figures supplied by the state taxing agency or an outside valuation firm. These figures may or may not be reliable or up-to-date.

How to Determine the Replacement Cost of your Home

Once again, the best place to start is your local assessor's office. Normally the assessor employs the cost approach method to determine the assessment of your property. He is obligated by public records statutes to explain and reveal the dollar amounts employed and his source of these numbers. Ask to see and use the manual containing the official valuation standards and the official annual percentage rate of depreciation. Make certain that the dollar values used for the components of the building are current. Investigate whether the assessor is using a reputable, private cost expert company such as Marshall & Swift for his replacement values or a less dependable and not as current source, such as the state agency's set of numbers. It is also very important to verify the validity of the depreciation tables. Compare the rate of depreciation to the tables the larger local banks use, or the tables accountants use for tax purposes. Many times tax assessors depreciate a property at a far lower percentage rate than is normal practice in order to maintain a high value on the property. Remember that the assessor's valuation of your property will only be as good as the timeliness and reliability of the data he employs, the accuracy of his description of your home and the correctness of his arithmetical computations.

There is plenty of room here for the tax assessor to make mistakes. Take the time to search for these errors and personally validate all the dollar amounts he has used.

Researching the Cost Approach Method

Due to the complexity of the cost approach method, and the potential difficulty of obtaining satisfactory current cost figures, you may choose to use a professional valuation service to compile your analysis for you.

Exhibit F

RESIDENTIAL PROPERTY INFORMATION SHEET (for Cost Approach Method)

Name: _____   Tel: _____

Property Identification Number: _____

Address: _____

Legal Description of Property: _____

TYPE
- ☐ Single Family
- ☐ Multiple
- ☐ Town House
- ☐ Row House
- ☐ Manufactured
- ☐ Cabin, Dome, etc.

Age _____

HEAT/COOLING
- _____
- _____

FLOOR AREA
- 1st _____
- 2nd _____
- 3rd _____
- Total _____

QUALITY
- ☐ Low
- ☐ Fair
- ☐ Average
- ☐ Good
- ☐ Very Good
- ☐ Excellent

APPLIANCES
No. of _____
- ☐ Dishwasher
- ☐ Wash Mach.
- ☐ Dryer
- ☐
- ☐
- ☐

STYLE
No. Stories _____
- ☐ Bi-level
- ☐ Split level
- ☐ 1-1/2 story-fin.
- ☐ 1-2/2 story-unf.
- ☐ 2-1/2 story-fin.
- ☐ 2-1/2 story-unf.

EXTRA FEATURES
- ☐ End Row
- ☐ Inside Row

CLIMATE
- ☐ Mild
- ☐ Moderate
- ☐ Extream

REGION

GARAGE TYPE
Cars _____
- ☐ Detached
- ☐ Attached
- ☐ Built-in
- ☐ Subterranean
- ☐ Carport
- ☐ Gable, Shed or Flat

EXTRA FEATURES
- ☐ Patio _____ s.f.
- ☐ Deck _____ s.f.
- ☐ Pool _____ s.f.
- Bedrooms _____
- Bathrooms _____
- Fireplace(s) _____

TOTAL CONDITION

ROOF COVER
- ☐ Built-up
- ☐ Comp. Shingle
- ☐ Wood Shingle
- ☐ Shake
- ☐ Clay tile
- ☐ Concrete tile
- ☐ Slate
- ☐ Metal

FLOOR COVERING
- ☐ Carpet _____ s.f.
- ☐ Wood _____ s.f.
- ☐ Rugs _____ s.f.

BASEMENT AREA
- Unf. _____ s.f.
- Fin. _____ s.f.
- ☐ Separate Entrance
- ☐ To Outside
- ☐ To Garage

PORCHES
- ☐ Finished
- ☐ Unfinished
- ☐ How Many? _____
- ☐ Screen
- ☐ Glass
- ☐ Wooden
- ☐ Concrete

ATTIC
- ☐ Finished
- ☐ Unfinished

Lot size (length x width = square feet): _____ s.f.   Total size of home in square feet (see figure C, p. 21): _____ s.f.

Property Research Analysts
650 NE 126th Street, North Miami Florida 33161
Tel : (305)891-0000 • fax: (305)891-0000

Property Research Analysts, a professional real estate data research firm, uses the latest cost and depreciation values available. They generate a tailor-made, up-to-date complete computerized replacement cost report for your property. To use this service it is essential that you accurately complete and return the form represented in exhibit (F), page 35. The charge for this service is $100 per report. If they are unable to supply an accurate and timely report, your money will be refunded.

Figure G

REPLACEMENT COST REPORT

Property Owner:	Mr & Mrs Patrick Davis
Address:	1250 N E 137 Street
City, State, ZIP:	North Miami, FL 33161

Single Family Residence	Floor Area: 2,464 square feet
Effective Age: 10 years	Quality: Good
Cost as of 6/94	Condition:Very Good

Style: Two Story

Exterior Wall: Masonry Veneer

	Units	Cost	Total
Basic Square Foot Cost	2,464	37.25	91,784
Including 11 Plumbing Fixtures			
Composition Shingle	2,464	0.64	1,577
Warmed and Cooled Air	2,464	3.30	8,131
Floor Cover	2,464	3.08	7,589
Concrete Slab Floor	2,464	3.00	7,392
Appliance Allowance	2,464	1.11	2,735
Plumbing Fixture, Rough-In	1	295.00	295
Fireplace Double	1	4160.00	4,160
Subtotal Basic Structure Cost	2,464	50.19	123,663
Garage:			
Attached Garage	423	17.95	7,593
Extras:			
Open Slab Porch	345	3.38	1,166
Site Improvements			4,500
Subtotal			5,666
Replacement Cost New	2,464	55.57	136,922
Less Depreciation:			
Physical and Functional	<12.8		
Depreciated Cost	2,464	48.46	119,396
Miscellaneous:			
Land			35,000
Total	2,464	62.66	154,396

Cost data by Property Research Analysts
650 N.E. 126th Street, North Miami, Florida 33161
Telephone: (305) 891-0000 • Fax: (305) 891-0000

Using the same form as Figure G, page 36, it is possible for you to plug in the cost figures for each component of your home and deduct the proper total depreciation amount depending on the age of your home, thereby coming up with a satisfactory replacement cost figure. The key to doing this properly is using cost and depreciation figures that are accurate and timely. These figures are generally available from private fee appraisers, real estate brokers, property insurance appraisers, and bankers. You might also check with your local or county reference librarian to determine if they inventory any current books on costs or estimates of construction.

NOTES

The Equity Approach for Residential Property

This method of property analysis may be used in some states when recent sales of comparable property are not available. It is advisable to ask your local assessor if this is an accepted method to use in lieu of the comparative sales approach.

The basic premise of this technique is that the assessments of comparable homes should be the same, hence the term equitable. If by using the information available to you in the assessor's office (property record cards) you are able to locate three to six comparable properties that have significantly lower assessed values, then you will have a solid argument for a reduction in your valuation. It is necessary to adjust the value of unequal features (corresponding to the comparative sales approach) in the comparables that you are using. The three features that must be alike in order to have a valid comparison are the location of the property, the style of the home, and a similar type of basement. The allowable variables in each of the comparable homes, such as the difference in the numbers of bathrooms or the value of an extra fireplace, maybe adjusted up or down in value as required (just as in the comparable sales approach).

In the following example, figures (H) and (I), pages 40 and 41, using the equity approach the subject's property will be compared to similar properties using the residential equity approach form. Carefully note the adjustments up or down made to each comparable in order to reach a true valuation.

Equity Analysis

DATA ANALYSIS

The comparables used are similar in style, construction, age, and location. The range of assessed value per square foot of adjusted living space ranges from $53.67 to $78.47 with an average price established at $65.67 for eight comparables used. Comparable #7 and #8 (the low end of the value range) are larger in total square footage, and are most comparable to the appellants property. The results of this analysis supports the claim that a fair and equitable square foot assessed value for the appellant's property would be $65.67. Therefore the value of the appellant's assessment should be $203,248.65. This value is derived by multiplying the appellant's gross area square footage, 3,095, by the average assessed value per square foot of the eight comparables, $65.67. (Average Assessment value per square foot = 65.67 for the eight comparables used. 3,095 x $65.67 = $203,248.65). Therefore the reduction in assessed value should total $28,876.35 ($232,125.00 - $203,248.65 = $28,876.35).

Figure H

EQUITY ANALYSIS

Comp. #	Property ID #	Address	Age	Square Feet Gross Area	Assessment	Assessment Value per Sq. Ft.
1	13-2227-001-64	1350 98th St.	16	1820	$ 113,000	$ 62.09
2	13-2227-001-57	1270 97th St.	18	1552	$ 108,000	$ 69.59
3	13-2227-001-52	1311 100th St.	14	2061	$ 141,000	$ 68.41
4	13-2227-001-60	1260 95th St.	15	2235	$ 155,000	$ 69.35
5	13-2227-001-55	1211 98th St.	17	2492	$ 162,000	$ 65.00
6	13-2227-001-49	1250 102nd St.	14	2128	$ 167,000	$ 78.47
7	13-2227-001-66	1351 99th St.	18	3487	$ 205,000	$ 58.79
8	13-2227-001-48	1391 100th St.	21	3680	$ 197,500	$ 53.67
Appellant's	13-2227-001-36	1342 93rd St.	19	3095	$ 232,125	$ 75.00

Residential Equity Analysis

Explanation of Figure I

In order to compare apples with apples, it was necessary to adjust each of the comparable homes either up or down in value. After making the necessary adjustments the adjusted value per square foot and the adjusted total value represents a true comparable feature for feature. The average adjusted value per square foot is $15.33 (14.57 + 16.15 + 15.28 3 = 15.33).

Figure I

RESIDENTIAL EQUITY ANALYSIS REPORT

FEATURE	SUBJECT PROPERTY	COMPARABLE #1	COMPARABLE #2	COMPARABLE #3
Address	1342 93rd St.	1391 100th St.	1351 99th St.	1211 98th St.
Proximity		6 blocks away	5 blocks away	4 blocks away
Av.value/s.f.	$18.57	$15.80	$16.34	$14.27
Selling Price	$232,125 (Assessment)	$197,500	$205,000	$167,000
Construction	Concrete, Brick, Stone	CBS	CBS	CBS
Design	Single level, ranch	s.l. ranch	s.l. ranch	s.l. ranch
Lot Size	100 x 125 (12,500 s.f.)	100x125 (12,500)	98 x 128 (12,544)	90x130 (11,700)
Condition	Good	Good	Good	Average -$7,000‡
Age	19	21	20	23
Total number of Rooms, Bedrooms, Baths	8 rooms, 3 bedrooms, 2 bath	8/3/2	9/3/3 +$13,000‡	8/3/2
Air Conditioning	Central	Central	Central	Central
Garage	Detached	Detached	attached -$18,000‡	semi-attached -$9,000‡
Living-Area s.f.	3,025 s.f.	3,680 s.f. - $10,349‡	3,487 s.f. -$7,549‡	2,128 s.f. +$12,800‡
Basement	no	no	no	no
Extra (i.e.pool..)	1 fireplace, patio	patio - $5,000‡	patio, pool fireplace +$15,000‡	patio, pool, fireplace +$15,000‡
Comparative adj.		more s.f. no fireplace -$15,349‡	more land, garage, room, pool -$2,451‡	cond. & garage, lot size, pool +$11,800‡
Total value adj.	$191,625 (Adj. Assessment)	$182,151	$202,549	$178,800
Adjusted value per sq. ft.	$15.33	$14.57	$16.15	$15.28

‡ = Adjustment +/- $

Comparative Data Compiled by:
Property Research Analysts
650 N.E. 126th Street North Miami, Florida 33161
Telephone: (305) 891-0000 • Fax: (305) 891-0000

Therefore the assessment on the subject property should be $191,625 (15.33 x 12,500 s.f. = $191,625). The reduction in assessed value should be $40,500 ($232,125 - $191,625 = $40,500).

Explanation of adjustments made:

a) Comparable #1 Adjustments - living area larger by 655 s.f. causing a deduction of $10,349 (655x 15.80, price per unadjusted s.f.). Comparable # 1 does not have a fireplace which, for sake of this example, we arbitrarily valued at $5,000. Therefore we deduct $15,349 from the assessment of $197,500 giving a total adjusted value of $182,151 or adjusted value per square foot of $14.57 ($182,151 ÷ 12,500sq. ft = $14.57).

b) For Comparable #2, we add $13,000 for an extra bathroom, and add $15,000 for a swimming pool. We add these two amounts because both features are extras which our subject property does not have. We deduct $7,549 because of a larger adjusted living area and $18,000 because of an attached garage, giving us a total adjusted value of $202,549 or $16.19, adjusted value per square foot ($202,549 ÷ 12,544 sq.ft = $16.15).

c) For comparable #3 we add $12,800 for a smaller adjusted living area than our subject's home and $15,000 for a pool. We deduct $7,000 because the overall condition of the comparable home is average as compared to good for the subject's home. We deduct $9,000 for the garage which is semi-attached as opposed to the fully detached garage of our subject's home. Therefore we have a total adjusted value of $178,800 divided by a lot size of 11,700 sq. ft. which equals $15.28 of adjusted value per square foot.

Sales To Assessment Ratio Studies

The purpose of a sales ratio study is to help insure fairness of the assessments and point out any inequities. This study is conducted by either the state, the province, or the local assessor. It compares the actual sales prices of verified, arms-length transactions to the assessed value placed on that property. Sales ratio studies may be conducted by dividing the properties into different classifications:

1. Properties may be divided by their usage code such as residential, commercial, agricultural, vacant land, etc. For example, we may compare the sales to assessment ratio for the sales of all the industrial property in your town for the last year.

2. Real estate may be categorized by the amount of dollars the property sold for. For example we may compare all the residential properties that sold in your taxing jurisdiction between $35,000 and $75,000 for the past year.

3. In larger communities it may be more practical to conduct this analysis by the location of the property. We might divide the community into neighborhoods and do an analysis of residential property within each section.

Using the Sales Ratio Approach

If you can conclusively demonstrate that the ratio for your property is 15% to 20% higher than the sales assessment ratio established by the government, then you have sufficient grounds to appeal your property's valuation. If your state or province conducts this study, the figures will be available at your local assessor's office and must be supplied upon demand. For example, if you recently purchased your home for $150,000 and the assessor valued your home for $150,000, then your ratio is 1.000 (sales price divided by assessed value equals sales ratio). Exhibit (J), page 43, lists other properties that sold during the last tax year in your neighborhood. Their sales ratio was .856. The average ratio is approximately 15% lower than yours. This is satisfactory grounds to appeal your assessment. This is a particularly useful technique for comparing assessments and sales in a large condominium complex.

Sales Ratio Analysis

Exhibit J

SALES RATIO ANALYSIS

Comparable. Number	Property ID Number	Address	Date of Sale	Selling $	Assessment	% Assessment to Selling $
1	13-2227-001-64	1350 98th St.	04/27/93	$133,500	$113,750	0.852
2	13-2227-001-57	1270 97th St.	07/10/93	$127,900	$108,000	0.844
3	13-2227-001-52	1311 100th St.	08/16/93	$165,000	$141,000	0.854
4	13-2227-001-60	1260 95th St.	01/20/93	$180,000	$155,000	0.861
5	13-2227-001-55	1211 98th St.	03/1/93	$190,000	$162,000	0.852
6	13-2227-001-49	1250 102nd St.	05/27/93	$195,000	$167,000	0.856
7	13-2227-001-66	1351 99TH St.	06/7/93	$237,500	$205,000	0.863
8	13-2227-001-68	1391 100th St.	08/12/93	$227,900	$197,500	0.866
9	13-2227-001-73	1201 96th St.	09/11/93	$233,000	$201,500	0.864
Appellant	13-2227-001-36	1342 93rd St.	12/10/93	$260,000	$232,000	0.892

DATA ANALYSIS

Explanation of Exhibit J

The mean average assessment to sales price percentage for the nine sales is .856 or 85.60% . The mean average is determined by adding up the percentage of assessment to selling price and dividing by the number of sales, in this case nine. The appellant's assessment to sales price percentage is 89.20%, or 3.6% higher than the area's mean percentage. Consequently the appellant's revised assessment should be $222,560, a reduction of $9,440 of assessed valuation. (Selling price x mean average assessment to sales price percentage, or $260,000 x .856 = $222,560.)

The Appeal
Process

How to Win Your Appeal

After investing hours of your time researching your property tax, you uncover what you believe to be valid evidence of overassessment. To effectively challenge the assessor's opinion regarding the value of your property and have your assessment lowered, it is necessary to go through the appeal process. Each state, province, and locality has its own distinctive statutes and regulations specifying the necessary procedural steps that must be followed by a taxpayer who wishes to appeal. The summaries in the second half of this book have detailed information pertaining to the appeal process in your state or province. It is necessary, however, to verify this material with your local assessor to be certain of the accuracy of the current deadlines and information. The following example is a generic approach to the appeal process. It serves as guide on how to appeal successfully.

INFORMAL APPEAL

Normally the appeal process starts with an informal conference between you and the assessor. Shortly after receiving your tax bill (or notice of change of assessment), and after completing your research, you may arrange an informal meeting with your local assessor or his representative. The procedure for arranging this meeting is usually printed somewhere on your tax bill or published in the local newspaper.

It is the assessor's principal job to place an estimated value on your home and defend it. You will not win your informal appeal unless you can convincingly prove to the assessor that the assessment is overstated. Therefore, do your research prior to your meeting and be prepared to present your evidence in a calm, sensible manner.

Generally it is easier to have a clerical, mathematical, or procedural mistake corrected than it is to have an assessment reduced. A mistake on the property record file is glaring and generally insupportable, but a request for reduction in the assessment is a challenge to the assessor's method of operation and the mass appraisal techniques he employs. Having a clear understanding of the problem you are up against, go to this conference with a positive attitude, and present your evidence in a logical, direct manner using only the facts necessary to support your case. Regardless of the tact or lack thereof that the assessor employs, never become emotional or abusive. Stick to the facts and complete your presentation in a courteous manner. The informal appeal with the assessor is very difficult to win because you are putting him on the defensive by challenging his valuation of your property, and asking him to be his own impartial judge. If it becomes apparent that you have reached an impasse, do not become angry or insulting. Thank the assessor for his time and ask him for the necessary forms required to file a formal appeal to the local appeal board.

THINGS NOT TO DO

1. Never complain about property taxes being too high. This is not the concern of the assessor. He does not establish the dollar amount of your property tax, he simply assists in its determination.

2. Do not bring up the question of tax rates. The tax rate is not decided by the assessor and the subject has no place at these hearings.

3. A statement such as "I can't afford these high taxes!" by the homeowner is not appropriate at these hearings. *Ad Valorem property tax is levied according to the current value of the property regardless of your ability to pay. Not being able to afford to pay the taxes is immaterial to the appeal.*

4. Do not get into a shouting match or otherwise become offensive with the assessor or his representative. It will not help, and generally it will hurt your appeal. Remember the old adage that you catch more flies with honey than you do with vinegar.

5. Do not fall for any of the trick questions the assessor may ask you. Maintain a clear understanding of the appraisal methods the assessor used to arrive at his assessments and refute any questions which stray from those methods. For example, the assessor might ask you one or more of the following questions:

• **How much did you pay for your home and when did you buy it?**

If you purchased your property within the last two years the question is valid and the assessment should be close to the purchase price if the purchase was an arms-length transaction. Otherwise, the question is totally irrelevant. Remind the assessor that valuation is established on current value regardless of the method he employs.

- **Would you be willing to sell your home for the current assessment price?**

This question is totally immaterial. Assessments must be based on valid sales comparisons, or the replacement cost less depreciation, relative to similar homes in the same area.

- **How much is your property insured for?**

Once again, this question is totally irrelevant. What the home is insured for is not the basis by which the assessor values property. He must operate by the mass appraisal techniques that he normally uses for arriving at market value.

- **Have you made any improvements to your home recently? What type of improvements were they? How much did they cost?**

Do not lie, even if you did the work yourself without drawing a permit. The assessor may be aware of the construction and you will end up perjuring yourself. Generally, the assessor is aware of any improvements which were made to the home during the tax year by the building permits that were drawn and filed with the clerk's office. If the construction improved the value of the home (add-on of a room, swimming pool, etc.) as opposed to normal and routine maintenance (new roof, remodeling old kitchen, etc.), the assessor probably already added the extra value into his estimate. Therefore answer his question honestly, point out what type of construction it was and what it cost, and ask him if he was already aware of the improvement. This will defuse this potentially troublesome issue.

Appealing to the
Local Appeal Board

The local appeal boards are known by a number of different names such as the Board of Review, Equalization Board, Tax Commission, etc. In most cases their operating procedures, filing date deadlines, and scheduled times in which they conduct public hearings to address property tax grievances, are governed by state or provincial statutes and local regulations. Generally they begin their hearings shortly after change of assessment notices or property tax invoices are mailed out. Only taxpayers who file a properly completed written application during the prescribed filing period are allowed to appear in front of the board. The board is normally made up of local officials or their designated representatives who have a working knowledge of property tax law and the appraisal techniques utilized by the assessor.

The assumption by the local appeal board is that the assessor's valuation of your property is accurate and the burden of proving the assessor's valuation incorrect is on the appellant. The advantage of appearing in front of this board is that they are a third party willing to listen and act upon a well-founded, well-documented argument.

The key to winning your appeal is to be completely prepared and have your evidentiary material fully documented. Using one or more of the techniques we have previously considered (comparative sales, cost, equity, or the sales to assessment ratio approach), be sure to present your case in a clear, calm and concise manner. Stick to the facts relevant to the your case. Do not give in to the temptation of stating your negative opinion of the tax, the assessor's office, or the value of the current proceedings. This might make you feel better by relieving stress, tension, and frustration, but it will not help you win your case.

Have enough photocopies of the evidence you are submitting to support your argument to be able to present one to each of the members of the board and the assessor. This will make it easier for all parties concerned to follow your argument.

After you have finished presenting your testimony to the board, it is entirely possible that one or more board members may ask questions or ask for clarification on some points. Be ready to answer any question which conceivably could be asked regarding your case. Answer these questions as concisely and politely as possible without furnishing any unnecessary facts, details, or personal opinions.

Next, the board will allow the local assessor to present information which substantiates his valuation. Prior to the commencement of the assessor's testimony, you should ask for a photocopy of the material he intends to use to support his opinion. Listen to his testimony carefully and write down any points which you may want to address. Never, under any circumstance, interrupt the assessor while he is giving his deposition. It is considered very bad manners and it will definitely work against you. Sit quietly in a dignified manner without showing any emotion. After the assessor finishes giving his statement you have the right to cross-examine and try to refute his testimony.

HOW TO CROSS-EXAMINE THE ASSESSOR

Your case will be won or lost depending upon how effectively you cross-examine the assessor. At this point the board has heard both arguments and now it is important for you to discredit the assessor's information. This may be done by considering the following reasons to question the validity of the assessor's information.

1. What approach is the assessor using to arrive at his opinion of value? Is this the standard approach his office normally uses? If it is a different approach, why did he decide to use it? Is it legal based on state agency guidelines and statutes?

2. If the assessor is using recent sales comparables to substantiate his assessment, is he comparing similar type homes? Are the homes he is comparing the same type, same age, same neighborhood, same square-footage, same lot size, etc.? If he isn't comparing similar properties, be sure to point this out to the board.

3. Are there significant differences between the features of the properties he is using as comparables and your home? Has the assessor adjusted the assessments to reflect the differences? Whose cost figures is he using? Are the numbers current? How valid is the source of his numbers?

4. If he is using the cost approach, whose dollar amounts is he using? Are they current? Are they realistic? What percentage rate of depreciation is he using? Is it reasonable in the market-

place? Are his replacement values based on an accurate description of the property?

5. If the assessor is using the equity approach, has he chosen valid comparisons? Are the properties similar to appellant's property in style, age, living square footage, land size, neighborhood, etc.? If there are differences, has he adjusted the value to reflect the differences? Whose dollar amounts has he used? Are they current? Are they realistic? How valid is the source?

6. If the assessor has chosen the sales to assessment ratio approach, how old is the survey? What type of properties does it cover? How large a section of the taxing district does it survey? Who conducted the survey? Are there other surveys available that are more narrow in scope?

THE RULING FROM THE LOCAL BOARD

Normally the board hears a number of cases during each session but does not immediately render a decision. In each case the board listens to the testimony of the taxpayer and the assessor, takes notes, retains copies of the evidence submitted by opposing parties, and may have the entire proceeding recorded on tape or transcribed by a court stenographer. The time allotted for a ruling to be issued by the board to interested parties is regulated by state statute or local regulation.

Even though you might have presented a convincing argument for a reduction of your assessment, you may not win your appeal on the local level. Many times local monetary or political considerations influence a ruling. For example, for the tax year 1993 I appealed four properties. In each instance my argument was valid and I won my case, but I was not granted the full reduction I had requested. I was given a partial reduction which the board hoped would pacify me. This practice of partially placating appellants is often used because the board knows that most taxpayers will not go through the trouble and expense of filing another appeal. My recourse was to continue my appeal on a higher level, in my case, judicial review, which I am presently doing. (Please refer to Appendix C which shows a copy of my complaint used in Circuit Court.)

If you are not satisfied by the findings of the local board you may continue your appeal on a higher level. Each state or province has its own hierarchy of appeal boards and judicial review (refer to the state and provincial summaries for in depth details pertaining to your area). It is important to comply with the filing date deadlines prescribed by the various appeal boards, and the state and provincial courts.

Since the proceedings at any of the appeal boards are public record, you are legally entitled to review and photocopy your case file, including any subsequent documents or reports which were used to arrive at a ruling. You might find something of value among these documents, or they may be helpful if you would like to show your case to someone else for a second opinion prior to your next appeal.

The higher up the appeal ladder you climb, the more impartial the boards become. The county board (if one exists) is more impartial than the local board because it is further removed from local political influences and financial concerns. The state board is even further removed and will hopefully be even more objective. If after all administrative remedies are exhausted you are still dissatisfied with the final ruling, you have further recourse through the judicial system.

The standard, cautious advice at this point is to hire an attorney in order to successfully navigate the legal waters. This is safe, solid advice that quickly resolves a difficult question and gets the author off the proverbial hook.

I, however, choose to disagree. You don't need a lawyer to go to court. The law clearly allows you to file an appeal on your own behalf, go to court, and present your case. Each state or province has its specific rules governing how and when to file an appeal, but I don't believe it is so complicated or difficult that the average citizen can't comply. It requires that you spend enough time and effort to do the proper research and seek out and ask public agencies the right questions, thereby finding the correct procedural answers.

I am presently approaching the court for the first time in order to continue my 1993 appeals. I am doing all of the work myself, hoping to prove that this legal system of ours is still open and available to John Q. Public. As of yet, I do not see the need to hire a two hundred dollar per hour attorney who really doesn't care about my insignificant case and is probably too overloaded with other cases to give me the attention I deserve. In subsequent editions of this book, I promise to include a chapter on how to successfully go to court and win.

THE APPEAL PROCESS

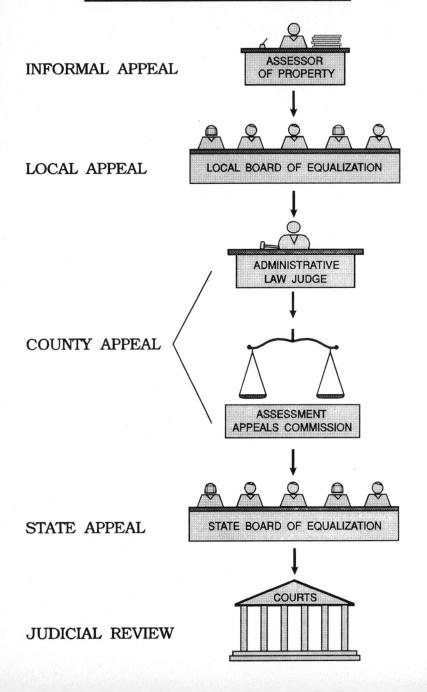

INFORMAL APPEAL

LOCAL APPEAL

COUNTY APPEAL

STATE APPEAL

JUDICIAL REVIEW

Dealing with Your Bank   8

If you gain no other valuable information at all, this section alone will be worth the purchase price of this book. It also involves what I personally believe may be one of the biggest rip-offs presently being perpetrated on the North American public.

Most people who buy a residential property initially outlay somewhere between 5% and 10% of the purchase price of the property as a down payment, and the balance of the cost of a home is financed by large financial institutions, normally banks and mortgage companies. This type of collateralized loan is known as a mortgage, which is defined as "a conditional conveyance of property to a creditor as security, as for repayment of money." Mortgages are expensive loans to obtain. There are application fees, procedural fees, administrative fees, closing fees and interest on the principal amount you borrow. These are expected costs and you must anticipate these expenses when purchasing a home.

Let's look at a home that Mr.& Mrs. John Q. Public purchased at a cost of $100,000. Let's assume that they put down $10,000 and have a fixed-rate mortgage for thirty years. Let's also assume that their annual total property tax bill is $5,000. Therefore the owners of this property, from the very beginning of their ownership, have twice as much equity (cash value) in the property as the total amount of the property tax.

Besides collecting the fees, interest, and principal they are entitled to, the banks and mortgage companies collect the homeowner's property tax. This is normally done by dividing the previous year's tax amount into twelve equal payments and collecting a payment each month. When the property tax is due, the bank is holding enough funds and pays the tax to the local tax collector. This type of an account is called an escrow account. The bank, if questioned about this account, will reply that this insures that the tax will be paid.

My problem with these property tax escrow accounts is that they are not interest bearing. During the course of the entire year, banks and mortgage companies all over the United States and Canada collect billions of dollars that they use and make money with without paying any interest! If the financial institutions insist on collecting money to protect their investment, shouldn't they be forced to pay us interest? Don't we have to pay them interest when we borrow money from them? Of course we do!

To add fuel to the flame, let's go back and look at the equity (cash value) the property owners have in their residences. In our example, Mr. & Mrs. Public had $10,000 worth of equity (down payment) in their home at the onset. As the years progressed and they paid their mortgage, their equity slowly increased. If suddenly Mr. & Mrs. Public had a financial crisis, wouldn't the equity in their residence be enough to cover the property tax due? Even if they had to refinance their mortgage or the house had to be sold, wouldn't the equity cover the property tax? Besides, if they were responsible enough to qualify for a mortgage in the first place, wouldn't they be responsible enough to make the yearly property tax payment? What I am saying is that this whole concept of financial institutions requiring trustworthy people to make monthly payments into non-interest bearing escrow accounts for property tax may be unjustified.

My suggestion is when you are negotiating your mortgage, to either insist on making your own yearly property tax payment, or insist on placing your money in an account with the financial institution that bears interest. The key here is being aware of the possibility of negotiating this type of arrangement and insisting upon it. If the bank or mortgage company you are trying to do business with refuses to pay you interest, they are trying to rip you off and you should look for another lender. The problem is that at this point in time, you may not be able to find one!

Discounts

Many taxing districts offer a discount for early payment of the property tax. In my county you can get as much as a 4% discount for early payment (see figure Metro-Dade Combined tax bill under section Disc Amount Due if Paid In, exhibit (K), page 55). To find out if your tax district offers a discount for early payment, check with your local assessor or tax collector.

If your taxing district offers a discount on your total property tax bill for early payment be sure that your bank takes advantage of the program, and more importantly credits your account with the savings. Taking advantage of this discount program should not be a problem because

Exhibit K

COMBINED TAX BILL
1993 AD VALOREM TAXES 1993

MILL CD 3000   FOLIO   30 2000 000 0000   NAME: JANE DOE

SCHOOL AND STATE DISTRICTS

AUTHORITY	RATE	AMOUNT	AUTHORITY	RATE	AMOUNT	AMOUNT DUE IF PAID IN	
SCH OP	9.2830000	524.49			0.00	NOV 4%	1,988.74
SCH DEB	0.6400000	36.16			0.00	DEC 3%	2,009.46
FIND	0.0510000	2.88			0.00	JAN 2%	2,030.17
WM DIST	0.5970000	33.73		SUB TOT	597.26	FEB 1%	2,050.89

CITY-TYPE SERVICES PROVIDED BY COUNTY
MAR 0%   2,071.60

MUN SVC	2.3740000	134.13			0.00
		0.00			0.00
		0.00			0.00
		0.00		SUB TOT	134.13

DADE COUNTY DISTRICTS
PRIOR YEARS TAXES DUE

CNTY WD	7.3050000	412.73	MDCC	0.7500000	42.38
DEBT SVC	0.8300000	46.89			0.00
LIBRARY	0.3510000	19.83			0.00
FIRE RE	2.3440000	132.44		SUB TOT	654.28

VALUATIONS
TOT VALUE   82,000
HMSTD EX   25,000

NON-AD VALOREM ASSESSMENTS

SPECIAL ASSESSMENT	DIST	RATE	FT/UNIT	AMOUNT
WASTE MANAGEMENT	T123	399.00	1.00	399.00
COLONIAL DRIVE	LO018	0.4520	64.00	28.93
MIAMI LAKES	M183	0.0212	12170.00	258.00
				0.00
				0.00
				0.00
			SUB TOT	685.93

WID EX   500
TAXABLE VALUE   56,500

IMPROVEMENT DIST.	DIST	INT/RATE	YEARS	INTEREST	INSTALLMENT AMOUNT

COMMENTS

DETACH HERE

MAIL THIS PORTION WITH PAYMENT

COMBINED TAX BILL
1993 REAL PROPERTY TAXES

VALUATIONS		Mill Code	Folio Number	DISC AMOUNT DUE IF PAID IN	
TOT VALUE	82000	3000	30 2000 000 0000	4% NOV	1,988.74
HMSTD EX	25000	MTG		3% DEC	2,009.46
WID EX	500			2% JAN	2,030.17
				1% FEB	2,050.89
				0% MAR	2,071.60

SEQ 000001-000003   PRIOR YEAR TAXES DUE   DELINQUENT AFTER MARCH 31

JEFF ESTATES
JANE DOE   PB-66-13
1957 METRO LN   LOT 1 BLK 10
MIAMI FL 33016   LOT SIZE SQU   12170

you have been making monthly payments into an escrow account and at tax time the money should be there. I have run into a number of instances where the bank has been credited for the discount but has failed to pass all or some of the savings on to the property owner, who is the rightful owner of those funds. This is tantamount to theft, but that does not mean the practice does not go on. It is vital that you as the mortgagor be aware of your bank's policy and monitor them to be sure that you are properly credited.

Condominiums 9

Challenging the assessor's valuation of a condominium requires a few extra considerations which I shall cover in this section. Using the comparative sales approach, I would first compile all the sales in my building or complex of similarly featured apartments, regardless of the floor on which they are located or their selling prices. If I found two or three comparables that were lower in price than my assessment, my case would be solid. If that were not the case, I would go to the county clerk and look up the details of the sales individually. At the very least, I would obtain the name of the buyer and seller of each unit I was interested in investigating. At best, I would find a transfer document that specifically listed all items included with the sale, if such a document exists in your state or province. What I am looking for is the sale of personal property (furniture, drapes, appliances, etc.) along with the sale of the condominium. The value of all the personal property should be deducted from the selling price of the real property, the condominium. In some instances this can add up to thousands of dollars, depending on the extent and quality of the personal property sold with the apartment.

Another valid technique is the sales to assessment ratio approach. For a specific period of time (your last tax year) collect the actual sales prices of apartments similar to yours in the same or a nearby condominium development. Divide each apartment's sales price by its assessed value in order to obtain a percentage. Then add up all of your percentage figures and divide by that number. If the ratio on your property is significantly above the collective sales to assessment ratio, you have a valid reason to have your assessment reduced. Refer to exhibit (J), on page 43, for an example of the sales ratio technique.

Another interesting possibility is to compare the sales to assessment ratio study the state or local authorities issue. In order to achieve a degree of equality in assessments, the state government normally collects data from the counties and statistically measures and manipulates that data to determine a common multiplier which renders an official equalized sales to assessment ratio between townships and/or counties within the state. There may be a state statute prescribing the maximum percentage deviation allowable between taxing districts. If the sales of similar apartments in the same area are significantly above the state equalized sales to assessment ratio (15% to 20%), this becomes valid grounds for a reduction in assessment.

Lastly, the cost approach opens up some interesting possibilities. Assume that the common areas (lobby, garage, grounds) are properly valued, but you are comparing similarly featured apartments on different floors of the condominium. What is each ascending story worth? What is a superior view (ocean front, golf course) worth as opposed to a street view? In such large buildings, the possibilities of errors and inequities abound.

Conclusion 10

If you have carefully read the material and analyzed the examples included, you will no longer be intimidated by what you don't understand about your property taxes. You are now armed with sufficient knowledge about this ever escalating tax to thoroughly be able to investigate the government's alleged facts pertaining to your property. You can protect yourself against the abuses of omissions, errors, fallacious interpretations, and the manipulation of mass data. Certainly you should have a clear understanding of why you are taxed, how you are taxed, and who is doing the taxing. You should be able to clearly comprehend the different information on your tax bill and know how to go about determining whether or not that information is correct. You should have a clear understanding of the techniques employed by the assessor to value your property, and where to look for information to either verify or dispute that valuation. Lastly, you are now equipped to intelligently gather conclusive evidence to support your argument and to make a comprehensive, compelling appeal. In short, if you have put forth a sincere effort, you should have accomplished the stated purposes of this book:

1. To be able to determine whether or not you are paying more than your fair share of ad valorem real property tax; and

2. if you are paying too much, how to successfully appeal and have your taxes reduced.

During the course of this discussion I have stressed the negatives of the property tax and, to a certain extent, the officials who are responsible for maintaining the system. I would like to point out however, in all fairness, that we as people and as nations are indeed blessed.

We are fortunate to live in countries which have developed powerful enough economies to enable so many of their citizens to become property owners. We are twice blessed to live in nations which are democracies, that allow us the freedom to investigate and gather together information deemed to be public for the purpose of peacefully and legally protesting the amount of tax the government contends we owe.

When objectively examining the majority of nations around the globe, one quickly discovers that most governments repress most, if not all, of the personal freedoms and human rights of its citizens.

We living in the United States and Canada should be eternally grateful that the laws, traditions, and institutions exist that allow us the freedom and luxury to peacefully and legally protest without fear of governmental oppression or bodily harm.

By taking the time and making the effort to exercise your freedom, such as the right to thoroughly examine your property tax bill and to lodge an appeal when it seems appropriate, you are helping to ensure that the government will never attempt to take away your rights and freedoms. Our rights and freedoms are like a complicated machine. If not regularly used and routinely maintained, they will become non-functional and eventually discarded.

Definitions of Terminology Used in the State & Provincial Summaries

Name of Real Property Tax: Name of the tax on real property in this state or province.

Official Valuation Standard: The definition of real property value for assessment purposes used by this state or province.

Annual Assessments of Real Property: Are annual assessments of real property required?

Reassessment Cycle: How often reassessments are required as prescribed by law in this state or province.

Assessment Date: The day of the year that this state or province uses to establish the monetary value of real property for assessment purposes.

Classification of Property: The manner in which property is categorized in this state or province.

Exemptions Available to Homeowners: The qualifications and restrictions on a variety of tax-relief exemptions available to homeowners in this state or province.

Statutory Exemptions: Catagories of properties that by state or provincial statute, or local regulation, are either entirely or partially excused from paying property taxes.

Appeal Procedures: A detailed explanation of the types of appeals available to the property owner who wants to protest his/her assessment in this state or province.

Appeal Calendar: The deadline dates for taxpayers to file appeals.

Level of Government Responsible for Assessment: Examples are village, town, city, township, county, state and province. This is the level at which a property owner begins his/her research and appeal.

Tax Assessor:

1. Is your local assessor elected or appointed?

2. What is the length of time that the tax assessor serves?

3. What is the minimum formal education required for employment?

4. Is the assessor required to have special educational credentials or be certified?

State Issued Assessor's Manuals: Titles of the manuals used by the tax assessor in this state or province.

Equalization: Adjustment of assessments on the local, county, state, or province level to achieve equality in valuations of real property. This is done to assure that each taxpayer is bearing only his fair share of the tax burden.

Property Tax Maps Mandatory: Does this state or province require the local tax assessor to provide the taxpayer with a detailed map specifying property location, lot dimensions, and corresponding property identification number?

Allow Real Property to be Assessed at Financially Better Use Rather Than Current Use:

YES means that your property can be valued at its "best use" value as opposed to what it is presently used for. For example if you own a property which is zoned industrial and it is presently used as residential, it may be valued at the higher or more expensive value.

NO means it may only be valued at its present use regardless of its potential.

Frequency of State Ratio Studies: How often, if at all, is the assessment to sales ratio study conducted by this state or province.

Are State or Province Ratio Studies Accessible to the Public: Are the results of the latest ratio studies available to the public in this state or province?

State or Provincial Agency Address: The name and address of the state or provincial agency or department that is responsible for regulating the ad valorem property tax in this area. Also included is the name of the person to contact, and his/her telephone and fax number when available.

NOTES

UNITED STATES

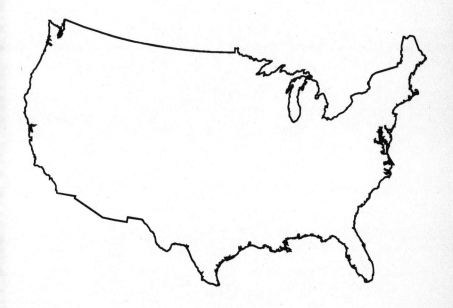

NOTES

ALABAMA

Name of real property tax: *Ad Valorem Tax*

Official valuation standard: *"The fair and reasonable market value of such property" Code of Alabama 40-8-1.*

Annual assessment of real property: *Yes*

Reassessment cycle: *Not required by Alabama law.*

Assessment date: *October 1*

Classification of property:

Class I   All properties owned by public utilities and used in the business of such utilities.

Class II   All properties not otherwise classified.

Class III   All agricultural, forest, residential property, and historical buildings and sites.

Assessment rate:

Class I   30% of market value

Class II   20% of market value

Class III   10% of market value

Tax relief available to homeowners:

(See chart on page 70)

1. Over 65 years of age: For residents over 65 years of age the State of Alabama has no maximum amount of assessed value exemption and has no income requirement. The county exemption has a maximum deduction of $5,000 on assessed value and the taxpayer must not have an adjusted gross income of more than $11,999 for the taxing period.

2. Under 65 years of age: Maximum $6,000 deducted from assessed value and no income requirement.

3. Permanent & total disability regardless of age:
   Minimum $5,000 deducted from assessed value.

4. Blind regardless of age: Minimum $5,000 deducted from assessed value.

5. Over 65 years old & totally disabled: No maximum / minimum.

Exemptions:

- Government property

- Religious property

- Charitable property

- Educational property

- Cemeteries

Appeal procedure:

Step 1   Immediately after receiving notice of assessment, have an informal meeting with the local tax assessor and try to resolve the problem. If after the meeting you are not satisfied with the decision, go to step 2.

Step 2   Within 10 days of receipt of the notice of assessment, and after an unsuccessful informal meeting with the tax assessor, file a written notice with the County Board of Equalization.

Step 3   If after presenting all of your evidence before the County Board of Equalization you are dissatisfied with their decision, you may appeal to the Circuit Court of Appeals.

Step 4   If after presenting all of your evidence before the Circuit Court of Appeals you are dissatisfied with their decision, you may appeal to the Supreme Court of Alabama.

In accordance with state statutes, once started all administrative appeals must be exhausted before an appeal may be filed with the Supreme Court of Alabama. In addition, the current property tax the state alleges you owe must be paid (under protest) before the courts will hear your case.

Appeal calendar:

1. Ten days after receiving the notice of assessment, the taxpayer must file a written notice of appeal with the County Board of Equalization.

2. The County Board of Equalization will start hearings on the first Monday in June.

3. If the taxpayer chooses to continue the protest, an appeal must be filed at the Circuit Court within 30 days after receiving the final written decision of the County Board of Equalization.

4. If the taxpayer chooses to continue the protest, an appeal must be filed with the Supreme Court of Alabama within 42 days after receiving the final judgement of the Circuit Court.

Level of government responsible for assessment:
County

Tax assessors:

- Elected for a six year term.

- High school education is required.

- Special education or certificate is not required but recommended.

State issued assessor's manual: *Alabama Assessor's Manual*

Equalization: *No*

Property tax maps mandatory: *Yes*

Allow real property to be assessed at financially better use rather than current use: *Yes*

Frequency of state ratio studies: *Yearly*

Are state ratio studies accessible to the public: *No*

Exhibit AL

ALABAMA HOMESTEAD EXEMPTIONS

Type	Eligibility Requirements	STATE EXEMPTION		COUNTY EXEMPTION		CITY EXEMPTION	
		Maximum Exempt. (Assessed Value)	Income Requirements	Maximum Exemption (Assessed Value)	Income Requirements	Maximum Exemption	Income Requirements
HS #1 (Reg.HS)	Not over 65	$4000	None	$2,000*	None	*	None
HS #2a. (Act 91)	Over 65	No Maximum	None	$5,000	Adjusted Gross Income of less than $12k (State Tax Return)	None	None
HS #2b.	Permanent & Total Disability Regardless of Age	No Maximum	None	$5,000	None	None	None
HS #2c.	Blind Regardless of Age	No Maximum	None	$5,000	None	None	None
HS #3	Over 65 or Totally Disabled (Act 48 Princple Residence Exemption)	No Maximum	Not more than $7,500 Combined Taxable Income (Federal Tax Return)	No Maximum	Not more than $7.5k Combined Taxable Income (Federal Tax Return)	No maximum	Not more than $7.5k Combined Taxable Income (Federal Tax Return)
HS #4 (Act 91)	Over 65	No Maximum	None	$2,000	None		None

Homestead Exemptions are limited to land areas of not more than 160 acres.
*NOTE: The County, Municipalities, or other taxing authority may grant a Homestead Exemption up to $4,000 in assessed value on HS#1 & HS#4. County and City School Taxes are not exempted under HS#1 & HS#4.

State agency information and contact person:

State of Alabama
Department of Revenue
Ad Valorem Tax Division
Montgomery, Alabama 26132
Mr. Kenneth E. King
Telephone: (205) 242-1525 • Fax: (205) 242-0145

NOTES

ALASKA

Name of real property tax: *Property Tax*

Official valuation standard: *Alaska Statute 29.45.110 specifies that the full and true value is "the estimated price that the property would bring in an open market and under the then prevailing market conditions in a sale between a willing seller and a willing buyer both conversant with the property and with the prevailing general price levels."*

Annual assessment of real property: *Not required by statute*

Reassessment cycle: *Not specified by statute*

Assessment date: *January 1*

Classification of property:

Class I   Real and personal property

Class III   Oil & gas property

Assessment rate:

Class I   100% of market value

Class III   100% of market value

Tax relief available to homeowners:

Alaska Statute 29.45.030 (e)-(i)

1. Over 65 years of age: First $150,000 of assessed value on primary residence is exempt.

2. Widow/widower: unremarried surviving spouse of senior qualifying homeowner and at least 60 years old. First $150,000 of assessed value on primary residence is exempt.

3. Veterans with a service related 50% permanent disability or greater: first $150,000 of assessed value on primary residence is exempt.

4. Renters rebate: Alaska Statute 29.45.040

This program rebates eligible applicants for that portion of their yearly rent on their permanent place of abode that goes toward the payment of real property taxes. To be eligible a person must be 65 years of age or older the entire year in which he/she applies, or a disabled veteran with 50% or greater service connected disability rating. Applicants must apply directly to their municipality before January 15th each year.

Exemptions:

- Government property
- Religious property
- Charitable property
- Educational property
- Non-profit hospitals
- Some utility co-ops
- Cemeteries

Appeal procedure:

Step 1   Informal administrative review. Immediately after receiving notice of assessment, a taxpayer with a grievance should have an informal meeting with the local tax assessor and try to resolve the problem. If after the meeting the taxpayer is not satisfied with the decision, go to step 2.

Step 2   Within 30 days of receipt of the notice of assessment, and after an unsuccessful informal meeting with the tax assessor, file a formal appeal form or written letter with the Board of Equalization in your taxing jurisdiction. Almost all cases are resolved at this level.

Step 3   If the taxpayer is dissatisfied with the final decision of the Board of Equalization, the taxpayer may appeal to the Superior Court of Alaska.

> *Once started, all administrative appeals must be exhausted before an appeal may be filed with the Superior Court of Alaska. In addition, the current property tax the state alleges you owe must be paid (under protest) before the courts will hear your case.*

Appeal calendar:

1. Thirty days after receiving the notice of assessment the taxpayer must file a written notice of appeal with the Board of Equalization.

2. If the taxpayer chooses to continue the protest, an appeal must be filed at the Superior Court of Alaska within 30 days after receiving the final decision of the Board of Equalization.

Level of government responsible for assessment:

With certain limitations, all cities, boroughs, and unified municipalities in the State of Alaska may choose to levy a property tax. Property tax is not mandatory or even generally practiced. If a municipality chooses to levy a property tax, it may only levy on property that is "taxable."

Tax assessors:

- Appointed to an indefinite term.

- High school education is required.

- Special education or certificate is not required but recommended.

State issued assessor's manuals: *Alaska Statute 29.45 and the Municipal Code*

Equalization: *Not mandatory*

Property tax maps mandatory: *Yes*

Allow real property to be assessed at financially better use rather than current use: *Yes*

Frequency of state ratio studies: *Yearly*

Are state ratio studies accessible to the public: *Yes*

State agency information and contact person:

State of Alaska Department of Revenue
Income & Audit Division
P.O. Box 110420
Juneau, Alaska 99811-0420
Mr. Paul E. Dick
Telephone: (907) 465-3691 • Fax: (907) 465-2375

NOTES

ARIZONA

Name of real property tax: *Property Tax*

Official valuation standard:

> *The Arizona property tax system is based upon the principle of uniform valuation of property at its full cash value. Full cash value is "... that estimate of value that is derived annually by the use of standard appraisal methods and techniques," if no statutory valuation method is prescribed. Full cash value determined by use of standard appraisal methods and techniques equates to market value (Arizona Statute 42-201).*

Annual assessment of real property: *Yes*

Reassessment cycle: *Not required by Arizona law.*

Assessment date: *November 1*

Classification of property:

Class I	Producing mines
Class II	Utilities
Class III	Commercial / Industrial
Class IV	Agricultural / Vacant
Class V	Residential Property
Class VI	Rented Residential
Class VII	Railroad
Class VIII	Historic Property

Assessment rate:

Class I	30% of market value
Class II	30% of market value
Class III	25% of market value
Class IV	16% of market price
Class V	10% of market price

Class VI   14% of market price

Class VII   20% of market price

Class VIII   5% of market price

Tax relief available to widows, widowers, disabled persons, and disabled veterans:

Within limits, property of qualifying widows, widowers, and disabled persons is exempted from property tax by the State Constitution (Article 9, Sections 2 and 2.1). The limitations include a scale of exemption benefits based upon assessed value of property owned by the person seeking the exemption. For example, an exemption of $2,340 assessed value may be claimed by a person with a total assessment of $5,460 or less. The amount of exemption decreases in steps until, at $7,800 total assessment, there is no exemption.

An income test must be met for qualification. A widow, widower, or disabled person may meet that test if his/her income does not not exceed $8,400 for the prior year if none of his/her children under the age of 18 reside in the home. The income can be a maximum of $12,000 if one or more of his/her children under 18 reside in the home, or if a child who is totally and permanently disabled resides with him/her.

Exemptions for veterans and disabled veterans were invalidated by the Arizona Court of Appeals, Division Two, in 1989. Disabled veterans may qualify for the disabled persons exemption described above, however.

Exemptions:

- Government property
- Religious property
- Charitable property
- Educational property
- Hospitals
- Cemeteries

Appeal procedure:

Step 1   Immediately after receiving notice of assessment, have an informal meeting with the local tax assessor and try to resolve the problem. If after the meeting you are not satisfied with the decision, go to step 2.

Step 2   Within 15 days of receipt of the notice of assessment, and after an unsuccessful informal meeting with the tax assessor, file a written appeal with the County Board of Equalization.

Step 3   If after presenting all of your evidence before the County Board of Equalization you are dissatisfied with their decision, you may appeal to the State Board of Tax Appeal.

Step 4   If after presenting all of your evidence before the State Board of Tax Appeal you are still not satisfied with their decision, you may appeal to Tax Court (Superior Court).

All administrative appeals must be exhausted before an appeal may be filed with the Tax Court. In addition, you must pay the current property tax (under protest) the state alleges you owe before the Tax (Superior) Court will hear your case.

Appeal calendar:

1. By December 31, or 45 days after the mail date on the notice of valuation, whichever is later, the taxpayer must file a written notice of appeal with the county assessor. The county assessor must respond to all appeals by April 1.

2. Appellant must file a petition (appeal) with the County Board of Equalization within 15 days of the notification of the County Assessor's decision. The County Board of Equalization will decide appeals within 10 days of the hearing date. All hearings must be complete by May 10.

3. If the taxpayer is not happy with the decision of the County Board of Equalization and chooses to continue the protest, an appeal must be filed with the State Board of Tax Appeals within

15 days of the notification of the decision of the County Board of Equalization. All appeals before the State Board of Tax Appeals must be completed no later than July 25.

4. Any taxpayer who files an administrative appeal may appeal to the Tax Court (Superior Court) for a judicial decision within 60 days of the mailing date of the most recent administrative decision relating to the petition.

Level of government responsible for assessment:
County

Tax assessors:

•   Elected for a four year term.

•   High school education is required.

•   State certificate is required.

State issued assessor's manuals: *Agricultural Manual Mines and Natural Resources Manual, Assessment Procedures Manual, Personal Property Manual, Construction Cost Manual, Property Use Code Manual, Land Manual, Sales Ratio Statistical Summary*

Equalization: *Yes*

Property tax maps mandatory: *Yes*

Allow real property to be assessed at financially better use rather than current use: *No*

Frequency of state ratio studies: *Yearly*

Are state ratio studies accessible to the public: *Yes*

State agency information and contact person:

State of Arizona Department of Revenue
Division of Property Valuation & Equalization
1600 West Monroe
Phoenix, Arizona 85007-2650
Mr. Seth I. Franzman, Manager
Manuals and Certification Unit
Telephone: (602) 542-3529 • Fax: (602) 542-5667

ARKANSAS

Name of real property tax: *Property Tax*

Official valuation standard: *Market value defined as "what a willing buyer would pay a willing seller for the property in an open, competitive market."*

Annual assessment of real property: *Yes*

Reassessment cycle: *Not specified by statute*

Assessment date: *January 1*

Classification of property:

Class I	Real property
Class II	Personal property
Class III	Utility & carrier

Assessment rate:

Class I	20% of market value
Class II	20% of market value
Class III	20% of market value

Tax relief available to homeowners:

The following refunds are available to low income real property owners and any person 62 years of age or older who has been a resident of this state for 2 years or more, who owns and has resided in a homestead in this state for a period of 1 year or more.

If your income is:	The maximum refund is:
$0 to $7,000	$250.00
$7,000.01 to $8,000.00	$200.00
$8,000.01 to $9,000.00	$150.00
$9,000.01 to $10,000.00	$100.00
$10,000.01 to $11,000.00	$ 75.00
$11,000.01 to $15,000.00	$ 50.00

Disabled veterans with service connected 100% total and permanent disability, shall be exempt from payment of all state taxes on homestead and personal property owned by such disabled veteran. Upon the death of such disabled veteran, the surviving unremarried spouse and minor dependent children of such disabled veteran shall be exempt from payment of all state taxes on the homestead and personal property owned by the surviving spouse and minor dependent children of such deceased disabled veteran. (Ars 84-209)

Exemptions:

- Government property
- Religious property
- Charitable property
- Educational property
- Non-profit hospitals
- Some utility co-operatives
- Cemeteries

Appeal procedure:

Step 1   Informal administrative review. Immediately after receiving notice of assessment, a taxpayer with a grievance should have an informal meeting with the local tax assessor and try to resolve the problem. If after the meeting the taxpayer is not satisfied with the decision, go to step 2.

Step 2   Within 30 days of receipt of the notice of assessment, and after an unsuccessful informal meeting with the tax assessor, file a formal appeal form or written letter with the Equalization Board in your taxing jurisdiction. Almost all cases are resolved at this level.

Step 3   If the taxpayer is dissatisfied with the final decision of the Board of Equalization, the taxpayer may appeal to the County Court.

Step 4   If the taxpayer is dissatisfied with the final decision of the County Court, the taxpayer may appeal to the Circuit Court.

Step 5   If the taxpayer is dissatisfied with the final decision of the Circuit Court, the taxpayer may appeal to the Supreme Court of Arkansas.

> *Once started, all administrative appeals must be exhausted before an appeal may be filed with the Supreme Court of Arkansas. In addition all current property taxes must be paid (under protest) before the court will hear the case.*

Appeal calendar:

1. Assessment date: January 1

2. Assessment notices received by taxpayers by August 1.

3. All applications to the County Equalization Board shall be made on or before the third Monday in August.

4. All applications shall be made to and considered by the County Board of Equalization on or before the first Saturday preceding the third Monday in September.

5. Appeals to County Court must be filed on or before the second Monday in October.

6. A ruling by County Court shall be made on or before the first Monday in November.

Level of government responsible for assessment:
County

Tax assessors:

- Elected to a two year term.

- High school education is required.

- Special education or certificate is not required.

State issued assessor's manuals: *Arkansas Assessor's Real Estate Replacement Manual (1986), Marshall & Swift*

Equalization: *Not mandatory*

Property tax maps mandatory: *Not mandatory*

Allow real property to be assessed at financially better use rather than current use: *No*

Frequency of state ratio studies: *Yearly*

Are state ratio studies accessible to the public: *Yes*

State agency information and contact person:

State of Arkansas
Assessment Coordination
Division of the Public Service Commission
1614 West Third
Little Rock, Arkansas 72201
Mr. John B. Zimpel
Telephone: (501) 324-9240 • Fax: (501) 324-9242

CALIFORNIA

Name of real property tax: *Property Tax*

Official valuation standard: *Article XIII-a of the California Constitution.*

Annual assessment of real property: *Not required by law.*

Reassessment cycle: *Not required by law.*

Assessment date: *March 1*

Classification of property:

Class I	Land
Class II	Improvements
Class III	Personal Property
Class IV	Utilities and Railroad Property

Assessment rate:

Article XIII-a of the California Constitution rolled back most property assessments to 1975 market value levels and limited the property tax rate on that value to 1 percent plus the rate necessary to fund local voter-approved bond indebtedness. Further, it limited future property tax increases to no more than 2 percent a year on properties that were not involved in a change in ownership or did not undergo new construction.

However, properties that are newly constructed, have had significant renovations, or have changed ownership are assessed at market value.

Tax relief available to homeowners:

Homeowners Exemption: If you own a home and occupy it as your principal place of residence on March 1, you are eligible for an exemption of $7,000 off the assessed value of that residence.

Disabled Veterans Exemption: If you are a California veteran who is rated 100% disabled, blind, or paraplegic due to a service-connected disability (or if you are the unmarried widow of such a veteran), you may be eligible for an exemption of up to $150,000 off of the assessed value of your home.

Veterans Exemption: Veterans receive an exemption of up to $4,000 off the assessed value of their home for their service to the nation.

Disaster Relief: If a major calamity, such as fire or flooding, damages or destroys your property, you may be eligible for property tax relief. In such cases, the assessor's office will immediately reappraise the property to reflect its damaged condition. In addition, when the owner rebuilds the property in a like or similar manner, the property will retain its pre-damage assessed value.

Eminent Domain (Proposition 3): State law provides that if a government agency acquires property through condemnation, owners may have the right to retain that property's existing assessed value by transferring it to a replacement property.

Decline in Value (Proposition 8): If the actual current market value is less than the assessment, the assessor's office may reduce the assessment value of any real property.

Parent & Child Exclusion (Proposition 58): The transfer of real property between parents and children may be excluded from reappraisal for property tax purposes.

Exclusion for Seniors (Propositions 60 & 90): A senior citizen over 55 years of age, who buys a residence of equal or lesser value may be able to have his/her old assessed value transferred to the new home.

Severely and Permanently Disabled Exclusion (Prop 110): A severely and permanently disabled person, who buys a new home, may be able to have his/her old assessed value transferred to the new home.

Exemptions:

- Government property
- Religious property
- Charitable property
- Educational property
- Household furnishings and personal effects
- Business inventories
- Cemeteries

Appeal procedure:

Step 1   Immediately after receiving notice of assessment on July 1, arrange an informal meeting with the local tax assessor and try to resolve the problem. If after the meeting you are not satisfied with the decision, go to step 2.

Step 2   Between July 2 and September 15 and after an unsuccessful informal meeting with the tax assessor, file a written notice of appeal with the Assessment Appeal Board.

Step 3   If after presenting all of your evidence before the Assessment Appeal Board you are still dissatisfied, you may appeal to the courts, but only under certain circumstances. The courts will only hear a case for the following reasons: arbitrariness, lack of due process, abuse of discretion, failure to follow standards prescribed by law (e.g. using an erroneous method of valuation), or other questions of law. The court will not receive new evidence of value; the court will only review the record of the hearing before the County Board. If the court finds that the County Board's decision is supported by credible evidence, it will uphold the Board.

Taxpayers must exhaust their administrative remedies before seeking judicial relief.

Appeal calendar:

1. Assessment date is March 1.

2. Assessment notices are received by taxpayers by July 1.

3. Written notices of appeal must be filed with the County Assessment Appeal Board between July 2 and September 15.

4. If the taxpayer chooses to continue the protest, an appeal must be filed at the Circuit Court within 60 days after receiving the final decision of the County Assessment Appeals Board.

Level of government responsible for assessment:
County, State

Tax assessors:

- Elected for a four year term.

- College degree or high school education with four years of experience is required.

- Special education or certificate is not required.

State issued assessor's manuals: *Letter to Assessors (guidance documents), Property Tax Law Guide, Assessor's Handbook*

Equalization: *No*

Property tax maps mandatory: *Yes*

Allow real property to be assessed at financially better use rather than current use: *Yes*

Frequency of state ratio studies: *Not required*

Are state ratio studies accessible to the public: *No*

State agency information and contact person:

State of California
State Board of Equalization
Property Tax Department
P.O. Box 942879 (450 N Street)
Sacramento, Ca 94279-0001
Mr. John W. Hagerty, Deputy Director
Telephone: (916) 445-1516 • Fax: (916) 323-8765

COLORADO

Name of real property tax: *General Property Tax*

Official valuation standard: *Valuations for assessment based on actual value of the property in accordance with state statutes.*

Annual assessment of real property: *No*

Reassessment cycle: *Every two years*

Assessment date: *January 1*

Classification of property:

Class I	Vacant land
Class II	Residential
Class III	Commercial
Class IV	Industrial
Class V	Agricultural

Assessment rate:

Class I	29% of actual value
Class II	15% of actual value
Class III	29% of actual value
Class IV	29% of actual value
Class V	29% of actual value

Tax relief available to homeowners:

Senior Citizen Property Tax Rebate Program

Up to $500 rebate if:

1. Either husband or wife is 65 years old or older, or if applicant is a surviving spouse, the applicant must be 58 years old.

2. Applicant has paid property tax on his personal residence.

3. Applicant resided in Colorado during the entire taxable year claimed.

4. Applicant is not claimed as a dependent on any other person's federal income tax return.

5. Applicant must meet the following income limitations:

If single—your total income for the taxable year did not exceed $7,500.

If married—your total combined income for the taxable year did not exceed $11,200.

Permanent & Total Disability Regardless of Age:

Up to $500 rebate if:

1. Applicant was disabled (regardless of age) for the entire taxable year claimed.

2. Applicant received full disability payments from a bona fide public or private plan based solely on such disability. Examples of public plans would be Social Security or Veterans Administration.

3. Applicant must submit a statement from the agency or source providing the applicant's disability benefits.

Exemptions:

- Government property
- Religious property
- Charitable property
- Educational property
- Household personal property
- Agricultural products and livestock
- Computer software
- Cemeteries

Appeal procedure:

Step 1   Immediately after receiving notice of valuation, schedule an informal meeting with the local tax assessor and try to resolve the problem. If after the meeting you are not satisfied with the decision, go to step 2.

Step 2   As soon as possible after receipt of notice of valuation, and after an unsuccessful decision from the tax assessor, file a written notice of appeal with the County Board of Equalization.

Step 3   If after presenting all of your evidence before the County Board of Equalization you are not satisfied with their decision, you may appeal to either the State Board of Assessments, the District Court, or go to binding arbitration. If you elect binding arbitration, this will be the final step.

Step 4   If after presenting all of your evidence before the District Court or State Board of Assessment you are not satisfied, you may appeal to the Court of Appeals.

Step 5   If after presenting all of your evidence before the Court of Appeals you are still not satisfied, you may appeal to the Colorado Supreme Court.

You must pay the current property tax (under protest) the state alleges you owe or the courts will not hear your case.

Appeal calendar:

1. May 1: The assessor mails a notice of any change in valuation to real property owners along with a protest form. The assessor also gives public notice to all taxpayers concerning their right to protest the value placed on their property.

2. Last working day in June: Decisions are issued by the local assessor.

3. July 1: First day of hearings by the County Board of Equalization.

4. July 15: Last day to file an appeal with the County Board of Equalization.

5. August 10: Last day for County Board of Equalization to render decisions.

6. Within 30 days of the decision of the County Board of Equalization, a taxpayer may file an appeal with either the State

Board of Assessment Appeal, District Court, or request binding arbitration.

7. A taxpayer may file an appeal with the Court of Appeals within 45 days after the Board of Assessment Appeal or District Court renders its decision.

8. The Court of Appeals hears appeals when the calendar permits.

9. Lastly, a taxpayer may file an appeal with the Colorado Supreme Court if he/she is unhappy with the decision of the Court of Appeals.

Level of government responsible for assessment:
County

Tax assessors:

*   Elected for a four year term.

*   High school education is not required.

*   Special education or certificate is not required.

State issued assessor's manual: *Assessor's Reference Manual (volumes 1-5)*

Equalization: *Yes*

Property tax maps mandatory: *Yes*

Allow real property to be assessed at financially better use rather than current use: *No*

Frequency of state ratio studies: *Yearly*

Are state ratio studies accessible to the public: *Yes*

State agency information and contact person:

Colorado Department of Local Affairs
Division of Property Taxation
1313 Sherman Street, Room 419
Denver, Co 80203
Mr. Paul N. Brown
Telephone: (303) 866-2371 • Fax: (303) 866-4000

CONNECTICUT

Name of real property tax: *Property Tax*

Official valuation standard: *"The general statutes provide that the present true and actual value of property must be deemed by all assessors and Board of Tax Review to be its fair market value and not its value at a forced or auction sale."*

Annual assessment of real property: *No*

Reassessment cycle: *Every ten years*

Assessment date: *October 1*

Classification of property:

Class I	Real Property
Class II	Personal Property
Class III	Motor Vehicles

Assessment rate:

Residential property assessed at 70% of market value.

Class I	70% of market value
Class II	70% of market value
Class III	70% of market value

Tax Relief:

State-Mandated Relief Programs

1. Elderly/Disabled Homeowner Program

    A. Eligibility: *Homeowners, over age 65* (or surviving spouses over 50) and the *disabled of any age* (all of whom must have been *state residents for at least one year*), are eligible. Certain residents of continuing care communities are also eligible.

    B. Income:
        *   Married taxpayers with an *income less than $25,400.*
        *   Single/widowed taxpayer with an *income less than $20,700.*

C. Description: Those meeting the eligibility requirements receive
a *credit of up to 50 percent of their residential property tax*, but
no more than a *maximum credit of $1,250*. The percentage
reduction and maximum/minimum credits are based on income.
For 1994-95 (the income brackets are adjusted each year for
inflation), the credits are shown in figure below.

D. Statutory reference: Connecticut General Statutes section 12-
170(aa) through 12-170(cc)

CONNECTICUT
PROPERTY TAX

Income Limitations for Participation in the Elderly Homeowners,
Renters, and Persons with Disabilities Program

Income	Cut by:	Minimum	Maximum
MARRIED HOMEOWNERS			
$ 0 - 10,300	50%	$400	$1,250
10,300 - 14,000	40%	300	1,000
14,000 - 17,300	30%	200	750
17,300 - 20,700	20%	100	500
20,700 - 25,400	10%	100	250
UNMARRIED HOMEOWNERS			
$ 0 - 10,300	40%	$300	$1,000
10,300 - 14,000	30%	200	750
14,000 - 17,300	20%	100	500
17,300 - 20,700	10%	100	250
MARRIED RENTERS*			
$ 0 - 10,300		$400	$900
10,300 - 14,000		300	700
14,000 - 17,300		200	500
17,300 - 20,700		100	250
20,700 - 25,400		50	150
UNMARRIED RENTERS*			
$ 0 - 10,300		$ 300	$700
10,300 - 14,000		200	500
14,000 - 17,300		100	250
17,300 - 20,700		50	150

** Special note: Upon proper application filed with local assessors, the State sends
tax-relief grants directly to the eligible renters. Municipalities must certify the
eligibility of homeowners and renters.*

*In 1992-93, the State paid $17,967,067 to 40,955 eligible homeowners and
$11,034,119 to 26,799 eligible renters.*

2. Veteran's Exemption Program

   A. Eligibility: *All honorably-discharged veterans who served in wartime* are eligible for the basic exemption. The *benefits are doubled if the veteran is below certain income levels*. There is a complicated set of additional exemptions based on the severity of disabilities. Special provisions apply to unremarried surviving spouses of veterans.

   B. Income: *No threshold is set for the basic exemption*. The *basic exemption is doubled* for *married* veterans with an *income less than $25,400* and *single/widowed* veterans with an *income less than $20,700*.

   C. Description: The basic exemption is $1,500 for all veterans. The basic exemption is doubled ($3,000) for low income veterans. Additional exemptions are added for disabilities—*the exemption can go as high as $30,000 for severely-disabled, low income veterans*.

   D. Statutory reference: CGS Sect. 12-62g; 12-81 [Numerous subsections]; 12-81g; 12-90(a).

3. Disability Exemption Program

   A. Eligibility: All *totally disabled (non-service connected) homeowners* are eligible.

   B. Income: *No income requirement*.

   C. Description: All disabled homeowners get a *$1,000 exemption*.

   D. In 1993-94, 11,036 eligible applicants received this aid. *The average benefit was $36*.

   E. Statutory reference: CGS Sect. 12-81 (55); 12-94; 12-94a.

4. Blind Exemption

   A. Eligibility: All *legally-blind homeowners* are eligible.

   B. Income: *No income requirement*.

   C. Description: All blind homeowners get a *$3,000 exemption*.

   D. Statutory reference: CGS Sect. 12-81 (17)

Local-Option Credit/Deferral/Exemption Programs

1. The tax-credit option for the elderly and disabled

Eligibility: *Homeowner, over age 65* (or surviving spouses over age 60) and the *disabled of any age* (all of whom have been *state residents for at least one year*), are eligible.

Income: *Municipalities are permitted to establish any income limit.* However, because the *total of the tax credits cannot exceed 10 percent of the grand levy on real property* and the *state does not reimburse municipalities* for the lost revenue, cities and towns have to set the income thresholds relatively low and/or keep the credit amounts relatively low to keep the taxes on every other taxpayer from rising too much.

Description: The credits can be generous, going *as high as 75 percent of total taxes owed.*

Statutory reference: CGS Section 12-129(n)

2. The tax-deferral option for the elderly and disabled

Exemptions:

Eligibility: *Homeowner, over age 65* (or surviving spouses over age 60) and the *disabled of any age* (all of whom have been *state residents for at least one year*), are eligible.

Income: *Municipalities are permitted to establish any income limit.* However, because the *total of the tax credits cannot exceed 10 percent of the grand levy on real property* and the *state does not reimburse municipalities* for the lost revenue, cities and towns have to set the income thresholds relatively low and/or keep the credit amounts relatively low to keep the taxes on every other taxpayer from rising too much.

Description: *Up to 100 percent of the property tax can be deferred.* A lien is filed against the property. Upon the sale of the property or the death of the taxpayer, the deferred tax (plus accrued interest) is paid out of the proceeds of the sale or out of the estate of the deceased taxpayer.

Statutory reference: CGS Section 12-129(n)

3. The Tax-Deferral Option For The Poor

Eligibility: Those who are "poor and unable to pay" or if "such property taxes exceeds *eight percent* or more of the total income from any source,...of such owner or owners,..."

Income: Municipalities determine the income limitations, if any.

Description: *Up to 100 percent of the property tax, or the interest on delinquent taxes, or both can be deferred.* A lien is filed against the property. Upon the sale of the property or the death of the taxpayer, the deferred tax (plus accrued interest) is paid out of the proceeds of the sale or out of the estate of the deceased taxpayer.

Statutory reference: CGS Section 12-124 and 12-124(a)

Exemptions:

- Government property
- Religious property
- Charitable property
- Educational property
- Hospitals
- Inventories
- Cemeteries

Appeal procedure:

Step 1   Immediately after receiving notice of assessment, schedule an informal meeting with the local tax assessor and try to resolve the problem. If after the meeting you are not satisfied with the decision, go to step 2.

Step 2   Before the last business day in February, file a written notice of appeal with the Board of Tax in your municipality.

Step 3   Within two months after receiving an unfavorable decision by the Board of Tax, you may appeal to the Connecticut Appeals Board.

Step 4   Within two months after receiving an unfavorable decision by the Connecticut Appeals Board, you may appeal to the Superior Court.

Step 5   If after presenting your evidence before the Superior Court you are still dissatisfied, you may appeal to the State Court of Appeals.

Step 6   After an unfavorable decision by the State Court of Appeals, you may appeal to the State Supreme Court.

> *You must exhaust each of the administrative appeals in proper sequence before asking for a judicial review. You must pay the current property tax (under protest) the state alleges you owe or the courts will not hear your case.*

Appeal calendar:

1. After receiving the notice of assessment, the taxpayer may have an informal meeting with the assessor between October 1 and January 31.

2. A taxpayer may appeal to the Board of Tax between January 21 and the last business day in February.

3. If the taxpayer receives an unfavorable decision from the Board of Tax, he/she may within 60 days of that decision file an appeal with the Connecticut Appeals Board.

4. If the taxpayer receives an unfavorable decision from the Connecticut Appeals Board and he/she chooses to continue the protest, an appeal may be filed with the Superior Court within 60 days after receiving the decision of the Connecticut Appeals Board.

5. State Court of Appeals

6. State Supreme Court

Level of government responsible for assessment:
Municipality

Tax assessors:

- 13 elected, 156 appointed

- Elected for 2 years; Appointment set by town charter

- High school education is not required.

- State certificate is required.

State issued assessor's manuals: *Statutes pertaining to the assessment & collection of local property taxes, Handbook for Connecticut Assessors*

Equalization: *No*

Property tax maps mandatory: *Yes*

Allow real property to be assessed at financially better use rather than current use:

1. Vacant land valued at highest and best use.

2. All other property valued at current use.

Frequency of state ratio studies: *Yearly*

Are state ratio studies accessible to the public: *Yes*

State agency information and contact person:

State of Connecticut
Office Of Policy and Management
Intergovernmental Policy
80 Washington Street
Hartford, Connecticut 06106
Ms. Marsha L. Standish, Municipal Assessment Advisor
Tel: (203) 566-8171 • Fax: (203) 566-3456

NOTES

DELAWARE

In Delaware, the state plays almost no role in levying property tax. Property tax assessment is the sole responsibility of County Government. The state imposes no requirements for periodic assessments, standardization of assessment practices, or valuation standards beyond the vague requirement that property be assessed at "true market value."

Name of real property tax: *Property Tax*

Official valuation standard: *True value in money (not interpreted by state statute).*

Annual assessment of real property: *Not required by state statute.*

Reassessment cycle: *Not required by state statute.*

Assessment date: *Varies by county/city*

Classification of property: Varies by county/city

Assessment rate: Varies by county/city

Tax relief available to homeowners:

- Senior citizens or disabled programs. The terms vary by county/city.

Exemptions:

- Personalty
- Government property
- Religious property
- Charitable property
- Educational property
- Forest/orchards

Appeal procedure:

Step 1 Immediately after receiving notice of assessment, have an informal meeting with the local tax assessor and try to resolve the problem. If after the meeting you are not satisfied with the decision, go to step 2.

Step 2   Depending on specific rules of the city/county,and after an unsuccessful informal meeting with the tax assessor, file a written notice of appeal with the County Board of Assessment.

Step 3   After receiving an unfavorable decision from the County Board of Assessment, you may appeal to the Superior Court in the county where the property is located.

Step 4   After receiving an unfavorable decision from the Superior Court, you may appeal to the State Court of Appeals.

Step 5   After receiving an unfavorable decision from the State Court of Appeals, you may appeal to the State Supreme Court.

You must exhaust all administrative appeals before asking for judicial reviews. You must pay the current property tax (under protest) the state alleges you owe or the courts will not hear your case.

Appeal calendar:

Appeal dates to protest county or municipal assessments vary. Contact the assessor in your county/city to obtain specific information regarding required filing dates.

Level of government responsible for assessment:
County/City

Tax assessors:

- Method of selection varies by county/city.

- High school education is required.

- Special education or certificate is not required but recommended.

State issued assessor's manuals: *No*

Equalization: *No*

Property tax maps mandatory: *No*

Allow real property to be assessed at financially better use rather than current use: *Yes*

Frequency of state ratio studies: *None*

Are state ratio studies accessible to the public: *No*

State agency information and contact person:

State of Delaware
Department of Finance
Division of Revenue
Carvel State Building
620 N. French Street
P.O. Box 8911
Wilmington, Delaware 19899-8911
David J. Blowman, Tax Policy Analyst
Telephone: (302) 577-3782• Fax: (302) 677-3689

NOTES

DISTRICT OF COLUMBIA

Name of real property tax: *Property Tax*

Official valuation standard:

> *"Estimated market value is the most probable price a willing buyer will pay a willing seller for a property on the open market. This means that neither the buyer nor the seller is forced to buy or sell the property; that no familial or other special relationship exists between them; and no unusual circumstances, such as divorce, affect the transaction."*

Annual assessment of real property: *Yes*

Reassessment cycle: *Yes - one year*

Assessment date: *January 1*

Classification of property:

Class I	Owner-Occupied Residential Properties
Class II	Multi-Family Residential
Class III	Hotels & Motels
Class IV	Commercial
Class V	Unimproved Properties & Mixed Use

Assessment rate:

Residential property is assessed at 100% of estimated market value.

Class I	100% of estimated market value
Class II	100% of estimated market value
Class III	100% of estimated market value
Class IV	100% of estimated market value

Tax relief available to homeowners:

Homestead Deduction

The program deducts, for tax purposes, an amount ($30,000 for tax year

1994) from the assessed value of the property you own and in which you live. Qualifying homeowners do not have to pay tax on $30,000 of assessed value of their real property for tax year 1994.

Cooperative Housing Association Homestead Deduction

For residential cooperatives to receive the homestead deduction, one or more of the units must be owner-occupied. If 50% or more of the units are owner-occupied, the cooperative will be placed in Class I. Otherwise, the property will be placed in Class II.

Senior Citizen Real Property Tax Relief

This program can reduce a senior citizen's property tax by one-half, if he/she can meet all of the following requirements:

1. You must have been 65 years of age or older by October 1, 1993 to qualify for the entire 1994 real property tax year, or by April 1,1994 to qualify for the second half of the 1994 real property tax year;

2. You must own and live in your property, and receive the homestead deduction;

3. The total adjusted gross income of all the people living in the property, excluding tenants, must be less than $100,000 for the previous calendar year; and

4. You or any other senior citizen owner-occupant must own 50% or more of the property.

Cooperative Housing Association
Senior Citizen Real Property Tax Relief

If you own a unit in a cooperative building that is taxed at the Class I rate, you may qualify for senior citizen homestead tax relief. Each qualified owner will receive a 50% refund of his/her proportionate share of the real property tax.

Property Tax Deferral

If you have lived in a Class I property for a year or more, have received the homestead deduction, and your tax has increased more than 10% from the previous year, you may defer payment on the amount over 10% through the property tax deferral program.

To be eligible for the property tax deferral program, you must file an application for tax deferral and meet all of the following conditions:

1. You must have owned your home for at least one year prior to the date of the application.

2. You must have occupied the property for the twelve-month period immediately preceding the date of the application.

3. You must currently occupy the property.

4. The tax for the current year must be more than 10% higher than the tax for the previous year.

5. The total of all taxes deferred, plus an annual interest rate of 8% accrued on the deferrals, must not exceed 25% of the property's assessed value for the tax year for which the deferral is requested.

Individual Income Property Tax Credit

This program gives a credit against your D.C. income tax or a rebate of up to $750 for eligible homeowners and renters. To be eligible for this program the total income of your household must be $20,000 or less.

Lower Income Home-Ownership Tax Abatement

This program helps first-time homeowners, including non-profit organizations and shared equity investors. It can abate or cancel taxes up to five years and exempt you from paying recordation and transfer taxes. The five-year period begins October 1 following the recordation of your deed. To qualify, you must meet all of the following conditions:

1. Be a first-time homeowner in the District of Columbia and occupy the property;

2. Have a certain income level; and

3. Submit an application for lower income/shared equity home-ownership exemption and a claim for exemption from real property recordation and transfer tax (fp-5) when your deed is recorded.

Exemptions:

*   Government property
*   Religious property
*   Charitable property
*   Educational property
*   Hospitals

- Museums
- Art galleries
- Cemeteries

Appeal procedure:

Step 1   Immediately after receiving notice of assessment, have an informal meeting with the local tax assessor and try to resolve the problem. If after the meeting you are not satisfied with the decision, go to step 2.

Step 2   File a written appeal with the Board of Real Property Assessment and Appeal (BRPAA). Your real property assessment form must be submitted on or before April 30th.

Step 3   If you do not agree with BRPAA's decision you may appeal to the D.C. Superior Court. To appeal you must:
- pay all taxes due;
- file a petition with the tax division of the D.C. Superior Court.

Appeal calendar:

1. January 1: assessment day

2. March 1: notice for proposed assessment for real property mailed to taxpayers.

3. March 1: filing period for appeal to the Board of Real Property Assessments and Appeals (BRPAA) begins.

4. April 30: filing deadline for real property assessment appeals.

5. July 7: conclusion of all appeals heard by BRPAA.

6. October 15: deadline for filing appeals with the Superior Court for assessments.

7. November 1: deadline for requesting review of reclassification of real property.

Level of government responsible for assessment: Municipal

Tax assessors:

- Civil service appointment.

- High school education is required.

- Special education or certificate is not required.

State issued assessor's manual: *Real Property Assessment Manual* published and compiled by District of Columbia

Equalization: *No*

Property tax maps mandatory: *Yes*

Allow real property to be assessed at financially better use rather than current use: *No, current use*

Frequency of state ratio studies: *Yearly*

Are state ratio studies accessible to the public: *Yes*

State agency information and contact person:

District of Columbia
Office of Economic & Tax Policy
Real Property Tax Administration
One Judiciary Square
441 4th Street N.W. Room# 400
Washington, D.C. 20001
Ms. Julia Friedman
Telephone: (202) 727-6027 • Fax: (202) 727-9069
or
Mr. David B. Jackson
Chief, Real Property Assessment Division
441 4th Street N.W. Suite# 450
Washington, D.C. 20001
Telephone: (202) 727-0867 • Fax: (202) 727-4001

NOTES

FLORIDA

Name of real property tax: *Ad Valorem Tax*

Official valuation standard:

> *Just value "means the price at which a property, if offered for sale in the open market, with a reasonable time for the seller to find a purchaser, would transfer for cash or its equivalent, under prevailing market conditions between parties who have knowledge of the use to which the property may be put, both seeking to maximize their gains and neither being in a position to take advantage of the exigencies of the other."*

Annual assessment of real property: *Yes*

Reassessment cycle: *Yes, one year*

Assessment date: *January 1*

Classification of property:

Class I	Residential
Class II	Commercial and Industrial
Class III	Agricultural
Class IV	Exempt, wholly or partially
Class V	Leasehold Interest (government-owned)
Class VI	Other
Class VII	Centrally Assessed
Class VIII	Non-Agricultural Acreage

Assessment rate:

Class I	100% of just value
Class II	100% of just value
Class III	100% of just value
Class VI	100% of just value
Class VII	100% of just value

Class VIII   100% of just value

Tax relief available to homeowners:

1. $25,000 Homestead Exemption: Every person who has legal or equitable title to real property in the state of Florida and who resides thereon and in good faith makes it his or her permanent home is eligible.

2. $500 Widow's Exemption: Any widow who is a permanent Florida resident may claim this exemption.

3. $500 Widower's Exemption: Any widower who is a permanent Florida resident may claim this exemption.

4. $500 Disability Exemption: Every Florida resident who is totally and permanently disabled qualifies for this exemption.

5. $500 Exemption For Blind Persons: Every Florida resident who is blind qualifies for this exemption.

6. Service-connected total and permanent disability exemption: Any honorably discharged veteran with service-connected total and permanent disabilities is entitled to exemption on real estate used and owned as a homestead less any portion thereof used for commercial purposes.

7. Exemption for totally and permanently disabled persons:

    A. Any real estate used and owned as a homestead less any portion thereof used for commercial purposes by any quadriplegic shall be exempt from taxation.

    B. Any real estate used and owned as a homestead less any portion thereof used for commercial purposes by a paraplegic, hemiplegic or other totally and permanently disabled person, as defined in section 196.012(10). F.S., who must use a wheelchair for mobility or who is legally blind, shall be exempt from taxation.

        • Persons entitled to the exemption under number two (2) above, must be a permanent resident of the State of Florida as of January 1st of the year of assessment. Also, the prior year gross income of all persons residing in or upon the homestead shall not exceed $14,500 adjusted annually by the percentage change of the average cost of living index issued by the United States Department of Labor. Gross income shall include Veterans Administration and any Social Security benefits paid to the persons.

Eligibility Criteria To Qualify for Property Tax Exemption

When to File:

Application for all exemptions must be made between January 1 and March 1 of the tax year. However, at the option of the property appraiser, original homestead exemption applications for the succeeding year may be accepted after March 1. Initial application should be made in person at the Property Appraiser's office. Subsequent yearly renewal of exemption status may be made by mail. Failure to make application by March 1 of the tax year shall constitute a waiver of the exemption privilege for that year.

$25,000 Homestead Exemption:

Every person who has legal or equitable title to real property in the State of Florida and who resides thereon and in good faith makes it his or her permanent home is eligible. First time applicants should have available evidence of ownership; i.e.,deed, contract, etc.

If title is held by the husband alone, a wife may file for him, with his consent, and vice versa.

If filing for the first time, be prepared to answer these and other questions:

1. In whose name or names was the title to the dwelling recorded as of January 1st?

2. What is the street address of the property?

3. Are you a legal resident of the State of Florida? (A Certificate of Domicile or Voter's Registration will be proof if dated prior to January 1st.)

4. Do you have a Florida license plate on your car and a Florida driver's license?

5. Were you living in the dwelling being claimed for homestead exemption on January 1st?

$500 Widow's Exemption:
Any widow who is a permanent Florida resident may claim this exemption. If the widow remarries, she is no longer eligible. If the husband and wife were divorced before his death, the woman is not considered a widow. You may be asked to produce a death certificate when filing for the first time.

$500 Widower's Exemption:
Any widower who is a permanent Florida resident may claim this exemption. If the widower remarries he is no longer eligible. If the husband and wife were divorced before her death, the man is not considered a widower. You may be asked to produce a death certificate when filing for the first time.

$500 Disability Exemption:
Every Florida resident who is totally and permanently disabled qualifies for this exemption. Furthermore, any serviceman disabled at least 10% in war or by service-connected misfortune is entitled to a $500 exemption.

If filing for the first time, please present at least one of the following as proof of your disability:

1. If totally and permanently disabled, a certificate from two professionally unrelated licensed Florida physicians or from the Veterans Administration.

2. If claiming at least 10% wartime or service-connected disability, a certificate from the United States Government.

$500 Exemption For Blind Persons:
Every Florida resident who is blind qualifies for this exemption. If claiming exemption based on blindness, a certificate from the Division of Blind Services of the Department of Education or the Federal Social Security Administration or the Veterans Administration certifying the applicant to be blind is required. "Blind person" is defined as an individual having central vision acuity 20/200 or less in the better eye with correcting glasses, or a disqualifying field defect in which the peripheral field has contracted to such an extent that the widest diameter or visual field subtends and angular distance is no greater than twenty degrees.

Eligibility Criteria To Qualify For Property Tax Exemption

Service-connected Total And Permanent Disability Exemption:
Any honorably discharged veteran with service-connected total and permanent disabilities is entitled to exemption on real estate used and owned as a homestead less any portion thereof used for commercial purposes.

Persons entitled to this exemption must have been a permanent resident of this state as of January 1st of the year of assessment.

Under certain circumstances the benefit of this exemption can carry over to the veteran's spouse in the event of his/her death. Consult your appraiser for details.

If filing for the first time, please bring proof of your service-connected disability, such as a letter from the U.S. Government, United States Veterans Administration.

Exemption for Totally And Permanently Disabled Persons:

1. Any real estate used and owned as a homestead less any portion thereof used for commercial purposes by any quadriplegic shall be exempt from taxation.

2. Any real estate used and owned as a homestead less any portion thereof used for commercial purposes by a paraplegic, hemiplegic or other totally and permanently disabled person, as defined in Section 196.012(10),F.S., who must use a wheelchair for mobility or who is legally blind, shall be exempt from taxation.

A person entitled to the exemption under number two above, must be a permanent resident of the State of Florida as of January 1st of the year of assessment. Also,the prior year gross income of all persons residing in or upon the homestead shall not exceed $14,500 adjusted annually by the percentage change of the average cost of living index issued by the United States Department of Labor. Gross income shall include Veterans Administration and any Social Security benefits paid to the persons. A statement of gross income must accompany the application.

If filing for the first time, please bring a certificate from two licensed doctors of this state or a letter from the Veterans Administration or an award letter from the Social Security Administration.

Exemptions:

- Government property
- Religious property
- Charitable property
- Educational property
- Homes for the aged
- Fraternal & benevolent organizations
- Cemeteries

Appeal procedure:

Step 1   Immediately after receiving the notice of proposed assessment, have an informal meeting with the local tax assessor and try to resolve the problem. If after the meeting you are not satisfied with the decision, go to step 2.

Step 2   Within 25 days of receipt of the notice of proposed assessment, and after an unsuccessful informal meeting with the tax assessor, file a written notice of appeal with the County Value Adjustment Board.

Step 3   After presenting your evidence before the County Value Adjustment Board and after receiving an unfavorable decision, you may appeal to the Circuit Court of Appeals.

Step 4   If after presenting your evidence before the Circuit Court of Appeals you are still not satisfied with the ruling, you may appeal to the Supreme Court of Florida.

> *You must exhaust all of your administrative appeals before asking for a judicial review. You must pay the current property tax the state alleges you owe (under protest) or the courts will not hear your case.*

Appeal calendar:

1. 25 days after receiving the notice of proposed assessment, the taxpayer mst file a written notice of appeal with the County Value Adjustment Board.

2. The County Value Adjustment Board will render its decision in writing within 20 calendar day of the last day the Board is in session.

3. An appeal must be filed at the Circuit Court within 60 days after the final meeting of the County Value Adjustment Board.

Level of government responsible for assessment: *County*

Tax assessors:

- Elected for a four year term.

- High school education is required.

- Certificate is required.

State issued assessor's manual: *Florida Manual of Instruction For Ad Valorem Tax Administration*

Equalization: *Yes*

Property tax maps mandatory: *Yes*

Allow real property to be assessed at financially better use rather than current use: *No*

Frequency of state ratio studies: *Yearly*

Are state ratio studies accessible to the public: *Yes*

State agency information and contact person:

State of Florida
Department of Revenue
Division of Ad Valorem Tax
P.O. Box 3000
Tallahassee, Florida 3315-3000
Mr. John R. Everton
Fax: (904) 488-9482 • Telephone: (904) 488-9483

NOTES

GEORGIA

Name of real property tax: *Ad Valorem Taxation of Property*

Official valuation standard: *Fair market value is interpreted as "the amount a knowledgeable buyer would pay for the property and a willing seller would accept for the property at an arm's length, bona fide sale."*

Annual assessment of real property: *Yes*

Reassessment cycle: *Yearly*

Assessment date: *January 1*

Classification of property:

Class I	Residential (including residential transitional and historic)
Class II	Agricultural (including preferential, conservation use and environmentally sensitive)
Class III	Commercial
Class IV	Industrial
Class V	Utility

Assessment rate:

Residential property assessed at 40% of fair market value.

Class I	40% of fair market value
Class II	40% of fair market value
Class III	40% of fair market value
Class IV	40% of fair market value
Class V	40% of fair market value

Tax relief available to homeowners:

1. Each resident of Georgia is entitled to the regular homestead exemption of $2,000 on the property the resident owns and occupies as his or her permanent residence on January 1 of each year. The $2,000 is deducted from the 40% assessed value of the homestead property.

2. Homeowners 65 years of age or older with a net combined income (taxpayer and spouse) not exceeding $10,000 annually, are allowed an exemption of $4,000.

3. Homeowners 65 years of age and older with a gross combined income (taxpayer and spouse) of less than $10,000 annually are allowed a $4,000 exemption on the assessed value county and school property tax.

4. Certain disabled veterans are entitled to a homestead exemption of $38,000.

Homestead exemptions are allowed as indicated below:

GEORGIA HOMESTEAD EXEMPTIONS

Qualifications	County M&O	County Bond	School M&O	School Bond
Owner/occupied	$2,000	-0-	$2,000	-0-
Age 65, net income less than $10,000	4,000	4,000	4,000	4,000
Age 62, net income less than $10,000	2,000	-0-	10,000	-0-
Age 65, gross income less than $10,000	4,000	4,000	10,000	10,000
Disabled Veteran	38,000	38,000	38,000	38,000

Explanation of chart:

M&O = maintenance and operation

Dollar values represent exemption from assessed value

Example: A homeowner's residence has a fair market value of $100,000. The assessed value is determined by multiplying the fair market value ($100,000) by 40% yielding an assessed value of $40,000.

Exemptions:

* Government property
* Charity
* Non-profit homes for elderly
* Places of worship and burial

- All personal property used in home (if not held for sale or other commercial use)

- All tools and implements of trade of manual laborers

- Cemeteries

Appeal procedure:

Step 1   Immediately after receiving the notice of assessment, have an informal meeting with the local tax assessor and try to resolve the problem. If after the meeting you are not satisfied with the decision, go to step 2.

Step 2   After an unsuccessful informal meeting with the tax assessor, file an appeal with the County Board of Assessors within 45 days of the mailing or notice of assessment.

Step 3   If after presenting all of your evidence before the County Board of Assessors you are still not satisfied, you may appeal to the County Board of Equalization within 21 days of mailing of decision of the County Board of Assessors.

Step 4   The County Board of Equalization will set a date for a hearing within 15 days of receipt of the notice of appeal.

Step 5   The hearing will be held by Board of Equalization within 30 days of the date of notification to the taxpayer (appellant).

Step 6   Notice of decision of the County Board of Equalization shall be given to each party (taxpayer and County Board of Assessors) by sending a copy of the decision by registered or certified mail to the appellant (taxpayer) and by filing the original copy of the decision with the County Board of Assessors.

Step 7   Within 30 days from the date on which the decision of the County Board of Equalization is mailed, the taxpayer may appeal to the Superior Court of the county in which the property lies.

Step 8   Each hearing, before the court sitting without a jury, shall be held within 40 days following the date on which the appeal is filed with the clerk of the Superior Court.

Step 9   Court of Appeals

Step 10   State Supreme Court

You must exhaust all of the administrative appeals prior to asking for a judicial review. You must pay the current property tax (under protest) the state alleges you owe or the courts will not hear your case.

Level of government responsible for assessment:
County

Tax assessors:

- Appointed for six year term by county governing authority.

- No minimum education is required.

- State certification is required.

State issued assessor's manuals: No state issued manual used by assessors.

Equalization: *No*

Property tax maps mandatory: *No*

Allow real property to be assessed at financially better use rather than current use: *Yes*

Frequency of state ratio studies: *Yearly*

Are state ratio studies accessible to the public: *Yes*

State agency information and contact person:

State of Georgia
Department of Revenue
405 Trinity-Washington Building
Atlanta, Georgia 30334
Sha P. Hester, Revenue Section Supervisor
Telephone: (404) 656-4108 • Fax: (404) 651-8689

HAWAII

Hawaii's four counties have full control over their property tax system since voters approved a constitutional amendment transferring the responsibility for property valuation, exemptions, and tax collections from the state to the counties.

Name of real property tax: *Real Property Taxation*

Official valuation standard: *Fair market value (not defined by state statute) the price most people will pay for your property, is the standard used to measure equity in assessments.*

Annual assessment of real property: *No*

Reassessment cycle: *Not defined by state statute*

Assessment date: *January 1*

Classification of property:

Class I   All properties owned by public utilities and used in the business of such utilities.

Class II   All properties not otherwise classified.

Class III All agricultural, forest, residential property, and historical buildings and sites.

Assessment rate:

Residential property assessed at 100% of fair market value. Each county determines its own level.

- See figure A

Tax relief available to homeowners:

- Homeowner Exemptions - Principal residence as of January 1, $40,000.00 exemption from total assessed value.

- Senior Citizen Multiple Home Exemption:

- 55 - 59 years of age: $ 60,000.00 exemption

- 60 - 64 Years of age: $ 80,000.00 exemption

- 65 - 69 Years of age: $100,000.00 exemption

- 70 Years or older: $120,000.00 exemption

- Totally disabled veterans due to injuries received while on active duty with U.S. Armed Forces are totally exempt from all property taxes except for $100.00 (minimum tax).

- Hansen Disease Victims: $25,000.00 maximum exemption

- Blind, deaf, and totally disabled: $25,000.00 maximum exemption

Exemptions:

- Personal property
- Government property
- Religious property
- Charitable property
- Educational property
- Historical property
- Residential property (partially exempt)
- Utility property
- Cemeteries
- Hospitals

Appeal procedure:

Step 1   Immediately after receiving notice of assessment, schedule an informal meeting with the local tax assessor and try to resolve the problem. If after the meeting you are not satisfied with the decision, go to step 2.

Step 2   Before the deadline of April 9th, and after an unsuccessful informal meeting with the tax assessor, file a written notice with the Board of Review.

Step 3   If after presenting all of your evidence before the Board of Review you are still not satisfied, you may appeal to the Tax Appeal Court. This should be done 30 days after decision by Board of Review or by April 9th.

Step 4 You can go before the small claim procedure of Tax Appeal Court if the amount of tax in dispute is less than $1,000.00.

Step 5 Supreme Court - Within thirty days after decision of Tax Appeal Court (if you use small claims procedure you waive your right to appeal to the Supreme Court), you may make a written appeal to the Supreme Court of Hawaii.

You must exhaust all of the administrative appeals prior to asking for a judicial review. The appeals must be made in proper sequence. You must pay the current property tax (under protest) the state alleges you owe or the courts will not hear your case.

Appeal calendar:

1. March 15: Assessment notices mailed.

2. April 9: Deadline for assessment appeals to either the Board of Review or the Tax Appeal Court.

Level of government responsible for assessment:
County

Tax assessors:

• Appointed for an indefinite time.

• College degree is required.

• No certificate program.

State issued assessor's manuals: *No*

Equalization: *No*

Property tax maps mandatory: *Property maps provided by county assessor.*

Allow real property to be assessed at financially better use rather than current use: *Yes, assessed at highest and best use.*

Frequency of state ratio studies: *Not performed by state, but by county.*

Are state ratio studies accessible to the public: *Yes*

REAL PROPERTY TAX RATES IN HAWAII
Fiscal Year July 1, 1993 to June 30, 1994

	Class	Tax Rate Per $1,000 Net Taxable Building	Tax Rate Per $1,000 Net Taxable Land
	HONOLULU		
A 1	Improved Residential	$3.92	$3.12
B 8	Unimproved Residential	3.92	3.92
C 2	Apartment	3.52	3.52
D 7	Hotel and Resort	9.64	9.64
E 3	Commercial	8.51	8.51
F 4	Industrial	8.51	8.51
G 5	Agricultural	9.00	9.00
H 6	Conservation	9.00	9.00
	MAUI		
A 1	Improved Residential	$4.75	$4.75
B 8	Unimproved Residential	4.75	4.75
C 2	Apartment	4.75	4.75
D 3	Commercial	6.50	6.50
E 4	Industrial	6.50	6.50
F 5	Agricultural	4.75	4.75
G 6	Conservation	4.75	4.75
H 7	Hotel and Resort	8.00	8.00
I 9	Homeowner	3.50	3.50
	HAWAII		
A 1	Improved Residential	$8.50	$8.50
B 2	Apartment	8.50	10.00
C 3	Commercial	8.50	10.00
D 4	Industrial	8.50	10.00
E 5	Agricultural	8.50	10.00
F 6	Conservation	8.50	10.00
G 7	Hotel and Resort	8.50	10.00
H 8	Unimproved Residential	8.50	10.00
I 9	Homeowner	4.45	4.45
	KAUAI		
A 1	Single Family Residential	$3.94	$4.93
B 2	Apartment	7.59	7.99
C 7	Hotel and Resort	7.59	7.99
D 3	Commercial	7.59	7.99
E 4	Industrial	7.59	7.99
F 5	Agricultural	3.94	7.39
G 6	Conservation	3.94	7.89
H 8	Homestead	3.18	4.04

Administration/Technical Branch
Real Property Assessment Division
Department of Finance
City and County of Honolulu
July 1, 1993

State agency information and contact person:

There is no state agency. Write to county officials.

Hawaii County
Mr. Gary M. Kiyota
Real Property Tax Administrator
Department of Finance - Real Property Tax
865 Piilani Street
Hilo, Hawaii 96720
Tel: (808) 961-8354, Fax: (808)961-8415

Honolulu County
Mr. Raymond T. Higa, Administrator
Real Property Assessment Division
Department of Finance
City and County of Honolulu
842 Bethel Street, 2nd Floor
Honolulu, Hawaii 96813

Kauai County
Real Property Assessment Division
Department of Finance - Real Property Tax
4396 Rice Street
Lihue, Hawaii 96766

Maui County
Real Property Assessment Division
Department of Finance - Real Property Tax
200 South High Street
Wailuku, Hawaii 96793

NOTES

IDAHO

Name of real property tax: *Ad Valorem Tax*

Official valuation standard: *Idaho Code 63-202 states:*

> *"An open market value concept is that amount of United States money or its equivalent that in all probability a property would exchange hands between a willing seller under no compulsion to sell, and an informed capable buyer; a reasonable time being allowed to consummate the sale and substantiated by a reasonable down payment or full cash payment."*

Annual assessment of real property: Yes

Reassessment cycle: Every 5 years as defined by state statute.

Assessment date: January 1

Classification of property:

Class I	All properties owned by public utilities and used in the business of such utilities.
Class II	All properties not otherwise classified.
Class III	All agricultural, forest, residential property, and historical buildings and sites.

Assessment rate

Residential property assessed at 100% of current full market value.

Class I	Real and Personal Property 100%
Class III	Operating Property 100%

Tax relief available to homeowners:

Homestead Exemption: Idaho Code 63-105d gives every owner-occupied residence a 50% or $50,000.00 exemption, whichever is less, if the residence is owned and owner-occupied on or before January 1 of the year in which application is being made. Application must be filed with the assessor's office between January 1, and April 15. You need not re-apply each year if you received the exemption the previous year and still live in the same house.

Circuit Breaker Program: The Circuit Breaker Program reduces property tax for qualified applicants. The amount of reduction is based on total household income for the previous calendar year. If you qualify, the property taxes on your home and up to one acre of land may be reduced by as much as $800. To qualify for the Circuit Breaker Property tax reduction you must meet the following requirements:

1. You owned and lived in a house or mobile home in Idaho that was your primary residence (you may qualify if you lived in a care facility or nursing home).

2. Your total household income for 1993 was $16,990 or less after deducting:

    A. Expenses that were not reimbursed by medicare or other insurance

    B. Business and farm losses

    C. Capital gains

    D. You were in one or more of the following categories:
        - Over 65 years of age
        - Motherless or fatherless child under 18
        - Widow or widower
        - Veterans with at least 10% service-connected disability
        - Former prisoners of war/hostages
        - Disabled veterans
        - Other qualified disabled persons with a limited income

Exemptions:

- Government property
- Religious property
- Charitable property
- Educational property
- Hospitals

Appeal procedure:

Step 1   Immediately after receiving notice of assessment, have an informal meeting with the local tax assessor and try to resolve the problem. If after the meeting you are not satisfied with the decision, go to step 2.

Step 2   After an unsuccessful informal meeting with the tax assessor, make a written request for a hearing before the County Board of Equalization.

Step 3   If after presenting all of your evidence before the County Board of Equalization you are still dissatisfied you may request a hearing before the State Board of Tax Appeal.

Step 4   If after presenting all of your evidence before the State Board of Appeals you are still unhappy, you may appeal to the District Court in the county where the property is located.

Step 5   If after presenting your evidence to the District Court you are still not satisfied, you may request a hearing before the Supreme Court.

> *You must exhaust all administrative appeals prior to requesting a judicial review. You must also pay the current property tax (under protest) the state alleges you owe or the courts will not hear your case.*

Appeal calendar:

1.   May to June 15, the assessor mails assessment notices which state the value of the property in the opinion of the assessor.

2.   The County Board of Equalization begins two week session on the fourth Monday in June to hear value appeal.

3.   The second Monday of July is the last day to file appeals with the Board of Equalization.

4.   During October and November, the treasurer mails the current year's property tax bill.

5. On the fourth Monday of November, the Board of Equalization begins a one week session to hear appeals to subsequent tax roll.

6. The first Monday of December is the last day to file appeal with the Board of Equalization.

Level of government responsible for assessment: *County*

Tax assessors:

- Elected for a four year term.

- No education requirement.

- Special education or certificate is not required.

State issued assessor's manuals: *Idaho State Tax Commission Rules, Idaho State Tax Assessors Manual.*

Equalization: *Yes*

Property tax maps mandatory: *Yes*

Allow real property to be assessed at financially better use rather than current use: *No - current use (actual & functional)*

Frequency of state ratio studies: *Yearly*

Are state ratio studies accessible to the public: *Yes*

State agency information and contact person:

Idaho State Tax Commission
Ad Valorem Tax Division
800 Park Plaza IV
Boise, Idaho 83722
Mr. Alan S. Dornfest, Tax Policy Specialist - Ad Valorem
Telephone: (208) 334-7530 • Fax: (208) 334-7844

ILLINOIS

Name of real property tax: *Property Tax*

Official valuation standard: *Property must be appraised at fair cash value as required by statute.*

Annual assessment of real property: *Yes*

Reassessment cycle: *All counties reassess every four years except Cook County, which reassesses every three years.*

Assessment date: *January 1*

Classification of property for all counties except Cook County:

Class I   Residential assessed at 33% of fair cash value

Class II   Farm assessed at 33% of fair cash value

Class III   Commercial assessed at 33% of fair cash value

Class IV   Industrial assessed at 33% of fair cash value

Class V   Railroad assessed at 33% of fair cash value

Class VI   Mineral assessed at 33% of fair cash value

Cook County Classifications:

Class I   Agricultural & Residential (less than 7 units): 16%

Class II   Unimproved Real Estate: 22%

Class III   Residential other than Class II: 33%

Class IV   Real Estate owned by non-profit corporations: 30%

Assessment rate:

33% of cash value for all classifications of property except in Cook County. Percentage assessment rates listed individually under classification of property section.

Tax relief available to homeowners:

The Homestead Exemption Limited
The Homestead Exemption Limited benefits homeowners of any age

and is given to owner-occupied residential property or to leased single family residential property when the lessee is responsible for the property tax. This exemption equals the increase in the equalized assessed value over the equalized assessed value of a property for 1977 to a limit of $3,500 ($4,500 in Cook County). County clerks deduct these homestead exemptions from each property's equalized valuation before computing tax rates. County assessors or supervisors of assessments identify which properties qualify for this exemption; some counties may require an application to aid in the identification of eligible properties.

Senior Citizens Homestead Exemptions

Senior citizens may also qualify for a reduction of $2,000 ($2,500 in Cook County) in equalized assessed value. This reduction is provided for homes owned and occupied by persons who will be at least 65 years of age by December 31st and for single-family dwellings leased by persons that age who are liable for taxes. Homeowners must apply for this exemption to their assessor or chief county assessment officer. In counties of less than 3,000,000 inhabitants, homeowners may be required to file an annual application.

Homestead Improvement Exemption

Homeowners who have made improvements to properties used exclusively for residential purposes may also qualify for the "Homestead Improvement" exemption of up to $30,000 of the value of the improvements if an assessment increase has resulted. This exemption can continue for four years from the completion of the improvement. Owners must apply to their Board of Review or Board of Appeals (Cook County) for this exemption.

Special Homestead Exemption for Disabled Veterans

In addition to the above homestead exemptions, "special adapted housing" (as defined by federal law) owned and used by disabled veterans or their unremarried spouses may be exempt up to an assessed value of $50,000. The Illinois Department of Veterans' Affairs determines eligibility for this exemption.

Solar Energy Equipment Exemption

Owners of property which is heated or cooled by solar energy equipment may apply to have a property valued as though it used conventional heating or cooling equipment, even though the special equipment has added value to the property. Pollution control equipment also receives a preferential assessment.

The Circuit Breaker

Another type of property tax relief which is available to senior citizens and disabled persons is the "Circuit Breaker." To qualify, a person must be at least 65 years old, or totally disabled and at least 16 years old. If the eligible claimant becomes deceased prior to filing for a Circuit Breaker grant, the surviving spouse may file and be eligible if that spouse is at least 63 years old at the time of the eligible claimant's death. Also, the total household income must be less than $14,000 for the year. The grant is based on the amount of property tax and household income. The maximum grant is $700, minus 4 1/2 percent of the household income; the amount of the grant decreases as the household income increases to $14,000. Renters can also benefit from this program as 25 percent of the rent is considered payment for property taxes. Under Circuit Breaker legislation, senior citizens pay their tax bills in the normal fashion, then apply to the state for a grant.

Senior Citizens Real Estate Tax Deferral Program

The Senior Citizen Tax Deferral Program allows qualified senior citizens to defer part or all of the property tax on their personal residences. Under the program, the state pays the property tax due, charges the owner 6 percent interest per year on the amount paid and the state acquires a lien on the property which must be repaid after the taxpayer's death or when the property is sold. To qualify, an applicant must:

1. Be 65 or over by June 1 of the year application is made;

2. Have a total household income of less than $25,000;

3. Have lived on the property or on other qualifying property for at least three years;

4. Own the property (the property must be used exclusively for residential purposes) and;

5. Have no delinquent property taxes on the property.

Eligible applicants may defer all or part of their property taxes each year they qualify. The maximum total amount which can be deferred (including interest and fees) is 80 percent of the taxpayer's equity in the property. Any taxes deferred are considered as paid for the purpose of calculating the Circuit Breaker grant amount. Tax deferral can be continued by a surviving spouse who is at least 55 years of age within six months of the taxpayer's death.

Exemptions:

- Personal property
- Government property
- Religious property
- Charitable property
- Educational property
- Residential (partial homestead exemption)
- Hospitals
- Cemeteries

Appeal procedure:

A taxpayer who is not a resident of Cook County begins the appeal process with his *County Board of Review*. If dissatisfied with the board's decision, the taxpayer has a choice with regard to his next step. He may take his complaint to the *State Property Tax Appeal Board*, a five member board appointed by the governor. The State Property Tax Appeal Board's decisions are subject to administrative review in Circuit Court, should the property taxpayer so desire. The other alternative for the dissatisfied taxpayer is to pay the property tax under protest and appeal the decision of the County Board of Review directly to the *Circuit Court*. When a taxpayer goes to court to challenge the assessment, however, he must prove either fraud on the assessor's part, or that the assessment is so high it is "constructively" fraudulent, whereas if the taxpayer takes his case to the State Property Tax Appeal Board, his case can be argued solely on the value of the property and the correctness of the assessment.

In Cook County, dissatisfied taxpayers may first file a complaint with the *county assessor* and, if dissatisfied with his ruling, may take their cases to the *County Board of Appeals*. Taxpayers may file directly with the County Board of Appeals, bypassing the county assessor, if they so desire. If dissatisfied with the board's ruling, the taxes may be paid under protest with an objection filed in the *Circuit Court of Cook County*.

If after presenting the taxpayer's supporting evidence before the Circuit Court he/she is dissatisfied with the ruling, the taxpayer may appeal to the Court of Appeals.

If after the taxpayer presents the case to the Court of Appeals and he is dissatisfied with the ruling, he/she may appeal to the Illinois Supreme Court.

Appeal calendar:

Taxpayers in counties with population of less than 150,000 should file their complaints with their Boards of Review by *August 10th*. In counties with populations of more than 150,000 but less than 1,000,000, the deadline is *September 10th*. Taxpayers dissatisfied with the decisions of the Board of Review may file appeals with the State Property Tax Appeal Board *within thirty days* after written notice of the Board of Review's decisions.

By law, Boards of Review must convene by the *first Monday in June*. Adjournment dates are also set by statute and depend on the population of the county. These dates range from *September 7th for counties with populations of less than 50,000 to December 31st for counties with populations over 100,000*.

In Cook County, after completing assessments in a township, the county assessor will publish a notice setting the time limit for taxpayers in that township to make application to the county assessor for review of their assessments. Taxpayers wishing to file complaints with the *Cook County Board of Appeals must do so within twenty days* after the Board has published a notice that it will hear appeals for the area in which they own property. The Board of Appeals in Cook County convenes by the *second Monday in September to hear complaints and stays in session until sixty days after receiving the last assessment book*.

Level of government responsible for assessment:
State, County, Township

Tax assessors:

- Some are elected for a four year term, and some are appointed for a four year term.

- College degree or equivalent is required.

- Certification is required by Illinois Property Assessment Institute and Illinois Department of Revenue.

State issued assessor's manual: *Illinois Real Property Appraisal Manual.*

Equalization: *Yes*

Property tax maps mandatory: *Yes*

Allow real property to be assessed at financially better use rather than current use: *Yes, highest & best use*

Frequency of state ratio studies: *Yearly*

Are state ratio studies accessible to the public: *Yes*

State agency information and contact person:

Illinois Department of Revenue
Office of Local Government Services
Replacement Tax Certification Division
101 West Jefferson Street
P. O. Box 19033
Springfield, Illinois 62794-9033
Ms. Barbara A. Moore, Research Section Manager
Telephone: (217) 782-3254 • Fax: (217) 782-9932

INDIANA

Name of real property tax: *Property Tax*

Official valuation standard: *True tax value as defined by rules of the State Board of Tax Commissioners. This is not market value.*

Annual assessment of real property: *No*

Reassessment cycle: *Yes - every four years*

Assessment date: March 1

Classification of property:

Class I	Real Estate 33%
Class II	Personal Property 33%
Class III	Public Utilities

Assessment rate:

Class I	33% of true tax value
Class II	33% of true tax value

Tax relief available to homeowners:

Homeowners Deduction/Credit:
If you're a homeowner and use it as your principal place of residence for the year proceeding March 1, your home and up to one acre of land qualify for a homeowners deduction.

The deduction is either one half of your assessed valuation or $2,000.00, whichever is less. The amount of the credit to which you are entitled equals 9% of your gross tax.

Mortgage Deduction:
If you own or are buying property that has a mortgage or a contract mortgage, and you are a resident of the State of Indiana, you may qualify for the mortgage deduction. The value of the deduction may not exceed the amount of indebtedness or one-half of the assessed valuation of the property.

Deductions for persons over the age of 65 or surviving spouses:
If you are a taxpayer over the age of 65 as of December 31 of the prior

year, have a combined adjusted income of less than $15,000.00, have property with an assessed value of no more than $19,000.00, and you owned the property one year prior to March 1 of the current year, you may be eligible for the over 65 deduction. If your assessed value is less than $1,000.00 the deduction will equal the amount of your assessment. This is also available for a surviving spouse over the age of 60 of a husband or wife who was over 65 at the time of death.

Deduction for Blind or Disabled:
If you are blind or disabled and own property that is used as your principal residence, you maybe eligible for a $2,000.00 deduction. Your gross taxable income must be less than $13,000.00 and proof of disability must be provided by a written statement of a physician, by records of a state/county Department of Public Welfare, or the Department of Human Services. If the assessed value is less than $2,000.00, the amount of the deduction would be the assessment.

Totally Disabled Veteran:
A veteran who owns property and is totally disabled with a disability unrelated to military service, with an assessed value that does not exceed $16,000.00, may qualify for a $2,000.00 deduction. The deduction is also available for a veteran's surviving spouse or a veteran who is at least 62 years of age who has a disability of at least 10%.

Veteran With Partial Disability:
A veteran who owns property with a service-connected disability of 10% or more, may qualify for a $4,000.00 deduction. The deduction is also available for a veteran's surviving spouse.

World War I Veterans:
If you served in the military or naval forces of the U.S. during W.W.I, are a resident of Indiana, and your assessment does not exceed $24,000.00, you may be eligible for a W.W.I deduction of $3,000.00. This deduction is also available to the veteran's surviving spouse without the assessed value limitation.

Exemptions:

- Government property
- Religious property
- Charitable property
- Educational property

- Historical property
- Hospitals
- Cemeteries

Appeal procedure:

Step 1   Meet informally with the assessor and try to resolve the problem. If after the meeting you are not satisfied with the results, go to step 2.

Step 2   After an unsuccessful informal meeting with the tax assessor, request a hearing before the County Board of Equalization.

Step 3   If after presenting all of your evidence before the County Board of Equalization you are still dissatisfied, you may request a hearing before the State Board of Tax Appeals.

Step 4   If after presenting your argument to the State Board of Tax Appeals you are still dissatisfied with the decision, you may appeal to the District Court.

Step 5   If after presenting all of your evidence before the District Court you are still not satisfied, you may appeal to the Court of Appeals.

Step 6   Finally, if you are still not satisfied, you may appeal to the State Supreme Court.

You must exhaust all of the administrative appeals before asking for a judicial review. You must also pay the current property tax (under protest) the state alleges you owe or the courts will not hear your case.

Appeal Calendar:

1. Assessment date: March 1

2. Township Assessor assesses property and issues a Notice of Assessment (Form 11) by mail.

3. The taxpayer may meet informally with the Town Assessor to discuss and clarify the assessment.

4. If no agreement is reached at the informal conference, the taxpayer may within 45 days of the date on the Assessment Notice or May 10th (of the year the assessment is effective), file a Petition for Review of Assessment (Form 130) with the County Auditor.

5. The County Board of Review sets a hearing date. A 10 day Notice to Appear is sent to the taxpayer as well as the township assessor. The County Board of Review will review the current assessment pursuant to Indiana Code 6-1.1-15-2.1.

6. Indiana Code 6-1.1-15-2.1 requires the Board of Review to process any petition relating to the reassessment of real property within 90 days.

7. The Board of Review hears the evidence and mails the taxpayer and the township assessor a written Notice of Determination.

8. If the taxpayer is dissatisfied with the decision of the Board of Review, the taxpayer has thirty (30) days to file an appeal with the State Tax Board pursuant with Indiana Code 6-1.1-15-4. The petition (form 131) should include a copy of the Board of Review's Notice of Determination (form 130) and should be filed with the County Auditors.

9. If the taxpayer is dissatisfied with the decision of the State Tax Board, the taxpayer may appeal to the Indiana Tax Court.

10. Lastly, if the taxpayer is dissatisfied with the decision of the Indiana Tax Court, the taxpayer may appeal to the Indiana Supreme Court.

Level of government responsible for assessment:
Township

Tax assessors:

*   Elected for a four year term.

*   High school education is required.

*   State certificate by state tax board is required.

State issued assessor's manual: *Indiana Real Estate Assessment Manual*

Equalization: *Yes*

Property tax maps mandatory: *Yes*

Allow real property to be assessed at financially better use rather than current use: *No*

Frequency of state ratio studies: *Every four years*

Are state ratio studies accessible to the public: *Yes*

State agency information and contact person:

State of Indiana
State Board of Tax Commissioners
Real Estate Division
100 N. Senate Ave. #N1058
Indianapolis, IN 46204
Dr. C. Kurt Zorn, Chairman
Tel: (317) 232-3782 • Fax: (317) 232-8779

NOTES

IOWA

Name of real property tax: *Property Taxes*

Official valuation standard: *Actual value (fair and reasonable market value), "the fair and reasonable exchange in the year in which the property is listed and valued between a willing buyer and a willing seller, neither being under any compulsion to buy or sell and each being familiar with all the facts relating to the particular property." (IC 441.21)*

Annual assessment of real property: *Yes*

Reassessment cycle: *No*

Assessment date: January 1

Classification of property:

Class I	Residential: 100%
Class II	Agricultural: 100%
Class III	Commercial: 100%
Class IV	Industrial: 100%
Class V	Personal: 100%
Class VI	Utilities: 100%
Class VII	Other: 100%

Assessment rate:

Residential property assessed at 100% of actual value.

Tax relief available to homeowners:

Homestead Credit

Must own and occupy the property as a homestead on July 1 of each year, declare residency in Iowa for income tax purposes and occupy the property for at least six months each year. Persons in the military or nursing homes who would otherwise qualify are also eligible. The current credit is equal to the actual levy on the first $4,850.00 of actual value.

Disabled and Senior Citizens Property Tax Credit
Must be 65 or older, be a surviving spouse on or before Dec. 31, 1988, or be totally disabled. Must have been a resident of Iowa during the entire preceding year and have household income of less than $14,000.00.

Mobile Home Credit
Must be 18 or older. Household income must be less than $14,000.00.

Exemptions:

- Personal property
- Government property
- Religious property
- Charitable property
- Educational property
- Historical property
- Forest & orchards
- Hospitals
- Cemeteries

IOWA LOCAL GOVERNMENT SERVICES

PROGRAM FY 93 Assistance Programs	DESCRIPTION	ELIGIBILITY	FILING REQUIREMENTS
Homestead Credit $93,571,831.00	Originally adopted to provide property tax relief and to encourage home ownership. The current credit is equal to the actual levy on the first $4,850 of actual value.	Must own and occupy the property as a homestead on July 1 of each year, declare residency in Iowa for income tax purposes and occupy the property for at least six months each year. Persons in the military or nursing homes who would otherwise qualify are also eligible.	Claim must be filed on or before July 1 of the first year for which the credit is claimed. Claims filed July 2 through Dec. 31 are considered a claim filed the following year. Claim is allowed for successive years without further filing as long as eligible.

IOWA LOCAL GOVERNMENT SERVICES

PROGRAM FY 93 Assistance Programs	DESCRIPTION	ELIGIBILITY	FILING REQUIREMENTS
Disabled and Senior Citizens Property Tax Credit $10,606,084.00	Incorporated into the Homestead Tax Law to provide additional relief to the elderly and persons with disabilities. Provides assistance for qualifying renters.	Must be 65 or older, surviving spouse 55 on or before Dec. 31, 1988, or totally disabled. Must have been a resident of Iowa during the entire preceding year and have household income of less than $14,000.	A property owner must file a claim with the county treasurer by June 1 preceding the fiscal year in which the property taxes are due. Renters must file with the Department of Revenue and Finance by Oct. 31 to claim reimbursement for the prior calendar year.
Mobile Home Credit $150,683.00	Enacted as a supplement to the Disabled and Senior Citizens Property Tax Credit. The objective is to provide mobile home owners with equivalent aid.	Must be 18 or older. Household income must be less than $14,000	On or before June 1 of each year, each mobile home owner eligible for a reduced rate may file a claim for such tax rate with the county treasurer.
Special Assessment Credit $31,079.05	Established in conjunction with the Disabled and Senior Citizens Property Tax Credit. The credit gives 100 percent assistance to qualified individuals who are required to pay special assessments.	Requirements parallel those for the disabled and senior citizens credit.	The claimant must file a claim with the county treasurer by Sept. 30 of each year.

IOWA LOCAL GOVERNMENT SERVICES

PROGRAM FY 93 Assistance Programs	DESCRIPTION	ELIGIBILITY	FILING REQUIREMENTS
Special Valuation for Machinery and Computers - $0 - Not Funded	Intended to provide tax relief for businesses which acquired industrial machinery and computer equipment after December 31, 1981. The property is assessed at fair market value. However, the liability is based on 30 percent on the acquisition cost.	All machinery used in manufacturing and computers as defined in 427A.1(ej). Certain limitations apply to acquired property previously leased or owned by a related person.	None.
Pollution Control Exemption Exemption only	Provides an exemption for certain pollution control equipment after the construction or installation is completed.	New installations or existing property if installed after Sept. 23, 1970. Exemption is limited to market value of property.	Application must be filed no later than Feb. 1 of the first year for which the exemption is requested.
Impounded Structures Exemption Exemption only	Provides an exemption for impoundment structures and land underlying an impoundment located outside any incorporated city or town.	Used for agricultural purposes.	Persons owning such structures must apply to the assessor each year before July 1.

IOWA LOCAL GOVERNMENT SERVICES

PROGRAM FY 93 Assistance Programs	DESCRIPTION	ELIGIBILITY	FILING REQUIREMENTS
Low-Rent Housing Exemption Exemption only	Provides an exemption for low-rent housing until the original housing development mortgage is paid in full or expires.	Property owned and operated by a nonprofit organization providing low-rent housing for the elderly and the physically and mentally disabled.	Must file with the assessor no later than July 1. The claim is allowed on the property for successive years without further filing as long as the property is used for purposes specified in the original claim.
Ag Land Credit $29,138,799.00	Credit established to partially offset the school tax burden borne by agricultural real estate. Current law allows a credit for any school general fund tax in excess of $5.40 per $1,000 of assessed value.	All land used for agricultural or horticultural purposes in tracts of 10 acres or more. Buildings or other structures are excluded.	Land owners are not required to file a claim. The county auditor determines the amount of credit applicable to each taxpayer.
Family Farm Credit $9,985,344.00	Credit established to partially offset the school tax burden borne by agricultural real estate. Current law allows a credit for any school general fund tax in excess of $5.40 per $1000 of assessed value.	All land used for agricultural or horticultural purposes in tracts of 10 acres or more. Buildings or other structures are excluded.	Claims filed between July 1 and October 15.

IOWA LOCAL GOVERNMENT SERVICES

PROGRAM FY 93 Assistance Programs	DESCRIPTION	ELIGIBILITY	FILING REQUIREMENTS
Recreational Lakes, Forest Covers, Rivers and Streams, River and Stream Banks and Open Prairies Exemption only	Provides an exemption as designated by the board of supervisors for the county in which the property is located.	Property not used for economic gain.	Application must be filed with the commissioner of the soil conservation district in which the property is located by April 15 of the assessment year.
Forest and Fruit Tree Reservations Exemption only	Provides an exemption to any person who establishes a forest or fruit tree reservation.	Forest Reserve:Minimum of two acres, contain not less than 200 trees per acre, not used for economic gain other than raising trees. Fruit tree:Not less than one nor more than 10 acres. Exemption for 8 years.	Application filed with assessor between Jan. 1 and April 15 of the year for which the exemption is first claimed.
Property Tax Replacement Replaces: Municipal Assistance, County Assistance, Liquor, Personal Property Monies and Credit $56,287,254.00	Provides a form of revenue sharing and payment for property tax not collected to local jurisdiction	Varies with type of program.	None.

IOWA LOCAL GOVERNMENT SERVICES

PROGRAM FY 93 Assistance Programs	DESCRIPTION	ELIGIBILITY	FILING REQUIREMENTS
Military Exemption $2,820,718.91	Serves to reduce the taxable value of property for military veterans who served on active duty during specified wartime periods.	The amount of exemption varies according to the wartime period of active duty.	A qualified veteran must file a claim with the local assessor by July 1 of the first year eligible. Subsequent claims need not be filed on the same property.

Appeal procedure:

Step 1   Appeal to the local assessor and try to resolve the problem. If after the meeting you are not satisfied with the decision, go to step 2.

Step 2   After an unsuccessful informal meeting with the local assessor, file a written notice to the Local Board of Review.

Step 3   If after presenting all of your evidence before the Local Board of Review you are still not satisfied, you may appeal to the District Court of the county.

Step 4   If after presenting all of your evidence before the District Court of the county you are still dissatisfied, you may appeal to the State Supreme Court.

> *You must exhaust all of the administrative appeals in proper sequence prior to asking for judicial review.*
> *You must pay the current property tax (under protest) the state alleges you owe or the courts will not hear your case.*

Appeal calendar:

1. April 15: Assessors complete their assessments and notify taxpayers.

2. Appeal to the local Board of Review on or after April 16 to May 5th of the year of the assessment.

3. Appeals may be taken from the action of the Board of Review with reference to protests of assessment, to the District Court of the county in which the Board holds its sessions, within twenty days after its adjournment or May 31, whichever date is later.

Level of government responsible for assessment: *County*

Tax assessors:

Appointed for 6 year terms.

*   Must be state certified.

State issued assessor's manual: *Iowa Real Property Appraisal Manual and Duties and Responsibilities of Iowa Assessors*

Equalization: *Yes*

Property tax maps mandatory: *No*

Allow real property to be assessed at financially better use rather than current use: *No, current use*

Frequency of state ratio studies: *Yearly*

Are state ratio studies accessible to the public: *Yes*

State agency information and contact person:

Iowa Department of Revenue and Finance
Local Government Services Division
Hoover State Office Building
Des Moines, Iowa 50319
Mr. Richard Stradley, Supervisor Assessment Section
Tel: (515) 281-3204 • Fax: (515) 242-6040

KANSAS

Name of real property tax: *Property Taxes*

Official valuation standard: *Fair market value in money. "The amount in terms of money that a well-informed buyer is justified in paying and a well-informed seller is justified in accepting for property in an open and competitive market, assuming the parties are acting without undue compulsion."*

Annual assessment of real property: *Yes*

Reassessment cycle: *Yes, every 4 years.*

Assessment date: *January 1*

Classification of property:

Class I	Residential
Class II	Agricultural
Class III	Vacant Lots
Class IV	Real Estate owned by not-for-profit organizations
Class V	Utilities (except railroad)
Class VI	Commercial and Industrial real property
Class VII	Other (not specifically categorized)

Assessment rate:

Class I	Assessed at 11½ % of fair market value.
Class II	Assessed at 30% of usage
Class III	Assessed at 12% of fair market value
Class IV	Assessed at 12% of fair market value
Class V	Assessed at 33% of fair market value
Class VI	Assessed at 25% of fair market value
Class VII	Assessed at 30% of fair market value

Tax relief available to homeowners:

Homestead Exemptions:

1. Senior citizens - must have been 55 years of age or older on January 1; or

2. Totally and permanently disabled or blind; or

3. One or more dependent children residing with you the entire year. At least one dependent must have been born on or before January 1 and must have been under 18 years of age the entire year.

   In addition to the above qualifications you must meet all of the following requirements:
   - You must have been a resident of Kansas for the entire year; and,
   - You must have owned, or rented, and occupied your homestead, or lived in a nursing home upon which general property taxes were assessed during the year;
   - You must not owe any delinquent taxes on your homestead, or if you are filing under the renter's provision, the rental property must be on the tax roll; and,
   - Your property tax or rent paid must not have been paid from public funds, on your behalf, directly to the county treasurer or landlord during the year.

4. Renters base their general property tax on 15% of the rent they pay for occupancy. They are also entitled to homestead exemption based on the amount paid in property and total household income.

Homestead and food sales tax claim forms will be mailed directly to individuals who filed a 1992 Kansas homestead and food sales tax refund claim and whose address has not changed. If you do not receive forms in the mail they are available at the office of county clerks, city clerks, banks, libraries, other places of convenience, and taxpayer assistance locations. You may also request forms from the Taxpayer Assistance Bureau, P.O. Box 12001, Topeka, Kansas 66612-2001.

The amount of refund is determined by law and based upon the amount of property tax or rent paid and the total amount of the combined household income.

The refund is the total amount of allowable general property tax paid and/or 15% of rent paid for occupancy compared to total household income for a refund not to exceed $600.00. (Line 13, form k-40h). A Kansas homestead refund cannot be issued for less than $5.00.

Exemptions:

- Government property

- Religious property

- Charitable property

- Educational property

- Hospitals

- Cemeteries

- Business aircraft

- Individual revenue bond properties

- Farm ponds & reservoirs

- Economic development

Appeal procedure:

Step 1   If after having an informal meeting with the county appraiser the taxpayer is dissatisfied with the results, he/she may go to step 2.

Step 2   File a formal appeal to a hearing officer or hearing panel. If the county does not have a hearing officer or hearing panel, or if the property owner is not satisfied with their decision, he may go to step 3.

Step 3   Fire a formal appeal to the County Board of Equalization. If the property owner is not satisfied with a decision from the County Board of Equalization, the taxpayer may go to step 4.

Step 4   Formally appeal to the State Board of Tax Appeal in Topeka, Kansas. If the decision by the Board is not satisfactory, the taxpayer may go to step 5.

Step 5   Legal proceedings may be initiated by the property
               owner with the District Court of the judicial district
               where the property in dispute is located.

Step 6   If the taxpayer is still not satisfied he may appeal to the
               Court of Appeals.

Step 7   Lastly, the property owner may appeal to the State
               Supreme Court.

> *You must exhaust each of the administrative appeals
> in proper sequence before asking the courts for a re-
> view. You must also pay the current property tax bill
> (under protest) the state alleges you owe or the courts
> will not hear your case.*

Appeal calendar:

1. Notice of value mailed between January 1 and March 1.

2. Informal hearings begin after January 1.

3. Informal hearings end April 1.

4. Hearing panel begins after January 15.

5. Hearing panel adjourns May 15.

6. Board of Equalization begins after February 1.

7. Board of Equalization adjourns by June 15.

Level of government responsible for assessment:
County, State

Tax assessors:

- Appointed to a four year term.

- Special education and certificate are required.

State issued assessor's manual: *Kansas Reappraisal Manual*

Equalization: *Yes*

Property tax maps mandatory: *Yes*

Allow real property to be assessed at financially better use rather than
current use: *Yes, highest and best use*

Frequency of state ratio studies: *Yearly*

Are state ratio studies accessible to the public: *Yes*

State agency information and contact person:

Kansas Department of Revenue
Division of Property Valuation
Robert B. Docking State Office Building
915 S.W. Harrison Street
Topeka, Kansas 66612-1585
Mr. Kimberly K. Moore, Chief Administrative Officer
Telephone: (913) 296-2365 • Fax: (913) 296-2320

NOTES

KENTUCKY

Name of real property tax: *Property Taxes*

Official valuation standard: *Fair cash value,*

> *"established as the price the property would bring at a fair, voluntary sale, except the following: real property qualifying for an assessment moratorium shall not have its fair cash value assessment changed while under the assessment moratorium unless the assessment moratorium expires or is otherwise canceled or revoked."*

Annual assessment of real property: *Yes*

Reassessment cycle: *Not required by Kentucky law*

Assessment date: *January 1*

Classification of property:

Class I	Real Property
Class II	Tangible Property
Class III	Intangible Property

Assessment rate:

Residential property assessed at 100% of fair cash value.

Tax relief available to homeowners:

The Kentucky Constitution has provided a homestead exemption for residents sixty-five (65) and older or those who have been classified as totally disabled. As stated in KRS 132.810, anyone applying for this exemption must own and maintain the property as his personal residence. Only one exemption may be obtained per residential unit regardless of the number of qualified applicants. The homestead exemption only applies to the value of real property.

Exemptions:

- Household personalty
- Government property
- Religious property (place of worship and parsonage)

- Charitable property

- Educational property

- Cemeteries

- Public libraries

- Crops in hand of farmer

- Bonds of state units of government

Appeal procedure:

Step 1   If you receive a notice of tax due or if the Revenue Cabinet notifies you that a tax refund or credit has been reduced or denied, you have the right to protest. To do so, submit a written protest within 45 days from the notice date.

Step 2   Conference
If you have not been able to resolve the tax matter through your protest, you have the right to request a conference to discuss the issue.

Step 3   Independent Informal Review
If you feel after the conference that you have not been treated in a fair and equitable manner, you have the right to request an independent informal review.

Step 4   Final Ruling
If you do not want to have a conference or if the conference did not resolve your protest, you have the right to request a final ruling of the Kentucky Revenue Cabinet (KRC) so that you can appeal your case further.

Step 5   Appeal

1. If you do not agree with the KRC's final ruling, you can file a written appeal to the Kentucky Board of Tax Appeals.

2. If you do not agree with the decision of the Kentucky Board of Tax Appeals, you have the right to appeal their ruling to the Kentucky courts:

    a.   First to the Circuit Court in your home county or in Franklin County;

    b.   Next to the Kentucky Court of Appeals;

    c.   Finally to the Kentucky Supreme Court.

> *You must exhaust all administrative appeals in proper sequential order prior to asking for a judicial review. You must pay the current property tax (under protest) the state alleges you owe or the courts will not hear your case.*

Appeal calendar:

KENTUCKY PROPERTY TAX CALENDAR

	REAL ESTATE	PERSONAL PROPERTY
Assessment Date	January 1	January 1
Listing Period	January 1 - March 1	January 1 - April 15
PVA* Estimate Of Net Assessment Growth To County Judge/Executive	April 1	n/a
PVA* Recap To Revenue Cabinet	First Monday In April	n/a
Public Inspection Of Tax Roll	12 Days Beginning First Monday In May (6 Days Per Week, Incl. Sat.)	n/a
Board Of Assessment Appeals	5 Days Beginning Third Monday In May	n/a
Final Recap To Revenue Cabinet	June 15	n/a
Revenue Cabinet Certification	Upon Completion Of Action By Revenue Cabinet	Upon Completion Of Action By Revenue Cabinet
Tax Bills Delivered To Sheriff	By September 15	By September 15
Pay With Discount	By November 1	By November 1
Pay Without Discount	November 2 - December 31	November 2 - December 31
Tax Bills Delinquent	January 1	January 1
Pay With 2 Percent Penalty	January 1 - January 31	January 1 - January 31
Pay With 10 Percent Penalty	After January 31	After January 31

PVA = Property Valuation Administrators

Level of government responsible for assessment:
County, state, municipal

Tax assessors:

- Elected for a four year term.

- No educational requirement.

- State certification is required.

State issued assessor's manual: *Boeckh*

Equalization: *No*

Property tax maps mandatory: *Yes*

Allow real property to be assessed at financially better use rather than current use: *The assessor must assess property at its highest and best use. However, farm land should be assessed according to its agricultural value, regardless of location.*

Frequency of state ratio studies: *Yearly*

Are state ratio studies accessible to the public: *Yes*

State agency information and contact person:

Kentucky Revenue Cabinet
Department of Property Taxation
Centrally Assessed Property
330 Versailles Road, Suite #6
Frankfort, Kentucky 40620
Mr. Jeffery K. Elam, Revenue Auditor II
Telephone: (502) 564-8175 • Fax: (502) 564-8192

LOUISIANA

Name of real property tax: *Property Tax*

Official valuation standard:

> *Title 33 of the Louisiana Revised Statutes of 1950, as amended, authorizes the levy of property taxes by municipalities and parishes. Actual cash value means the valuation at which any real or personal property is assessed for the purposes of taxation after the assessing authorities have considered every element of value in arriving at such valuation (LS 1702(7)). Property subject to ad valorem taxation shall be listed on the assessment rolls at its assessed value which shall be a percentage of its fair market value.*

Annual assessment of real property: *Yes*

Reassessment cycle: *Yes - every four years (realty)*

Assessment date: *January 1*

Classification of property:

Class I   Real Property: 10% of assessed value
Land: 10% of assessed value

Class II Personalty: improvements for residential purposes: 10% of assessed value

Class III   Public Service: 25% of assessed value
Other: 15% of assessed value

Assessment rate:

Residential 10%

Bona fide agricultural, horticultural, marsh and timber lands, as defined by general law, shall be assessed for tax purposes at 10% of use value rather than fair market value.

Tax relief available to homeowners:

- All homeowners are eligible for a $75,000 exemption on the fair market value of their home and 160 acres of land. This exemption is granted by the state, parish and district taxing authority but does not apply to municipal taxes.

- Homestead Exemption: $5,000 of assessed valuation

- Veterans: $5,000 of assessed valuation

- Surviving spouse or minor children : $5,000 of assessed valuation.

- Renters Relief: The legislature may provide tax relief for residential lessees in the form of credits or rebates.

- Persons 65 years of age and older: exemption of $5,000 of assessed valuation .

Exemptions:

- Government property

- Religious property

- Charitable property

- Non- profit educational property

- Transportation

- Non-profit hospitals

- Cemeteries

- Mines and mineral

- Household personalty

- Renovations to historical buildings

Appeal procedure:

Step 1   Appeal to parish governing authority, which is the local assessor. If after presenting your appeal you are not satisfied, go to step 2.

Step 2   If you did not resolve your tax matter with the parish governing authority, you may go in front of the Parish Board of Review. If you are still not satisfied, then go to step 3.

Step 3   Within 10 days of the Board of Review decision you may apply to the Louisiana Tax Commission. If you are still dissatisfied, proceed to step 4.

Step 4   If after presenting all of your evidence before the Louisiana Tax Commission you are still unhappy, you may within 30 days after the decision of the Tax Commission appeal to the District Court.

Step 5   If after presenting all of your evidence before the District Court you are dissatisfied with the ruling, you may appeal to the Appeals Court.

Step 6   Lastly, if you are still not satisfied, you may appeal to the State Supreme Court.

You must exhaust all of the administrative appeals in proper sequence before asking for a judicial review. You must pay the current property tax (under protest) the state alleges you owe or the courts will not hear your case.

Appeal calendar:

1. With notice of assessment and no earlier than August 15 and no later than September 15, an appeal form must be filed with the Board of Review within three working days (excluding legal holidays and weekends) after receiving notice.

2. The Board shall convene hearings within 10 working days of receipt of certified rolls from the assessor.

3. Fifteen days after the Board of Review shall have commenced public hearings, the corrected assessment lists will be certified and sent to the Louisiana Tax Commission.

4. The Louisiana Tax Commission within 10 days of receipt of certified assessment lists from Board of Review, shall conduct public hearings to hear appeals of taxpayers.

5. Decisions of the Tax Commission shall be made on or before October 15th.

Level of government responsible for assessment:
County (parish)

Tax assessors:

- Elected for a four year term.

- No minimum education required.

- Special education or certificate is not required.

State issued assessor's manual: *Louisiana Assessor's Manual*

Equalization: *No*

Property tax maps mandatory: *Yes*

Allow real property to be assessed at financially better use rather than current use: Highest price willing buyer would normally pay willing seller.

Frequency of state ratio studies: *Yearly*

Are state ratio studies accessible to the public: *Yes*

State agency information and contact person:

Louisiana Tax Commission
P. O. Box 66788
Baton Rouge, La 70896
Mr. Malcolm Price
Telephone: (504) 925-7830 • Fax: (504) 925-7827

MAINE

Name of real property tax: *Property Tax*

Official valuation standard: *Just value,*

> *"that value arising from presently possible alternatives to which the particular parcel of land may be placed. The just value of land is deemed to arise from and is attributable to legally permissible uses or uses only. (Title 36, part 2 of the Maine revised statutes annotated, 1964, as amended.) "Just value" is synonymous with true or market value which has been judicially equated with the price a willing buyer would pay a willing seller at a fair public sale; the market and place must be one where normal, as opposed to extraordinary conditions exist. (Frank V. Assessors of Skowhegan (1974) Maine 329a, 2nd 167).*

Annual assessment of real property: *Yes, physical inspection every 4 years; annual adjustment.*

Reassessment cycle: *No*

Assessment date: *April 1*

Classification of property: Varies by municipality

Assessment rate:

Assessment percentage varies by municipality.

Tax relief available to homeowners:

1. Residents 62 or older, unmarried 55 or older, receiving federal disability, married persons 55 or older both receiving federal disability who own or rent a home in Maine are eligible for the following benefits:

SENIOR BENEFITS AVAILABLE IN MAINE

Household Income	Benefits as % of "Benefit Base"	Max. Benefit
Single Member Households		
$ 0 - 6,800	100%	$400 max.
6,801 - 7,000	75%	300

SENIOR BENEFITS AVAILABLE IN MAINE

Household Income	Benefits as % of "Benefit Base"	Max. Benefit
7,001 - 7,200	50%	200
2,201 - 7,400	25%	100
Household With 2 or More Members		
$ 0 - 8,100	100%	$400 max
8,101 - 8,500	75%	300
8,501 - 8,800	50%	200
8,801 - 9,200	25%	100

"Benefit Base" is the amount of property tax accrued or rent constituting property tax accrued (25% of gross rent paid) less the equivalent tax value of any benefit received or to be received as a homestead property exemption. (Tit. 36, Secs 6201,6206)

2. Property of aged or disabled veterans, their unremarried widows, and mothers or minor children: up to $5,000 of assessed value.

Paraplegic veterans or unremarried widows of such veterans for specially adapted housing units: up to $47,500 of assessed value.

Legally blind residents of Maine: up to $4,000 of assessed value.

Veterans and unremarried widows and minor children: up to $5,000 of assessed value.

Exemptions:

- Government property
- Religious property
- Charitable property
- Educational property
- Hospitals
- Cemeteries
- Mines and minerals
- Railroads

- Motor vehicles
- Watercraft
- Inventories (stacks in trade)
- Municipal and fraternal organizations

Appeal procedure:

Step 1 Request an informal review with the local assessors. The assessor, within one year of assessment, may make abatements (TIT 36, Sec. 841).

Step 2 If you did not resolve your tax matter with the local assessor you may go in front of the Local Board of Assessment. If you are still not satisfied, then go to step 3.

Step 3 If you are still not satisfied after the decision of the Local Board of Assessment, appeal to the State Board of Property Tax Review.

Step 4 If after presenting all of your evidence before the State Board of Property Tax Review you are still dissatisfied, you may appeal to the Superior Court.

Step 5 If after presenting all of your evidence before the Superior Court you are still not satisfied with the ruling you may appeal to the Court of Appeals.

Step 6 Lastly, if you are still unhappy with the ruling, you may appeal to the State Supreme Court.

You must exhaust all administrative appeals prior to asking for a judicial review. You must pay the current property tax (under protest) the state alleges you owe or the courts will not hear your case.

Appeal calendar:

Informal Review With Assessor. The assessor shall give to any person applying to him for an abatement of taxes, notice in writing of his decision within 10 days after he takes final action thereon. If the assessor fails to give written notice of his decision within 60 days from date of filing, the application shall be deemed to have been denied. The same is true for the Local Board of Assessment.

Level of government responsible for assessment:
County, municipality, state

Tax assessors:

- Local option to elect or appoint.

- Associate degree and 2 years experience or college degree is required.

- Special education and certificate are required.

State issued assessor's manuals: *Marshall & Swift; State of Maine Assessment Manual.*

Equalization: *Yes*

Property tax maps mandatory: *Yes*

Allow real property to be assessed at financially better use rather than current use: *No, current use*

Frequency of state ratio studies: *Yearly*

Are state ratio studies accessible to the public: *Yes*

State agency information and contact person:

> *State of Maine*
> *Bureau of Taxation*
> *Property Tax Division*
> *State House Station 24*
> *Augusta, Maine 04333*
> *Mr. Larry Record, CMS Director*
> *Tel: (207) 289-2011 • Fax: (207) 287-4028*

MARYLAND

Name of real property tax: *Property Tax*

Official valuation standard: *Full cash value, defined as " fair market value" or " current value." (Article 81 of Annotated Code of Maryland, 1957, as amended)*

Annual assessment of real property: *No*

Reassessment cycle: *Every three years*

Assessment date: *January 1*

Classification of property:

Class I	Real Property - 50%
Class II	Operating Railroad
Class III	Public Utility
Class IV	Other

Assessment rate:

50% of full cash value

Tax relief available to homeowners:

1. Homeowners Property Tax Credit: This "circuit breaker" program limits the amount of property tax that any homeowner in Maryland must pay based on income, if he qualifies. The requirements for eligibility are:

    •   You must own or have a legal interest in the property.

    •   The dwelling on which you are seeking the tax credit must be your principal residence where you live at least six months of the year, including July 1, unless you are a new home purchaser or unless you are unable to do so on account of your health or need of special care.

    •   Your net worth, not including the value of the property on which you are seeking credit, must be less than $200,000.

    •   Only the taxes resulting from the first $60,000 of assessed valuation are eligible for tax credit.

MARYLAND TAX
CREDIT SCHEDULE

HOUSEHOLD INCOME	TAX LIMIT
$ 1- 4,000	$ 0
5,000	25
6,000	50
7,000	75
8,000	100
9,000	155
10,000	210
11,000	265
12,000	320
13,000	395
14,000	470
15,000	545
16,000	620
17,000	710
18,000	800
19,000	890
20,000	980
21,000	1,070
22,000	1,160
23,000	1,250
24,000	1,340
25,000	1,430
26,000	1,520
27,000	1,610
28,000	1,700
29,000	1,790
30,000	1,880
AND UP	*

For each additional $1,000 of income above $30,000 you add $90 to $1,880 to find the tax limit.

Example: If your combined household income is $12,000, you see from the chart that your tax limit is $320. You would be entitled to receive a credit for any taxes above the $320. If your actual property tax bill was $960, your would receive a tax credit in the amount of $640, this being the difference between the actual tax bill and the tax limit.

2. The Homestead Credit: To help homeowners deal with large assessment increases state law has established the Homestead Property Tax Credit. The homestead credit limits the increase in taxable assessments each year to a fixed percentage. Every county and municipality in Maryland is required to limit taxable assessment increases to 10% or less each year.

The homestead credit applies only to owner-occupied dwellings and is based on the total assessment for the dwelling and land associated with the dwelling. An assessment is 40% of the market value of that property.

3. Blind: up to $6,000 of assessed value exempt.

4. *100% Disabled Veterans*: totally exempt from property tax.

Exemptions:

- Government property
- Religious property
- Charitable property
- Educational property
- Cemeteries

Appeal procedure:

A new assessment on real property is made every three years. If a property owner believes the assessment valuation is too high, the property owner may appeal the assessment.

Step 1   Supervisor - level assessment appeal: After you fill out and file the appeal copy of the notice of assessment, a hearing will be scheduled within 45 days with a local assessor.

Step 2   Following the supervisor level hearing, the property owner will receive a final decision. Those disagreeing with the decision may appeal to the Property Tax Assessment Appeal Board.

Step 3   After due consideration of all the information brought forth, the Property Tax Assessment Board will render a decision and notify the property owner.

Step 4   Property owners who are still dissatisfied may appeal to the Maryland Tax Court. Property owners who are in disagreement with the decision of the Maryland Tax Court can appeal further through the judicial system.

Step 5   Appeal to the Circuit Court.

Step 6   Appeal to the Court of Appeals.

Step 7   Appeal to the Maryland Supreme Court.

You must exhaust each of the administrative appeals prior to asking for a judicial review. You must have paid the current property tax (under protest) the state alleges you owe or the courts will not hear your case.

Appeal calendar:

1. Assessment date: January 1

2. Supervisor level assessment appeal: Return appeal copy of notice of assessment within 45 days of the date of the notice.

3. Property Tax Assessment Appeal Board: File appeal within 30 days of the final notice from the Supervisor of Assessments.

4. Maryland Tax Court: File appeal within 30 days of the date of the Property Tax Assessment Appeal Board's decision.

Level of government responsible for assessment: *State*

Tax assessors:

• Unlimited appointment.

• Minimum high school graduate, college preferred.

• State certificate and special education are required.

State issued assessor's manuals: Commercial - *Marshall & Swift*, Residential - *Maryland State Cost Manual*

Equalization: *No*

Property tax maps mandatory: *Yes*

Allow real property to be assessed at financially better use rather than current use: *No, current value.*

Frequency of state ratio studies: *Yearly*

Are state ratio studies accessible to the public: *Yes*

State agency information and contact person:

State of Maryland
Department of Assessment and Taxation
Real Property Division, Room 511
300 West Preston Street
Baltimore, Maryland 21201
Ms. Sue Houff, Administrator
Telephone: (410) 225-1199 • Fax: (410) 333-7275

NOTES

MASSACHUSETTS

Name of real property tax: *Real Property Tax*

Official valuation standard: *"Full and fair cash valuation" for taxation purposes is the "fair market value," which is the price an owner willing but not under compulsion to sell ought to receive from one willing but not under compulsion to buy.*

Annual assessment of real property: *No, every three years.*

Reassessment cycle: *Every three years. Chapter 40, section 56 of the general laws provides that "the Commissioner shall triennially certify as to whether the Board of Assessors is assessing property at full and fair cash valuation."*

Assessment date: January 1

Classification of property:

Class I	Residential: 100%
Class II	Open Space: 100%
Class III	Commercial: 100%
Class IV	Industrial: 100%
Class V	Personal Property: 100%

Assessment rate:

Residential property is assessed at 100% full and fair cash valuation (fair market value).

Tax relief available to homeowners:

1. Cities and towns may grant residential exemption of up to 20 percent of the average assessed value of all residential properties.

2. Real property to the value of $2,000 or the sum of $175, whichever abates the greater amount of tax due, occupied by a surviving spouse or minor whose parent is deceased, or a person over age 70 who has owned and occupied the house for not less than 10 years, provided the value of the total estate, both real and personal, does not exceed $20,000 exclusive of any mort-

gage interest in property (g.L. Ch.59 S5 Cl.17). By local option (G.L.Ch.59 S5 Cl.17C) the total estate test is less stringent since real and personal property cannot exceed $40,000 exclusive of any mortgage interest and exclusive of the first $60,000 of value in the domicile. Under another local option statute (G.L. Ch59 S5 Cl.17C1/2) the total estate cannot exceed $40,000 exclusive of any mortgage and exclusive of the first $150,000 of value in the domicile. There is another local option statute (G.L. Ch59 S5 Cl.17D) and under its provisions a $175 exemption is granted to a surviving spouse or minor child with parent deceased or to a person over age 70 who has owned and occupied the property as a domicile for not less than five years. The total estate cannot exceed $40,000 exclusive of any mortgage interest and exclusive of the total value of the domicile except so much of the domicile as produces income and exceeds two dwelling units.

3. For real estate owned by a blind person, there is an exemption to the value of $5,000 or the sum of $437.50, whichever is greater (G.L. Ch.59 S5 Cl.37). By local option (G.L. Ch.59 S5 Cl.37A) a blind person would receive a $500 exemption on his home.

4. There is an exemption (G.L. Ch59 S5 Cl.41) for persons 70 years of age or over in the amount of $4,000 valuation or $500 in taxes, whichever will exempt the greater amount of taxes due, if the person (1) has had gross income of less than $6,000 ($7,000 if married) for the preceding year, (2) had a whole estate, real and personal, not over $17,000 ($20,000 if married) not including the realty occupied as a domicile except that portion which produces income, or not over $40,000 ($45,00 if married) if such real estate is included. By local option (G.L. Ch.59 S5 Cl.41B) the statutory requirements have been broadened. The property must be owned and occupied by a person at least 70 years of age who has been domiciled in Massachusetts for the ten preceding years and has owned and occupied such property or other property in the Commonwealth for 5 years or is a surviving spouse who inherits the property and has occupied such real property for 5 years. The taxpayer must have gross receipts in the preceding year of less than $10,000 ($12,000 if married) and a whole estate not exceeding $20,000 ($23,000 if married). The value of the domicile is excluded from the total

estate except that portion which produces income. Under another local option (G.L. Ch59 S5 Cl.41C), the ownership and occupancy requirements are the same as in clause 41b. However, the gross receipts must be less than $13,000 ($15,000 if married) and the whole estate must not exceed $28,000 ($30,000 if married). The value of the domicile is excluded from the total worth except so much of the domicile as produces income and exceeds two dwelling units.

5. Real estate owned and occupied by the surviving spouse or surviving minor children of a police officer or fire fighter killed in the line of duty is totally exempt from real estate taxes. (G.L. Ch59 S5 Cl.41A)

Exemptions:

6. A taxpayer who is at least 65 years of age who meets ownership and domiciliary requirements may defer real estate taxes provided the gross receipts for the preceding year did not exceed $20,000 (G.L. Ch.59 S5 Cl.41A).

7. Real estate of Massachusetts Veterans, their spouses, unremarried surviving spouses and fathers of veterans killed in such war times who served in the U.S. Armed Forces between February 15, 1898, and July 4, 1902; between April 6, 1917, and November 11, 1918; or who received WWI Victory Medal; between September 16, 1940, and December 31, 1946; between June 25, 1950, and January 31, 1955; or in Viet Nam between August 5, 1964, and the termination of the Viet Nam emergency or veterans serving at least 180 days active service between February 1, 1955, and August 4, 1964, when occupied at least in part as a domicile, to the amount of $2,000 or the sum of $175, whichever abates the greater amount of tax due.The exemption applies to veterans (and their spouses) who have a war time disability rating of 10% or more, veterans awarded the Purple Heart, and surviving spouses of World War I veterans, or veterans who were awarded the World War I Victory Medal who have not remarried and whose whole estate does not exceed $20,000 in value. An exemption to the amount of $4,000 or the sum of $350, whichever abates the greater amount of tax due, is allowed veterans (and their spouses) who have lost, or lost the use of one foot, one hand or one eye, or have been awarded the Congressional Medal of Honor, Distinguished

Service Cross, Navy Cross or the Air Force Cross. An exemption to the amount of $8,000 or the sum of $700, whichever abates the greater amount of tax due, is allowed veterans (and their spouses) who have lost, or lost the use of both feet, both hands, or one foot and one hand, or both eyes. An exemption to the amount of $10,000 or the sum of $875, whichever abates the greater amount of tax due, for veterans with a permanent and total disability (and their spouses). An exemption to the amount of $6,000 in the value of the sum of $525, whichever abates the greater amount of tax due, is allowed veterans who are 100% disabled due to a wartime injury and are incapable of working. A total exemption is granted to veterans who have been certified by the Veterans Administration as being "paraplegic." The surviving spouse, so long as he/she remains unmarried, will be entitled to the same exemption.

Exemptions:

- Religious property
- Charitable property
- Educational property
- Hospitals
- Cemeteries
- Residential personalty (furnishings)
- Machinery & equipment of manufacturing corporations
- Railroad rights-of-way

Appeal procedure:

Step 1   After receiving the notice of assessment, file a formal written appeal with the Board of Assessors or City Commissioners and try to resolve the problem. If after the meeting you are not satisfied with the decision, go to step 2.

Step 2   After an unsuccessful meeting with the Board of Assessors or City Commissioners, appeal to the State Appellate Tax Board.

Step 3   If after presenting all of your evidence before the State Appellate Tax Board you are still not satisfied, you may appeal to the Judicial Review (Appellate Court on matters of law only).

> You must exhaust all administrative appeals prior to requesting a judicial review. You must pay the current property tax the state believes you owe (under protest) or the courts will not hear your case.

Appeal calendar:

1. Assessment date: January 1

2. Notice of assessment: September 1

3. Within three months of notice, file a formal written appeal with the local Board of Assessors.

4. The Board of Assessors shall, within 10 days after their decision on an application for an abatement, give written notice thereof to the applicant. If the assessors fail to take action on such application for a period of three months following the filing thereof, they shall, within 10 days after such period, notify the applicant of such inaction in writing.

5. Within three months of the decision of the Board of Assessors, an aggrieved taxpayer may file a written appeal with the County Commissioner of the Appellate Tax Board.

Level of government responsible for assessment:
City & Town

Tax assessors:

- Elected for a three year term, unless charter, by- law, or ordinance provides otherwise.

- High school minimum education is required.

- Special courses and certificate are required.

State issued assessor's manual: *Massachusetts Assessor's Manual*

Equalization: *No*

Property tax maps mandatory: *Yes*

Allow real property to be assessed at financially better use rather than current use: *Yes, highest and best use.*

Frequency of state ratio studies: *Biennial*

Are state ratio studies accessible to the public: *Yes*

State agency information and contact person:

Massachusetts Department of Revenue
Division of Local Services
Property Tax Bureau
P.O. Box 9655
Boston, MA 02114-9655
Mr. Harry M. Grossman, Chief
Telephone: (617) 727-2300 • Fax: (617) 727-6432

MICHIGAN

Name of real property tax: *Ad Valorem Property Tax*

Official valuation standard: *True cash value "means the usual selling price that could be obtained for the property at private sale, and not at auction or at forced sale."*

Annual assessment of real property: *Yes*

Reassessment cycle: *Yes, every four years or less*

Assessment date: *December 1*

Classification of property:

Class I	Residential: 50% of assessed value
Class II	Personal Property: 50% of assessed value
Class III	Agricultural: 50% of assessed value
Class IV	Commercial: 50% of assessed value
Class V	Industrial: 50% of assessed value
Class VI	Timber Cutover: 50% of assessed value
Class VII	Developmental: 50% of assessed value

Assessment rate:

Residential: 50% of true cash value (market value)

Tax relief available to homeowners:

Homestead Property Tax Relief, also known as the "Circuit Breaker":

The homestead program establishes the following categories under which homeowners or renters can determine if they are eligible for a homestead property tax credit:

1. Citizens age 65 and older and the surviving spouses of senior citizens. A claimant or spouse must be age 65 by December 31 of the tax year for which he/she is filing. The property tax relief available to low-income persons in this category is much greater than the allowance granted to other taxpayers. If the

household income is $3,000 or less, then 100% of the property tax is refundable.

2. Paraplegic and quadriplegic persons.

3. Totally and permanently disabled persons who are not over age 65.

4. Eligible veterans, active military personnel, blind persons, and the surviving spouses of veterans.

5. All other homeowners and renters

Under this program, a credit/refund for property taxes paid is determined by placing homeowners and renters into one of the categories listed above and then relating their property taxes or percent of rent paid to their household income. Individuals must have resided in Michigan for at least six months of the calendar year for which they are applying for a credit.

Homeowners and renters who do not qualify for consideration under one of the special categories are granted a credit against their state income tax equal to 60% of the amount by which their property taxes exceed 3.5% of their household income. In lieu of property taxes paid by the homeowner, renters will base their claim on 17% of their yearly rent. If there is no income tax due or if the property tax credit exceeds the income tax, a refund will be made. The credit cannot exceed $1,200.

Since the 1982 tax year, there has been a phase-out of the property tax credit for taxpayers whose household income exceeded a certain amount. Your credit is reduced by 10% for each $1,000 or part of $1,000 by which household income is greater than $73,650. If your household income is $82,650 or more, you are not entitled to a property tax credit.

Persons whose household income consisted totally of Aid to Families with Dependent Children, State Family Assistance, or State Disability Assistance are not eligible for a property tax credit. For persons who received a part of their income from these programs, their credit will be reduced by the percentage by which their total household income was composed of ADC, SFA, or SDA benefits. This reduction shall not exceed the total of ADC, SFA, or SDA payments received during that year.

Exemptions:

- Government property

- Religious property
- Charitable property
- Educational property
- Fruit trees
- Hospitals
- Cemeteries
- Facilities of certain industries

Appeal procedure:

Step 1   After receiving a notice of assessment, have an informal meeting with the local assessor and try to resolve the problem. If after the meeting you are not satisfied with the decision, go to step 2.

Step 2   After an unsuccessful informal meeting with the tax assessor, file a formal appeal with the Local Governmental Board of Review.

Step 3   If after presenting all of your evidence before the Local Governmental Board of Review you are still dissatisfied, you may file a written appeal to the Michigan Tax Tribunal.

Step 4   If after presenting all of your evidence before the Michigan Tax Tribunal you are still not satisfied, you may appeal to the County Circuit Court.

You must exhaust all administrative appeals available in sequential order before asking for a judicial review. You must also pay the current property tax (under protest) the state alleges you owe or the courts will not hear your case.

Appeal calendar:

1. Assessment day: December 31 (tax day)
2. Notice of assessment sent to taxpayer. It must be sent at least ten days before the first meeting of the Local Board of Review.

3. Informal conference with assessor: any time before the first meeting of the Local Board of Review.

4. First meeting of Local Board of Review: first week in March.

5. Last meeting of Board of Review: first Monday in April (unless concluded earlier).

6. If the taxpayer is unhappy with the decision of the Board of Review, he may make formal appeal to the Michigan Tax Tribunal prior to June 30 in the year the assessment was received.

Level of government responsible for assessment:
Town, township, municipality.

Tax assessors:

*   1,527 units, 250 elected for a four year terms; balance appointed for indefinite term.

*   Minimum high school education is required.

*   Special course and certificate are required.

State issued assessor's manual: *Michigan State Tax Commission Assessor's Manual*

Equalization: *Yes*

Property tax maps mandatory: *Yes*

Allow real property to be assessed at financially better use rather than current use: *Yes, highest and best use.*

Frequency of state ratio studies: *Yearly*

Are state ratio studies accessible to the public: *Yes*

State agency information and contact person:

State of Michigan
Treasury Department/Property Tax Division
430 West Allegan
Lansing, MI 48922
Mr. Roland Anderson
Telephone: (517) 373-0674 • Fax: (517) 373-0633

MINNESOTA

Name of real property tax: *Property Tax*

Official valuation standard: *Market value,*

> *"the usual selling price at the place where the property to which the term is applied shall be at the time of assessment; being the price which would be obtained at a private sale or an auction sale, if it's determined by the assessor, that the price from the auction sale represents an arm's length transaction, the price obtained at a forced sale shall not be considered." Chapters 270-275 Minnesota Statutes, as amended.*

Annual assessment of real property: *Yes*

Reassessment cycle: *Yes. Every four years or less.*

Assessment date: *January 2*

Classification of property:

Class I	Residential
Class II	Personal Property
Class III	Agricultural
Class IV	Commercial
Class V	Industrial
Class VI	Timber Cutover
Class VII	Developmental

Assessment rate:

Residential property assessed at 100% of market value.

Tax relief available to homeowners:

The Regular Property Tax Refund

The regular property tax refund is income sensitive. This means that the larger the tax is compared to income, the greater the refund. The regular property tax refund has maximum income level requirements for both renters and homeowners. To be eligible for the regular property tax refund, renters must have a total household income of less than $35,000.

Homeowners applying for the regular property tax refund must have a total household income of less than $60,000. In addition, the taxpayer must have been a full - or part-year resident of Minnesota during the past tax year. If you are a homeowner, you must have owned and lived in your home on January 2 of the current tax year. If you are a renter, the building you live in must be one on which the owner:

1. was assessed property taxes; or

2. paid a portion of the rent receipts in place of property tax; or

3. made payment to a local government for such services as trash collection and street maintenance.

The Special Refund Program for Homeowners
The Special Refund Program is for homeowners with property tax increases of more than 12 percent from the previous year and whose increase was $300 or more. All homeowners are eligible for the refund, regardless of income. There is no maximum refund amount.

Levy Limits
Restrictions on the amount of property tax local governments can levy year to year are called levy limits. The limits are determined by the legislature and are the simplest and cheapest means of controlling property tax bills. No amounts have to be subtracted from property tax bills and no applications or refunds have to be filled out or processed.

Exemptions:

- Personal property (most)

- Government property

- Religious property

- Charitable property

- Educational property

- Public hospitals

- Cemeteries

- Native prairie

- Wetlands

- Certain property used in pollution control

- Certain domestic abuse shelters
- Certain hydroelectrical or hydromechanical power stations
- Certain transitional housing facilities
- Electric power lines from retail farm distribution

Appeal procedure:

One Step Appeal

A taxpayer may appeal directly to the regular division of the Minnesota Tax Court. The taxpayer is not required to employ an attorney, but since the proceedings are conducted according to the Minnesota Rules of Civil Procedure, he/she may wish to have one.

Four Step Appeal

Step 1   Schedule an informal meeting with local assessor's office to try to resolve the problem. If after the meeting you are not satisfied with the decision, go to step 2.

Step 2   After an unsuccessful informal meeting with the tax assessor, file an appeal with the city or town Board of Review.

Step 3   If after presenting all of your evidence before the Board of Review you are dissatisfied, you may appeal to the County Board of Equalization.

Step 4   If after presenting all of your evidence before the County Board of Equalization you are still unhappy, you may appeal to the Minnesota Tax Court.

If a taxpayer elects to use the four step appeal process he/she must exhaust all of the administrative appeals available in sequential order before asking for a judicial review. You must pay the current property tax (under protest) the state alleges you owe or the courts will not hear your case.

Appeal calendar:

1. Assessment date: January 2.

2. November 10: The last day for county auditors to mail notices of proposed tax increases to affected taxpayers.

3. December 1: The last day for county auditors to correct the valuation of undervalued properties or correct the classification.

4. March 31: The last day for the county treasurer to mail tax statements to owners of real and personal property, except manufactured homes.

5. April 1: First day for convening sessions of Local Boards of Review.

6. April 15: First day for convening sessions of State Board of Equalization.

7. May 15: Last day to file a petition in the Office of the Court Administrator of the District Court or Tax Court relating to objection of current taxes on real property.

Level of government responsible for assessment:
County, municipality, town and township

Tax assessors:

• Appointed for four years.

• Minimum high school education is required.

• Special course and certification are required.

State issued assessor's manual: *Minnesota Property Tax Administrators Manual*

Equalization: *Yes*

Property tax maps mandatory: *No*

Allow real property to be assessed at financially better use rather than current use: *Both current use and highest and best use are employed.*

Frequency of state ratio studies: *Yearly*

Are state ratio studies accessible to the public: *Yes*

State agency information and contact person:

Minnesota Department of Revenue
Property Tax Division
Mail Station 3340
St. Paul, MN 55146-3340
Ms. Gail L. Hiveley, Appraiser
Telephone: (612) 296-0334 • Fax: (612) 297-2166

NOTES

MISSISSIPPI

Name of real property tax: *Ad Valorem Taxes*

Official valuation standard: *"True value" shall mean and include but shall not be limited to market value, cash value, actual cash value, proper value and value for the purposes of appraisal for ad valorem taxation.*

Annual assessment of real property: *Yes*

Reassessment cycle: *Yes*

Assessment date: *January 1*

Classification of property:

Class I   Residential: 10% of assessed value

Class II   All other real property: 15% of assessed value

Class III   Personal: 15% of assessed value

Class IV   Public Utilities: 30% of assessed value

Class V   Motor Vehicle: 30% of assessed value

Assessment rate:

Residential (owner-occupied only) 10% of true value.

Tax relief available to homeowners:

Homestead Exemption
Based on current Mississippi statutes, qualified homeowners may be allowed a homestead exemption credit of up to $240.00 toward their total ad valorem taxes due. This credit is based on a maximum assessed value of $6,000.00.

Senior citizen or disabled exemption
Any qualified homeowner who has reached sixty-five (65) years of age on or before January 1 of the year for which the exemption is claimed or who is disabled, shall be exempt from ad-valorem taxes based on a maximum assessed valuation of $6,000.00.

Exemptions:

- Government property

- Religious property

- Charitable property

- Educational property

- Historical property

- Hospitals

- Cemeteries

- Mines and minerals

- Structures undergoing reconstruction in central business districts

- Garden clubs and patriotic organizations

Appeal procedure:

Step 1   If a taxpayer wishes to appeal his taxes, he may request an informal meeting with the local county tax assessor. If dissatisfied with the local assessor's decision, he can go to step 2.

Step 2   After an unsuccessful informal meeting with the local county tax assessor, file a written appeal to the County Board of Supervisors.

Step 3   If after presenting all of your evidence before the County Board of Supervisors you are still dissatisfied, you may appeal to the Circuit Court of Appeals in the county where the property is located.

> *You must exhaust all of the administrative appeals available in sequential order before asking for a judicial review. You must pay the current property tax (under protest) the state alleges you owe or the courts will not hear your case.*

Appeal calendar:

1. Tax lien date: January 1.

2. Taxes are due first day of February.

3. Objections to assessment (MS27-35-89). Beginning the first Monday in August of each year, the taxpayer may file objections with proper documentation for change in values with the County Board of Supervisors.

4. If the taxpayer is dissatisfied with the decision of the County Board of Supervisors, the taxpayer may appeal to the Circuit Court within ten (10) days after the adjournment of the meeting of the Board of Supervisors (MS27-35-119).

5. The local Board of Supervisors of each county shall have the power to change, cancel, or decrease an assessment upon application by the taxpayer or by the assessor on behalf of such party. This request may be submitted anytime after the assessment rolls have been approved by the tax commission and prior to the last Monday in August (MS27-35-143).

Level of government responsible for assessment: *County*

Tax assessors:

*   Elected for a four year term.

*   High school minimum education is required.

*   Special course and state certification are required.

State issued assessor's manual: *State of Mississippi Appraisal Manual*

Equalization: *No*

Property tax maps mandatory: *Yes*

Allow real property to be assessed at financially better use rather than current use: *No, current use*

Frequency of state ratio studies: *Yearly*

Are state ratio studies accessible to the public: *No*

State agency information and contact person:

Mississippi State Tax Commission
Property Tax Bureau/Ad Valorem Tax Division
Post Office Box 960
Jackson, Mississippi 39205-0960
Mr. Robert M. Megginson, Director Property Tax Bureau
Telephone: (601) 359-1076 • Fax: (601) 359-5519

NOTES

MISSOURI

Name of real property tax: *Property Taxes*

Official valuation standard: *The true value in money is the price the property would bring when offered for sale by a person who is willing but not obligated to sell it, and is bought by a person who is willing to purchase it but who is not forced to do so. The true value in money of agricultural/horticultural land is defined as its market or productive use.*

Annual assessment of real property: *No*

Reassessment cycle: *Yes, every two years, odd year*

Assessment date: *January 1*

Classification of property:

Class I   Residential: 19% of value

Class II   Agricultural: 12% of value

Class III   All other: 32% of value

Personal property is assessed at:

- Manufactured Homes: 19% of value

- Farm Machinery: 12% of value

- Livestock: 12% of value

- Historic Cars, Planes: 5% of value

- Crops (grain): .5% of value

- Vehicles, others: 33% of value

Assessment rate:

Residential: 19% of true value in money

Tax relief available to homeowners:

Missouri Property Tax Credit Claim
Senior citizens must pay their property taxes, but can receive credit for the taxes paid, or a portion of their rent, through the state income tax structure. Under the "circuit breaker," or Senior Citizens Tax Credit, senior citizens or disabled veterans can receive credit on their income

tax, or a check from the state if they owe no income tax. The amount of credit is determined by their income and the amount of tax or rent they paid on their home. The less their income, or the more they paid in property taxes or rent, the greater their credit. Rent credit is based on 20% of their gross rent.

Who may claim credit:

To qualify for this income tax credit or refund:

1. You or your spouse must be 65 years of age or over; and

2. You and your spouse must have been Missouri residents for the entire year; or

3. You or your spouse must be a veteran of any branch of the armed forces of the United States, or of this state who became one hundred percent disabled as a result of such service.

4. In addition to the above qualifications, the following two qualifications must also be met for all individuals:

    a. Your total household income cannot exceed $15,000. However, if your filing status is "married-filing combined," the total combined household income cannot exceed $17,000; and

    b. You must pay property tax on, or rent, the homestead during the calendar year.

Exemptions:

*   Government property
*   Religious property
*   Charitable property
*   Educational property
*   Mines & minerals
*   Non-profit cemeteries
*   Agricultural societies

Appeal procedure:

Step 1   Request an informal review with the local assessor. If after presenting all relevant facts you are not satisfied with the assessor's decision, you may file a formal written appeal with the Board of Equalization.

Step 2   If the taxpayer is dissatisfied with the decision of the Board of Equalization, the taxpayer may file an appeal with the State Tax Commission.

Step 3   If the taxpayer is still not satisfied with the decision of the State Tax Commission, the taxpayer may appeal that decision to the Circuit Court.

Step 4   Lastly, if still dissatisfied with the decision, the taxpayer can appeal to the State Supreme Court.

You must exhaust all the administrative appeals available before asking for a judicial review. You must pay the current property tax (under protest) the state alleges you owe or the courts will not hear your case.

Appeal calendar:

1.   Property is assessed as of January 1.

2.   By May 31 all assessors must have completed their real and personal property assessment rolls and turned them over to the county clerk.

3.   Local Boards of Equalization meet to hear valuation appeals by taxpayers beginning the third Monday in May, first Monday in June, or the second Monday in July, depending on the county's classification.

4.   Appeals from the Board of Equalization may be made to the State Tax Commission. They must be made: in first class counties and St. Louis City, by August 15 or 30 days after the Board's decision, whichever is later; in all other counties, by September 30 or 30 days after the Board's decision, whichever is later. An appeal must be made to the Board of Equalization, with an adverse ruling, before the Tax Commission may hear the appeal.

Level of government responsible for assessment:
County, State

Tax assessors:

- Elected to a four year term.

- Minimum high school education required.

- Special education and certificate are required.

State issued assessor's manual: *Missouri Assessor's Manual*

Equalization: *Yes*

Property tax maps mandatory: *No*

Allow real property to be assessed at financially better use rather than current use: *Yes, highest and best use*

Frequency of state ratio studies: *Yearly*

Are state ratio studies accessible to the public: *Yes*

State agency information and contact person:

State Tax Commission of Missouri
621 East Capitol Avenue
P. O. Box 146
Jefferson city, Missouri 652102-0146
Mr. Robert Van Ark, Property Tax Specialist
Tel: (314) 751-2414 • Fax: (314) 751-1341

MONTANA

Name of real property tax: *Property Taxes*

Official valuation standard: *Market value*

> *"the value at which property would change hands between a willing buyer and a willing seller, neither being under any compulsion to buy nor sell and both having reasonable knowledge of reasonable facts."*

Annual assessment of real property: Yes

Reassessment cycle: Yes, every five years

Assessment date: January 1

Classification of property:

Class I	Mines and Mining Claims (not including metal or coal mines)
Class II	Agricultural: 30% of assessed value
Class III	Residential: 3.86% of assessed value
Class IV	Machinery & Equipment: 11% of assessed value
Class V	Utilities: 12% of assessed value
Class VI	One Acre Farmsteads: 3.1% of assessed value
Class VII	Railroads: 10.6% of assessed value

Assessment rate:

Residential property is assessed at 3.86% of market value.

Tax relief available to homeowners:

Tax relief for elderly and low-income homeowners

Current Montana Statute (15-6-134 Amended) provides for tax relief for the elderly and others with low income. The 1992 Legislature amended the qualifying criteria for low income property tax reduction as follows: A recipient or recipients of employment income, retirement or disability benefits whose total income from all sources including gross business income less expenses and otherwise tax exempt incomes of all type, but not including Social Security income paid directly to a nursing home, and which totals no more than $12,974 for a single person or $15,569 for a married couple, are entitled to property tax relief. Proof of income is required, preferably in the form of federal or state income tax forms. This will simplify approval of your application.

The first $80,000 or less of market value of any improvement on real property, a mobile home affixed to the land, or mobile home, plus appurtenant land not exceeding five (5) acres: when such dwelling and land are owned or under Contract for Deed and actually occupied for at least 10 months per year as the primary residential dwelling, qualifies from the following table:

MONTANA TAX RELIEF TABLE

Income Single Person	Married Couple Income	Percentage Multiplier
$ 0 - 1,297	$ 0 - 1,557	0%
1,298 - 2,595	1,558 - 3,114	10%
2,596 - 3,892	3,115 - 4,671	20%
3,893 - 5,190	4,672 - 6,228	30%
5,191 - 6,487	6,229 - 7,785	40%
6,488 - 7,784	7,786 - 9,341	50%
7,785 - 9,082	9,342 - 10,898	60%
9,083 - 10,379	10,899 - 12,455	70%
10,380 - 11,677	12,456 - 14,012	80%
11,678 - 12,974	14,013 - 15,569	90%

Market Value in excess of $80,000 will be taxed at normal rates.

Residential property tax credit for the elderly
This benefit (Montana Statute 15-6-211) is a tax credit deducted from the Montana Income Tax owed, or a money amount sent by the state after the property tax has been paid.

Eligibility:
1. In order to be eligible an individual:

   a. must have reached age 62 or older during the tax year;

   b. must have resided in Montana for at least 9 months during the tax year;

    c.   must have occupied one or more dwellings in Montana as an owner, renter, or lessee for at least 6 months of the tax year.

2.   Property tax paid and rent-equivalent tax paid (15% of the gross rent paid) are reduced according to the following table:

MONTANA PROPERTY TAX CREDIT FOR ELDERLY

Household Income	Amount of Reduction
000 - 999	$0
1,000 - 1,999	$0
2,000 - 2,999	the product of .006 times the household income
3,000 - 3,999	.016
4,000 - 4,999	.024
5,000 - 5,999	.028
6,000 - 6,999	.032
7,000 - 7,999	.035
8,000 - 8,999	.039
9,000 - 9,999	.042
10,000 - 10,999	.045
11,000 - 11,999	.048
12,000 & over	.050

In no case may the state income tax credit exceed $400. This benefit is administered by the State of Montana, Income Tax Division. Their address is Mitchell Building, Helena, Montana 59620.

Certain disabled or deceased veterans residences exemption
(Montana Statute 15-6-211)

1.   A residence, including the lot on which it is built, owned and occupied by a veteran or a veteran's spouse is exempt from property taxation under the following conditions. The veteran must:

    a.   have been killed while on active duty or have died as a result of a service-connected disability; or

    b.   if living:

        •   have been honorably discharged from active service in any branch of the armed service:

- be rated 100% disabled due to a service-connected disability by the United States Department of Veterans Affairs or its successor; and

- have an annual adjusted gross income, as reported on the latest federal income tax return, of not more than $15,000 for a single person and $18,000 for a married couple.

2. Property shall continue to be exempt under this section so long as the property is the primary residence owned and occupied by the veteran or, if the veteran is deceased, by the veteran's spouse and the spouse:

    a. is the owner and occupant of the house;

    b. has an annual adjusted gross income, as reported on the latest federal income tax return, of not more than $15,000;

    c. has not remarried; and

    d. has obtained from the United States Department of Veterans Affairs a letter indicating that the veteran was 100% service-connected disabled at the time of death or that the veteran died while on active duty or as a result of a service-connected disability.

Exemptions:
- Government property
- Religious property
- Charitable property
- Educational property
- Certain agricultural property
- Hospitals
- Cemeteries
- Mines or minerals
- Public art galleries and observatories
- Agricultural and horticultural societies
- Household personalty
- Property used for non-profit athletic events

Appeal Procedure:

Step 1   Request an informal review with the local assessor by filing a written request (ab-26 form) for review.

Step 2   If the taxpayer is dissatisfied with decision of the local assessor, the taxpayer may file an appeal within 15 days from receipt of a decision from the local assessor with the County Tax Appeal Board.

Step 3   If the taxpayer is not satisfied with the decision of the County Tax Appeal Board, the taxpayer has 30 days to appeal that decision to the State Tax Appeal Board.

Step 4   The State Tax Appeal Board holds hearings and then issues a ruling on the taxpayer's complaint. If the taxpayer is dissatisfied with the decision, he has 60 days to appeal the State Tax Appeal Board's ruling to the District Court.

Step 5   The District Court rulings must be appealed to the State Supreme Court.

You must exhaust all of the administrative appeals before asking for a judicial review. You must pay the current property tax (under protest) the state alleges you owe or the courts will not hear your case.

Appeal calendar:

1. Assessment date: January 1

2. Receipt of notice of assessment or classification - In the spring, April through June.

3. Within 15 days of receipt of notice of assessment or classification, file a written appeal (form ab-26) with local assessor.

4. Within 15 days of receiving an unfavorable decision from the local assessor you must file an appeal with the County Tax Appeal Board.

5. Within 30 days of receiving an unfavorable decision from County Tax Appeal Board, you need to file an appeal with the State Tax Appeal Board.

6. Within 60 days after receiving unfavorable decision from the State Tax Appeal Board you need to file in District Court.

Level of government responsible for assessment:
County, State

Tax assessors:

- Elected to a four year term.

- Minimum high school education required .

- Special education and certificate are required.

State issued assessor's manuals: *Montana Appraisal Manual* and *Marshall & Swift Cost Manual.*

Equalization: *Yes*

Property tax maps mandatory: *No*

Allow real property to be assessed at financially better use rather than current use: *No, current use*

Frequency of state ratio studies: *Yearly*

Are state ratio studies accessible to the public: *Yes*

State agency information and contact person:

State of Montana
Department of Revenue
Property Assessment Division
Sam W. Mitchell Building
Helena, Montana 59620
Mr. Virgil F. Byford, Appraisal Specialist
Tel: (406) 443-0811 • Fax: (406) 443-1394

NEBRASKA

Name of real property tax: *Property Taxes*

Official valuation standard: *Actual value*

> *"the market value of the property in the ordinary course of trade. Actual value may be determined using professionally accepted mass appraisal techniques, including but not limited to: (1) earning capacity of the property; (2) relative location; (3) desirability and functional use; (4) reproduction cost less depreciation; (5) comparison with other properties of known or recognized values; (6) market value in the ordinary course of trade; and (7) existing zoning property."*

Annual assessment of real property: *Yes*

Reassessment cycle: *No*

Assessment date: *January 1*

Classification of property:

Class I   Residential: 100%

Class II   Commercial/Industrial: 100%

Class III   Agricultural: 80%

Class IV   Personal Property: 100%

Class V   Public Service: 100%

Class VI   Leased Land Improvements: 100%

Class VII   Motor Vehicles

Assessment rate:

Residential property assessed at 100% of actual value.

Tax relief available to homeowners:

NEBRASKA HOMESTEAD EXEMPTIONS

Application for exemption shall be filed after January 1 and on or before April 1 with the county assessor. Status Certification shall be filed annually after January 1 and on or before April 1 with the county assessor.

Category Requirements	Filing Requirements	Statute	Form	Exemption
(1) Qualified claimant 65 years or older before January 1 of the year application is made.	Original application only. Status certification required each year after exemption is granted.	77-3507 77-3514	458 458A	One hundred percent of the actual value of the homestead, up to the first $35,000 of value.
(2) † Veteran totally disabled by non-service-connected accident or illness.	Annual application required. Must include certification from either a qualified medical physician or the Department of Veterans' Affairs.	77-3508 (1a)	458 458B	% ‡Income Limit - of Relief 0 thru 10,400 - 100%
(3) Individuals: A) paralyzed in both legs so as to preclude locomotion without the regular aid of braces, crutches, canes, or wheelchairs. B) who have undergone amputation of both lower extremities such as to preclude locomotion without the regular aid of braces, crutches, canes wheelchairs, or artificial limbs. C) with progressive neuromuscular or neurological disease such as to preclude locomotion without the regular aid of braces, crutches, canes, wheelchairs, or artificial limbs. D) who have permanently lost the use or control of both arms. E) who have undergone amputation of both arms above the elbow.	Application must include certification from a qualified medical physician on forms prescribed by the Nebraska Department of Revenue. Status certification required each year after exemption is granted.	77-3508 (1b), (1c) (1d),(1e) 77-3514	458 458A 458B	
(4) † A) Veteran drawing compensation from the Department of Veterans' Affairs of U.S. because of 100 percent service-connected disability and not eligible for total exemption under Category 5, or the unmarried widow(er) of such veteran. B) Unremarried widow(er) of 1) any veteran who died because of service-connected disability. 2) a serviceperson whose death while on active duty was service connected. 3) a serviceperson who died while on active duty.	Application must include certification of eligiblility from the Department of Veterans' Affairs. Status certification required each year after exemption is granted.	77-3509 77-3514	458 458A	A percent of the actual value of the homestead, up to the first $35,000 of value. % ‡Income Limit - of Relief 0 thru 15000 - 100% 15001 thru 16000 - 80% 16001 thru 17000 - 60% 17001 thru 18000 - 40% 18001 thru 19000 - 20%

NEBRASKA HOMESTEAD EXEMPTIONS

Application for exemption shall be filed after January 1 and on or before April 1 with the county assessor. Status Certification shall be filed annually after January 1 and on or before April 1 with the county assessor.

Category Requirements	Filing Requirements	Statute	Form	Exemption
(5)Home substantially contributed by the Department of Veterans' Affairs of U.S. for a veteran who is a paraplegic or multiple amputee during lifetime of such veteran or until death or remarriage of veteran's widow(er). If home is sold and within one year proceeds are used to acquire another home for occupancy by veteran or unremarried widow(er), it is deemed to be substantially contributed to by the Department of Veterans' Affairs.	Annual application required. Original application for exemption must include certification of eligibility from the Department of Veterans' Affairs.	77-3526 through 77-3528458	458	Total Exemption
Any honorably discharged veteran of the United States Armed Forces who is disabled as follows: a)a veteran who has lost the use of or has undergone amputation of two or more extremities, or has undergone amputation of one or more extremities and has lost the use of one or more extremities b)a veteran whose sight is so defective as to seriously limit his ability to engage in the ordinary vocations and activities of life.	Application for exemption must be filed annually on or before April 1 with your county assessor for mobile homes. For properly registered motor vehicles, application for exemption must be filed with your county assessor not more than 15 days before nor 30 days after the registration date of the vehicle. A certificate of the veteran's condition from the Department of Veterans' Affairs must be attached to the application.	77-202.23 77-202.24	453	The following property shall be exempt from taxation: (1) A mobile home owned and occupied by a disabled or blind honorably discharged veteran of the United States Armed Forces whose disability or blindness is recognized by the Department of Veterans' Affairs of the United States as service connected; and (2) One motor vehicle owned and used for his or her personal transportation by a disabled or blind honorably discharged veteran of the United States Forces whose disability or blindness is recognized by the Department of Veterans' Affairs of the United States as service connected.

† For (2), (4A), and (4B3) veteran and serviceperson shall mean a person who had been on active duty in the armed forces of the U.S. at the time of service with military forces of a government allied with U.S. during the following years: April 21, 1898 to July 4, 1902; April 6, 1917 to November 1918; December 6, 1941 to December 31, 1946; June 25, 1950 to January 31, 1955; August 5, 1964 to May 7, 1975; and Persian Gulf War beginning August 2, 1990. (80-401.01)

‡The previous year's federal adjusted gross income, plus any Nebraska adjustments increasing the federal adjusted gross income, of the claimant, spouse, and all other persons who own and occupy the household.

All veterans must have received an honorable discharge or equivalent.

210

Exemptions:

- Government property
- Religious property
- Charitable property
- Educational property
- Cemeteries
- Agricultural machinery and equipment
- Railroad cars
- Household goods & personal effects
- Business inventories
- Livestock, grain, and seed

Appeal procedure:

Step 1   Request a review with the County Board of Equalization.

Step 2   If the taxpayer is dissatisfied with the decision of the Board of Equalization, the taxpayer may file an appeal with the District Court in the county in which the property is located.

Step 3   If the taxpayer is sill not satisfied with the decision of the District Court, the taxpayer may appeal that decision to the Court of Appeal.

Step 4   Lastly, if still dissatisfied with the decision, the taxpayer may appeal to the State Supreme Court.

> *You must exhaust all of the administrative appeals in sequential order before asking for a judicial review.*
> *You must pay the current property tax (under protest) the state alleges you owe before the courts will hear your case.*

Appeal calendar:

1. Appeal in writing to the County Board of Equalization within 30 days of the filing of the real property assessment roll (usually April 1 - May 31).

2. County Board of Equalization sessions begin on April 1 and end on May 31 of each year.

3. Within seven days after the final decision by the County Board of Equalization, the county clerk will notify the appellant (taxpayer) of the action taken.

4. An adverse decision of the County Board of Equalization may be appealed by the taxpayer to the District Court in the county in which the property is located. The appeal must be filed within 45 days after May 31, and an appeal bond must be filed with the protest petition.

Level of government responsible for assessment:
County

Tax assessors:

- Elected to a four year term.

- College degree or high school education with two years of experience is required.

- Special classes and state certification are required.

State issued assessor's manual: *Nebraska Assessor's Manual*

Equalization: *Yes*

Property tax maps mandatory: *Yes*

Allow real property to be assessed at financially better use rather than current use: *No, current use.*

Frequency of state ratio studies: *Yearly*

Are state ratio studies accessible to the public: *Yes*

State agency information and contact person:

State of Nebraska
Department of Revenue
Property Tax Division
301 Centennial Mall South
P. O. Box 94818
Lincoln, Nebraska 68509-4818
Mr. Dennis W. Donner, Administrator
Tel: (402) 471-2971 • Fax: (402) 471-5608

NEVADA

Name of real property tax: *Property Taxes*

Official valuation standard: *Taxable value,*

> *"(a) the full cash value of the land, based on the use to which the improvements are being put and (b) the value of any improvements made on the land determined by subtracting from the cost of replacement of the improvements all applicable deductions (i.e., straight-line depreciation and obsolescence). The computed taxable value of any property may not exceed its full cash value."*

Annual assessment of real property: *Yes*

Reassessment cycle: *Yes, 5 years or less*

Assessment date: *July 1*

Classification of Property:

Class I	Rural Land:	35%
Class II	Rural Improvements:	35%
Class III	Net Proceeds of Mines:	35%
Class IV	Mining Equipment:	35%
Class V	Mine/Mill Improvements	
Class VI	Mobile Homes	
Class VII	Personal Property	
Class VIII	Public Utilities	
Class IX	Urban Land	
Class X	Urban Improvements	

Assessment rate:

Residential property assessed at 35% of taxable value.

Tax relief available to homeowners:

Homestead Act
Nevada law protects and exempts your "homestead" (dwelling place or

mobile home) against attachment of your property, up to the amount of $95,000, in the event you should suffer a personal financial disaster.

The Nevada legislature provides exemptions and refunds to assist certain taxpayers who deserve consideration by the state. Some of these include veterans, disabled veterans, widows, blind persons, and senior citizens.

Widow's Exemption:
The widow's exemption applies to residents of the state of Nevada and is in the amount of $1,000.00 of assessed value. The exemption can be applied to real property, personal property (mobile homes) or used to exempt $1,000 assessed value from your vehicle privilege tax.

"Blind" Exemption:
The blind exemption is in the amount of $3,000 assessed value and is available to residents with visual acuity that does not exceed 20/200 in the better eye when corrected, or whose field of vision does subtend to an angle of 20 degrees. To qualify for this exemption, it is necessary to furnish a doctor's statement that the above requirements are met.

Veteran's Exemption:
The veteran's exemption applies to honorably discharged Nevadans who have served in the armed forces during one of the following periods:

- April 6, 1917 to November 11, 1918

- December 7, 1941 to December 31, 1946

- June 25, 1950 to January 31, 1955

- January 1, 1961 to May 7, 1975

- Desert Storm participants who were assigned to active duty or who served on active duty outside of the United States in connection with carrying out the authorization granted to the President of the United States in public law 102-1.

The veteran's exemption is in the amount of $1,000.

Disabled Veterans:
The disabled veterans exemption is provided for veterans who have a permanent service connected disability of at least 60%. The amount of exemption is dependent on the degree of disability incurred. The permanently disabled veteran with a 60% disability receives the exemption which ranges to a maximum of $10,000 assessed value for the 100% disabled veteran. The widow of a disabled veteran who was eligible for

this exemption at the time of death, may also be eligible to receive the benefits of this program.

Senior Citizen Tax Assistance Program:
Nevada offers a senior citizen tax assistance/rental rebate program to persons 62 years of age or older whose annual household income was $19,100 or less during the preceding year.

This program applies to any person meeting the age, residency, and income requirements regardless of whether he owns his home, rents an apartment or house, or lives in a mobile home.

The filing period for the tax assistance/rental rebate program is from January 15 to April 30 of each year. The amount of the benefit depends on household income and taxes or rent paid.

Exemptions:

- Government property
- Religious property
- Charitable property
- Educational property
- Cemeteries
- Household personalty

Appeal procedure:

Step 1   If after receiving a notice of change in assessment or a property tax bill, you have a question about your property's assessment, schedule an informal meeting with the assessor. If you are dissatisfied with the results of that meeting, go to step 2.

Step 2   Prior to January 15 file a written appeal with the County Board of Equalization.

Step 3   If after presenting all of your evidence before the County Board of Equalization you are dissatisfied with their decision, you may go to step 4.

Step 4   Prior to the first Monday in March, file a written appeal to the State Board of Equalization.

Step 5   If after presenting all of your evidence before the State Board of Equalization you are dissatisfied with their decision, you may go to step 6.

Step 6   Within 30 days after you have received a written decision from the State Board of Equalization, you may file a written appeal with the Circuit Court in the county in which the property is located.

Step 7   If after presenting all of your evidence before the Circuit Court you are dissatisfied with the ruling, you may go to step 8.

Step 8   You may elect to make an appeal to the State Supreme Court. This is the final appeal available to you and its decision is final.

You must exhaust all of the administrative appeals before asking for a judicial review. You must pay the current property tax (under protest) the state alleges you owe or the courts will not hear your case.

Appeal calendar:

1.   July 1: New fiscal year begins.

2.   December: Property value notice postcards are mailed to all real property owners. The tax roll is published in a local newspaper.

3.   January 15: Deadline for filing petitions to appeal property values with County Board of Equalization.

4.   February 28: Last meeting of the County Board of Equalization.

5.   First Monday in March: Filing deadline date for appeals to State Board of Equalization.

6.   February - March: State Board of Equalization meets.

7.   June - July: Property tax bills are mailed.

Level of government responsible for assessment:
County, State

Tax assessors:

•   Elected for a four year term.

- High school education is required.

- Special courses and state certification are required.

State issued assessor's manuals: *Nevada's Assessors Manual* and *Marshall & Swift valuation service*

Equalization: *Yes*

Property tax maps mandatory: *Yes*

Allow real property to be assessed at financially better use rather than current use: *No, current value*

Frequency of state ratio studies: *Yearly*

Are state ratio studies accessible to the public: *Yes*

State agency information and contact person:

State of Nevada
Taxation Department
Assessments Standards Division
Capitol Complex
Carson City, Nevada 89710-0003
Mr. Dave Pursell
Tel: (702) 687-4840 • Fax: (702) 687-5981

NOTES

NEW HAMPSHIRE

Name of real property tax: *Property Tax*

Official valuation standard: *Full and true value in money,*

> *"the same in payment of a just debt due from a solvent debtor, considering all evidence that may be submitted relative to the property value, the value of which cannot be determined by personal examination."*

Annual assessment of real property: *Yes*

Reassessment cycle: *No*

Assessment date: *April 1*

Classification of property:

Class I	Land (current use): 100%
Class II	Conservation Easements
Class III	Land (residential): 100%
Class IV	Land (commercial/industrial): 100%
Class V	Land (non-taxable)
Class VI	Buildings (residential): 100%
Class VII	Buildings (commercial/industrial): 100%

Assessment rate:

Residential property assessed at 100% of full and true value.

Tax relief available to homeowners:

Exemptions and Tax Credits:

An exemption is a reduction in the local assessed value of property, while a credit is a reduction of the amount of tax due.

Every municipality offers some form of an exemption for elderly property owners meeting certain qualifications. In addition, municipalities may adopt and grant the following exemptions: blind exemption, solar, wind-powered, and wood heating energy systems exemptions. In addition, property tax credits are available to qualifying veterans or their surviving spouses.

Application for an exemption or a credit must be made to the local assessing officials before April 15.

Exemptions:

- Personal property
- Government property
- Religious property
- Charitable property (some)
- Educational property
- Cemeteries

Appeal procedure:

Step 1   Taxpayer files a written appeal with the municipality within two months after receiving the notice of tax.

Step 2   Municipality has until six months after notice of tax to grant or deny the taxpayer's abatement application.

Step 3   Taxpayer may make written appeal to the Board of Tax and Land Appeals (RSA76: 16a) or to the Superior Court (RSA76: 17), but not to both:

1. No *earlier* than:

   a. receiving the municipality's decision on the abatement application; or

   b. six months after notice of tax, even if there has been no response from the municipality; and

2. No *later* than eight months from notice of tax.

Appeal calendar:

1. April 1: Assessment date
2. December: Property tax bills are mailed to property owners (notice of tax).

3. February: Deadline for taxpayer to file a written appeal with municipality.

4. August to October: Deadline for taxpayer to file a written appeal with either the Board of Tax and Land Appeals or the Superior Court.

Level of government responsible for assessment:
County, municipality, town

Tax assessors:

- Elected for a three year term.

- College (or associate degree with 2 years experience).

- Special education or certificate is not required.

State issued assessor's manuals: May choose assessment manual

Equalization: *Yes*

Property tax maps mandatory: *Yes*

Allow real property to be assessed at financially better use rather than current use: *Yes - highest and best use*

Frequency of state ratio studies: *Yearly*

Are state ratio studies accessible to the public: *Yes*

State agency information and contact person:

State of New Hampshire
Department of Revenue
61 South Spring Street
P. O. Box 457
Concord, N.H. 03302-0457
Ms. Linda C. Kennedy
Telephone: (603) 271-2687 • Fax: (603) 271-6121

NOTES

NEW JERSEY

Name of real property tax: *Property Tax*

Official valuation standard:

> *The assessor after ... examination and inquiry, determines the full and fair value of each parcel of property situated in the taxing district at such price as, in his judgement, it would sell for at a fair and bona fide sale by private contract on October 1. "Full and fair value" is defined as what a willing buyer would pay a willing seller for land, namely, the price property would sell for at a fair and bona fide sale by private contact. (Article 5 assessment of real estate sec 54:4-23)*

Annual assessment of real property: *Yes*

Reassessment cycle: *None prescribed by state statute*

Assessment date: *October 1*

Classification of property:

Class I	Residential
Class II	Farm (regular)
Class III	Farm (qualified)
Class IV	Vacant

Assessment rate:

For the purposes of assessment, the assessor shall compute and determine the taxable value of such real property at the level established for the county pursuant to law. (Article 5 section 54:4-23 assessment of real estate)

Tax relief available to homeowners:

Senior Citizen Deduction:

The New Jersey constitution authorizes an annual property tax deduction from the property taxes levied on a dwelling house owned and occupied by a person with an annual income of not more than a specified amount. To be eligible for this reduction a person must:

1. Be a resident of the State of New Jersey as of October 1 of the pre-tax year.

2. Be age of 65 or older as o _ ecember 31 of the pretax year.

3. Own the property as of October 1 of the pretax year.

4. Be a resident of New Jersey living on the property as of October 1 of the pretax year.

5. Have an income not in excess of a specified amount.

Disabled Person Deduction:
In order to qualify for a property tax deduction, a disabled person must meet the following requirements:

1. Be a resident of New Jersey as of October 1 of the pretax year.

2. Own the property as of October 1 of the pretax year.

3. Be a resident of New Jersey and living on the property as of October 1 of the pretax year.

4. Have an income not in excess of specified amount.

5. Disablement must be total and permanent resulting in an inability to engage in any substantial gainful activity as of December 31 of the pretax year.

Surviving Spouse:
In order to qualify for a property tax deduction, a surviving spouse of either a qualified senior citizen or disabled person must meet all of the following requirements:

1. Be a resident of New Jersey as of October 1 of the pretax year.

2. Own the property as of October 1 of the pretax year.

3. Be a resident of New Jersey and living on the property for which the deduction is claimed and upon which the deceased senior citizen spouse or disabled person spouse had received a property tax deduction.

4. Have an income not in excess of specified amount.

5. Age of the applicant must not be less than 55 on December 31 of pretax year, and was not less than 55 years of age at the time of death of the deceased spouse.

6. Is not remarried.

7. Is, in fact, the surviving spouse of a person who was receiving the property tax deduction as either a senior citizen or disabled person or the same property for which a claim is being made.

Veterans and Widows of Veterans:
In order to qualify for a property tax deduction, a veteran must apply for the deduction and must meet all of the following requirements as of October 1 of the pretax year.

1. Citizenship of the United States of America

2. Legal residence in New Jersey

3. Active service in the armed forces of the United States

4. Active service in time of war

5. Honorable discharge

6. Ownership of property

Surviving Spouse of Veteran:
In order to qualify for a property tax deduction as the surviving spouse of a veteran, the surviving spouse must have been married to the veteran at the time of death, and the veteran must have been qualified under all requirements listed above. *In addition*, the surviving spouse, as of October 1 of the pretax year:

1. Must not have remarried.

2. Must be a legal resident of New Jersey.

3. Must hold legal title or a fractional interest in the property.

4. Must prove that the deceased was a United States citizen and resident of New Jersey at the time of death.

5. Must apply for the property tax deduction.

Homestead Tax Rebate:
Any homeowner in New Jersey may qualify for payment of a homestead tax rebate if all of the following conditions are met:

1. Resident: The claimant must be a domiciliary of New Jersey.

2. Ownership: The claimant must be the owner of the property for which homestead tax rebate is claimed on October 1 of the pretax year.

3. Residence: A homestead tax rebate claimant must be a resident
    of New Jersey and a resident of the dwelling house for which
    the homestead tax rebate is claimed.

Additional homestead tax rebates are available to senior citizens, disabled persons, and surviving spouses.

Senior Citizens:

*   Age: The senior citizen must be 65 years of age or older prior
    to December 31 of the pre-tax year.

*   Income requirement: There is no restriction upon income level
    for this additional rebate.

Disabled Person:

To qualify the applicant must be permanently and totally disabled to the extent that he/she is unable to engage in any gainful employment.

Surviving Spouse:

1. The surviving spouse must have been married to a deceased
    citizen who received or was entitled to receive a senior or
    disabled person property tax deduction.

2. The surviving spouse must be 55 years of age or older.

3. The surviving spouse must remain unmarried.

4. The surviving spouse must establish status as a surviving
    spouse on or before December 31 of the pre-tax year.

Exemptions:

*   Personalty
*   Government property
*   Religious property
*   Charitable property
*   Educational property
*   Historical
*   Hospitals
*   Cemeteries

Appeal procedure:

Step 1   After receiving notice of assessment, appeal to assessor or revaluation firm for an informal review, and try to resolve the problem. If after the meeting you are not satisfied with the decision, go to step 2.

Step 2   After an unsuccessful informal meeting with the tax assessor, appeal to the County Board of Taxation.

Step 3   If after presenting all of your evidence before the County Board of Taxation you are still dissatisfied, you may appeal to the Tax Court.

Step 4   If after presenting all of your evidence before the Tax Court you are still not satisfied, you may appeal to the Superior Court.

Step 5   Lastly, you may appeal to the State Supreme Court.

You must exhaust all of the administrative appeals before asking for a judicial review. You must pay the current property tax (under protest) the state alleges you owe or the courts will not hear your case.

Appeal calendar:

1. Assessment day: October 1.

2. On or before December 31 of the pretax year: Informal review.

3. January 10: Tax list is filed with County Board of Taxation.

4. April 1: Deadline for filing formal appeal to County Board of Taxation.

5. November 15: Completion date for hearings by the County Board.

6. Within 45 days of decision from County Board of Taxation the aggrieved taxpayer may file a written appeal with the Tax Court.

Level of government responsible for assessment:
Municipality

Tax assessors:

- Appointed for a four year term.

- Minimum high school education is required.

- Special courses and certificates are required.

State issued assessor's manual: *Handbook for New Jersey Assessors*

Equalization: *Yes*

Property tax maps mandatory: *Yes*

Allow real property to be assessed at financially better use rather than current use: *Yes, highest and best*

Frequency of state ratio studies: *Yearly*

Are state ratio studies accessible to the public: *Yes*

State agency information and contact person:

State of New Jersey
Department of the Treasury
Division of Taxation
Property Administration
CN 251
Trenton, N.J. 08646-0251
Mr. Harris J. Adams, Chief LPB
Tel: (609) 292-7974 • Fax: (609) 292-9439

NEW MEXICO

Name of real property tax: *Property Taxes*

Official valuation standard: *Market value,*

> *"as determined by sales of comparable property or, if that method cannot be used due to lack of comparable sales data for the property being valued, then its value shall be determined using an income method or cost method of valuation. In using any method of valuation authorized by this subsection, the valuation authority shall apply generally accepted appraisal techniques."*

New Mexico Property Tax Code

Articles 35-38 NMSA, 1978

Annual assessment of real property: *Yes*

Reassessment cycle: *Yes, every two years*

Assessment date: *January 1*

Classification of property:

Class I	Land: 33.3%
Class II	Improvements: 33.3%
Class III	Personal property: 33.3%
Class IV	Mobile homes: 33.3%
Class V	Livestock: 33.3%

Assessment rate:

Residential property is assessed at 33.3 % of market value.

Tax relief available to homeowners:

Head of Household Exemption:

To qualify for head of family exemption an individual New Mexico resident must be either 1) married; 2) widow or widower; 3) head of household furnishing more than one-half the cost of support of any related person; or 4) a single person. The value of the exemption is $2,000 off the taxable value of the property.

Veterans Exemption:
The New Mexico Veteran's Service Commission determines all eligibility and issues a certificate to all qualifying veterans or their unremarried spouses. The New Mexico property tax exemption for veterans is up to $2,000 a year reduction from the taxable value.

Exemptions:

- Government property
- Religious property
- Charitable property
- Educational property
- Non-profit service organizations
- Licensed vehicles
- Licensed aircraft
- Private railroad cars
- Household personality

Appeal procedure:

Step 1   Immediately after receiving notice of assessment have an informal meeting with the field appraiser and try to resolve the problem. If after the meeting you are not satisfied with the decision, go to step 2.

Step 2   After an unsuccessful informal meeting with the field appraiser, file a formal written appeal with the Valuation Protest Board.

Step 3   If after presenting all of your evidence before the Valuation Protest Board you are dissatisfied with the ruling, you may appeal to the Court of Appeals.

Step 4   If after presenting your argument before the Court of Appeals you are in disagreement with their ruling, you may appeal to the State Supreme Court.

> You must exhaust all of the administrative appeals before asking for a judicial review. You must pay the current property tax (under protest) that the state alleges you owe before the courts will hear your case.

Appeal calendar:

1. January 1: Valuation date

2. April 1: Notice of value mailed to property tax

3. May 1, or no later than 30 days after receipt of notice of owners value, is the last day for filing a formal petition of protest with the Valuation Protest Board or:

4. If the taxpayer does not exercise the right to protest, he may file a claim for refund as a civil action in the District Court of the respective county. Action must be filed within 60 days after the first installment of the taxes are paid. New Mexico law allows taxes to be paid in halves. The first half is due November 1, and the second half April 1 of each year.

Level of government responsible for assessment:
County

Tax assessors:

• Elected for a four year term.

• Minimum high school education is required.

• No certification is required .

State issued assessor's manuals: *New Mexico Real Property Manual, New Mexico Manufactured Home Manual, New Mexico Personal Property Manual, New Mexico Land Manual*

Equalization: *Yes*

Property tax maps mandatory: *Yes*

Allow real property to be assessed at financially better use rather than current use: *No, current use.*

Frequency of state ratio studies: *Yearly*

Are state ratio studies accessible to the public: *Yes*

State agency information and contact person:

State of New Mexico
Taxation and Revenue Department
Property Tax Division
P. O. Box 25126
Santa Fe, New Mexico 87505
Mr. Domingo Martinez
Telephone: (505) 827-0870 • Fax: (505) 827-0782

NEW YORK

Name of real property tax: *Real Property Tax*

Official valuation standard: *Market value of property - what a willing buyer would pay a willing seller for a specific property at a certain price.*

Annual assessment of real property: *Yes*

Reassessment cycle: *Not required by New York law*

Assessment date: January 1 (in most taxing districts)

Classification of property:

New York City and Nassau County (Long Island) use four classes of real property:

Class I   One, two, and three-family residences

Class II   All other residential property

Class III   Utility

Class IV   All other taxable real property

All other municipalities in New York State use the following classification system:

Class A   Residential, Apartment, and Cooperative Apartment

Class B   Commercial, Apartment, Cooperative Apartment, Industrial, Misc.

Class C   Farm, Vacant

Class D   Utility

Assessment rate:

Must be uniform in the same taxing district but the percentage varies from municipality to municipality. The percentage is based on market value. Check with the assessor or the clerk of the municipality in which your residence is located to determine your assessment level and tax rate.

Tax relief available to homeowners:

Senior Citizen Exemption (section 467 of the real property tax law)
To qualify, seniors must be 65 years of age or older, have an income of

$16,500 or less, and the property must be their legal residence. The exemption is normally 50% of the assessed value, but may vary with each taxing unit.

Disabled Persons (section 459 of the real property tax law)
A partial exemption from real property taxes is granted to disabled persons for residential property which contains improvements intended to facilitate the use by, or accessibility of that property. The amount of the exemption is limited to the increase in the assessed value attributable to the improvement.

Veterans Exemptions (real property tax law section 458(57))
The veterans real property tax exemption has long provided a partial exemption where property owned by a veteran has been purchased with pension, bonus, or insurance monies, referred to as "eligible funds." This exemption generally has a $5,000 maximum reduction of the property's assessed value and is applicable to general municipal taxes, but not to school taxes or special district levies.

The Alternative Veterans Exemption (section 458-a of the real property tax law)
This new exemption only for residential real property of war veterans, was passed in 1984. It provides a property tax exemption of 15% of assessed value to veterans who served during wartime, and an additional 10% to those who served in a combat zone. The law also provides an additional exemption to disabled veterans equal to one-half of their service-connected disability ratings. The alternative exemption is applicable only to general municipal taxes and not to school taxes or special district levies.

Exemptions:
- Government property
- Personalty
- Non-profit religious property
- Charitable property
- Educational property
- Hospitals
- Cultural
- Cemeteries
- Residential (owner-occupied and rental)
- Business property improvements
- Railroads
- Agricultural and forest

Appeal procedure:

Step 1   After receiving notice of assessment, have an informal meeting with the local tax assessor and try to resolve the problem. If after the meeting you are not satisfied with the decision, go to step 2.

Step 2   After an unsuccessful informal meeting with the tax assessor, file a written notice with the Board of Assessment Review.

Step 3   If after presenting all of your evidence before the Board of Assessment Review you are still not satisfied, you have two choices.

> *1.* You may appeal to the small claims court for residential property. When a taxpayer files a petition for small claims assessment review, the taxpayer waives his/her right to judicial review of the assessment in the State Supreme Court pursuant to Title 1 of Article 7 of the real estate tax law (tax certiorari).

> *2.* Or you may appeal to the State Supreme Court, State Appellate Court or State Court of Appeals.

You must exhaust all of the administrative appeals before asking for a judicial review. You must pay the current property tax (under protest) the state alleges you owe or the courts will not hear your case.

Appeal calendar:

The dates mentioned in this calendar are not applicable uniformly throughout New York State. It is imperative that any resident of New York State check with his local municipal assessor or clerk to determine which dates are applicable in his locality.

1. Valuation date: January 1

2. Taxable status date: March 1

3. Informal review with local assessor: January 1 to April 31

4. Tentative roll date: May 1

5. Formal appeal to Board of Assessment Review: May 1 to Grievance Day

6. Grievance day: fourth Tuesday in May

7. Final assessment roll: July 1

8. Appeal to Small Claims Court or State Supreme Court: July 1 to August 1

Level of government responsible for assessment:
State, County, Municipality, Villages, Towns

Tax assessors:

*   Assessors may be appointed or elected.

*   Minimum education requirements exist, but experience may be substituted.

*   All assessors, with very few exceptions, must take special education courses and become state certified.

State issued assessor's manual: *New York State Division of Equalization and Assessment Assessor's Manual*

Equalization: *Yes*

Property tax maps mandatory: *Yes*

Allow real property to be assessed at financially better use rather than current use: *Yes, highest and best use*

Frequency of state ratio studies: *Yearly*

Are state ratio studies accessible to the public: *Yes*

State agency information and contact person:

State of New York
Division of Equalization and Assessment
16 Sheridan Street
Albany, New York 12210-2714
Mr. David Gaskell
Tel: (518) 474-5711 • Fax: (518) 474-9276

NORTH CAROLINA

Name of real property tax: *Ad Valorem Tax*

Official valuation standard: *True value in money,*

> *"the price estimated in terms of money at which the property would change hands between a willing and financially able buyer and a willing seller, neither being under any compulsion to buy or to sell and both having reasonable knowledge of all the uses to which the property is adapted and for which it is capable of being used."*

Annual assessment of real property: *No*

Reassessment cycle: *Yes, every eight years or less*

Assessment date: *January 1*

Classification of property:

Class I	Real Property: 100%
Class II	Personal Property: 100%
Class III	Utilities: 100%

Assessment rate:

Residential property is assessed at 100% of true value in money.

Tax relief available to homeowners:

Senior Citizen and Disabled Exemption:

The first twelve thousand dollars ($12,000) in assessed value of real property, or a mobile home owned by a North Carolina resident and occupied by the owner as his permanent residence shall not be assessed for taxation if, as of January 1 of the year for which the benefit is claimed:

1. The owner is either 65 years of age or older, or is totally and permanently disabled; and

2. The owner's disposable income for the preceding calendar year did not exceed eleven thousand dollars ($11,000); and

3. The owner makes the required application

4. The owner is a North Carolina resident

For married applicants residing with their spouses, the disposable income of both spouses must be included, whether or not the property is in both names.

Disabled Applicant:
Persons who are totally and permanently disabled may apply for this exclusion by a) entering the appropriate information on a form made available by the assessor, and b) furnishing acceptable proof of their disability.

Exemptions:

- Household personalty
- Government property
- Religious property
- Charitable property
- Educational property
- Livestock & poultry
- Pollution abatement equipment
- Recycling equipment
- Manufacturer, wholesale & retailer inventories
- Non-profit hospitals
- Non-profit cemeteries

Appeal procedure:

Step 1   Immediately after receiving notice of assessment have an informal conference with the local tax assessor and try to resolve the problem. If after the meeting you are not satisfied with the decision, go to step 2.

Step 2   After an unsuccessful informal meeting with the tax assessor, file a written appeal to the County Board of Equalization and Review.

Step 3   If you are not satisfied with the decision of the County Board of Equalization and Review, you may file a written appeal to the North Carolina Property Tax Commission.

Step 4   If after presenting all of your evidence before the Property Tax Commission you are still dissatisfied, you may appeal to the State Court of Appeals.

Step 5   If after presenting all of your evidence before the Court of Appeals you are still unhappy with the ruling, you may appeal to the North Carolina Supreme Court.

You must exhaust all of the administrative appeals before asking for a judicial review. You must pay the current property tax (under protest) the state alleges you owe or the courts will not hear your case.

Appeal calendar:

1. January 1: Assessment date

2. January 1 - April 1: Notices of assessment are mailed to the tax-payers and appeals are filed with the County Boards of Equalization and Review.

3. First Monday of April to first Monday of May: Commencement of hearings by the County Boards of Equalization and Review.

4. Appeals to the North Carolina Property Tax Commission must be filed within 30 days of receipt of the decisions of the County Boards of Equalization and Review.

5. Appeals from Commission decisions are made to the Court of Appeals and are based on the record made at the Commission hearings. Such appeals must be filed with the Court of Appeals within 30 days of the entry of the Commission's order (G.S. 105-345).

Level of government responsible for assessment:
County

Tax assessors:

• Appointed for a two or four year term depending on county.

• College degree is required.

• Special education and certificate are required.

State issued assessor's manuals: State publishes its own assessor's manual, the *Machinery Act of North Carolina.*

Equalization: *Yes*

Property tax maps mandatory: *Yes*

Allow real property to be assessed at financially better use rather than current use: *Yes, highest & best use.*

Frequency of state ratio studies: *Yearly*

Are state ratio studies accessible to the public: *No*

State agency information and contact person:

North Carolina Department of Revenue
Ad Valorem Tax Division
P. O. Box 25000
Raleigh, North Carolina 27640
Mr. John W. Erhardt, Real Property Appraiser
Tel: (919) 733-7711 • Fax: (919) 733-1821

NORTH DAKOTA

Name of real property tax: *Property Taxes*

Official valuation standard: *True and full value,*

> *"the value determined by considering the earnings or productive capacity if any, the market value of the property to be assessed."*

Annual assessment of real property: *Yes*

Reassessment cycle: *No*

Assessment date: *February 1*

Classification of property:

Class I	Agricultural
Class II	Residential
Class III	Commercial/Industrial
Class IV	Centrally assessed

Assessment rate:

Residential property is assessed at 4½% of true and full value.

Class I	taxable value = 5% of true and full value
Class II	taxable value = 4½% of true and full value
Class III	taxable value = 5% of true and full value
Class IV	taxable value = 5% of true and full value

Tax relief available to homeowners:

1. Personal property is exempt.

2. A three year exemption is available for the value added by rehabilitation or remodeling to property which is 25 years old or older.

3. A geothermal, solar or wind energy system may qualify for a five year exemption.

4. Homes owned and occupied by persons who are blind or disabled may be eligible for exemption or partial exemption from property taxes subject to annual review.

5. Qualifying new single-family residences and condominiums may be exempt for two years, provided the exemption is approved by the city or county. The exemption is limited to a maximum of $75,000 of the true and full value of the structure.

6. Homeowners who are 65 years of age or older, or who are certified as permanently and totally disabled regardless of age may be entitled to certain property tax credits under the homestead property tax credit program. Qualifications include an annual income from all sources of $13,000 or less and assets of $50,000 or less excluding the first $80,000 value of homestead. A qualifying homeowner may receive a credit to reduce the property's taxable value by up to $2,000. Application for these credits are filed with the local assessor.

7. In addition, homeowners who are 65 years of age and older may qualify for a property tax deferment plan, which is a special assessment credit which becomes a lien on the real property and must be repaid when the property is sold.

8. Renters who are 65 years of age or older, or who are certified as permanently and totally disabled regardless of age and who have an annual income from all sources of $13,000 or less, may be entitled to rent refunds under the homestead property tax credit program. Those who qualify may receive rent refunds of up to $230 if 20% of the rent they pay exceeds 4% of their income. Renters apply to the North Dakota Tax Department for this refund.

Exemptions:

- Government property
- Religious property
- Charitable property
- Educational property
- Farm, residential, agricultural improvements
- Forest & orchards

- Hospitals

- Mines & minerals

- Special exemptions for value added by residential or commercial rehabilitation

- Qualifying residential or business

- Personalty (except utility)

Appeal procedure:

Informal Appeal

In North Dakota there are two different types of procedures for appealing an assessment (valuation). The informal appeal allows a property owner to appeal the current year's assessment by contacting the local assessor and the various county Boards of Equalization before the assessment is finalized.

Step 1   If after receiving the property tax bill a homeowner has a question about his assessment (valuation), the owner should have an informal conference with his local assessor before
April 1.

Step 2   If after the conference the property tax owner is still dissatisfied, he should appeal to the Local Board of Equalization.

Step 3   If after presenting his evidence before the Local Board of Equalization the property owner is dissatisfied with their decision, he may appeal to the County Board of Equalization.

Step 4   If after presenting all the relevant facts before the County Board of Equalization the homeowner is still displeased, he may appeal to State Board of Equalization.

Step 5   The final step in the informal appeal process is the State Board of Equalization. The State Board may reduce an assessment only if an appeal has been made to both the local and county Board of Equalization. The decision of the State Board is final, however you may file a formal appeal.

Formal Appeal

The formal appeal allows a property owner to appeal either a current or prior year's assessment by completing and filing an application for abatement and refund of taxes. The formal appeal begins after the assessment is finalized, follows a strict schedule of hearings, and may result in a court action as the final step of appeal.

Step 1   Applications for abatement are available from the County Auditor or County Director of Equalization. By filing the application, the property owner agrees to allow assessment officials to inspect the property.

Step 2   Within 10 days after receiving the application from the County Auditor, the local governing body notifies the applicant of the time and place of the hearing.

Step 3   Within 60 days after the date of the hearing notice, the city or township board considers the application.

Step 4   The local board recommends either to grant or reject the application in whole or in part. The recommendation is sent to the County Auditor no later than 30 days after the local hearing.

Step 5   At least 10 days before the county hearing, the County Auditor notifies the applicant of the time and place of the hearing.

Step 6   At its next regular meeting, the county commission considers the application. The applicant has the opportunity to present information at the hearing.

Step 7   If the application is approved, the assessment is corrected. If the tax has been paid, a refund is issued. If the application is rejected, the reason(s) for rejection is (are) provided to the applicant.

Step 8   The decision of the county commission may be appealed to the North Dakota District Court. The notice of appeal must be filed with the Clerk of the Court within 30 days of the county decision. A copy of the notice to appeal must be served on the county commission and the state tax commissioner. A property owner may want to consult with an attorney if a court appeal is contemplated.

Appeal calendar: Informal Appeal

1. Before April 1: Informal conference with local assessor.

2. 2nd Monday (township), or
   2nd Tuesday in April: Deadline for an applicant appealing to the Local Equalization Board.

3. First Tuesday in June: Deadline for an applicant appealing to the County Board of Equalization.

4. Second Tuesday in August: Deadline for an applicant appealing to the State Board of Equalization.

Level of government responsible for assessment: *Municipality & Township*

Tax assessors:

- Either two year elected or two year appointed term.

- No minimum education is required.

- Special education and certificate are required.

State issued assessor's manuals: *North Dakota Tax Assessor Manual; Marshall & Swift*

Equalization: *Yes*

Property tax maps mandatory: *No*

Allow real property to be assessed at financially better use rather than current use: *Yes, highest and best use*

Frequency of state ratio studies: *Yearly*

Are state ratio studies accessible to the public: *Yes*

State agency information and contact person:

State of North Dakota
Office of State Tax Commission
State Capitol
600 E. Boulevard Ave
Bismarck, North Dakota 58505-0599
Mr. Barry Hasti, State Supervisor of Assessments
Telephone: (701) 224-2770 • Fax: (701) 224-3700

NOTES

OHIO

Name of real property tax: *Property Taxes*

Official valuation standard: *True value in money,*

> *"an arm's length sale between a willing seller and a willing buyer within a reasonable length of time, either before or after the tax lien date. However, the sale price in an arm's length transaction between a willing seller and a willing buyer shall not be considered the true value of the property subsequent to the sale if (a) the property loses value due to some casualty or (b) an improvement is added to the property."*

Annual assessment of real property: *No*

Reassessment cycle: *Yes, every six years*

Assessment date: *January 1*

Classification of property:

Class I	Residential: 35%	
Class II	Agricultural: 35%	
Class III	Industrial: 35%	
Class IV	Commercial: 35%	
Class V	Mineral: 35%	
Class VI	Business Personal Property	
Class VII	Public utility personal	

Assessment rate:

Residential property is assessed at 35% of true value.

Tax relief available to homeowners:

Homestead Exemption:

Homestead exemption property tax reductions are granted to qualified low-income homeowners who are at least 65 years of age or permanently and totally disabled, or to surviving spouses at least 59 years of age if the deceased had previously received the exemption. The reduction is equal to the gross millage rate multiplied by the reduction in taxable value shown in the following schedule:

Total Income of Owner and Spouse	Reduced Taxable Value by the Lesser Of
under $ 6,500	$5,000 or 75% of taxable value
$ 6,500 - 11,500	$3,000 or 60% of taxable value
$11,500 - 16,500	$1,000 or 25% of taxable value

Percentage rollback:
State law grants tax relief in the form of a 10 percent reduction in each taxpayer's real property tax bill. In addition, a 2.5 percent rollback of real property taxes is granted on a homestead for each homeowner. The state reimburses local governments for the cost of these tax credits.

Exemptions:

- Government property

- Religious property

- Charitable property

- Educational property

- Hospitals

- Cemeteries

Appeal procedure:

Step 1   A property owner who is unhappy with the assessment on his property must file a written complaint against the valuation with the County Auditor (assessor). The time period for filing the complaint starts when the official list of taxable property is prepared by the county auditor, and expires on March 31 of the following year. Generally, the period for filing is from January through March. The complaint will be heard by the County Board of Revision (BOR) which is a three member panel composed of the County Auditor, County Treasurer, and the president of the Board of County Commissioners.

Step 2   If the property owner wishes to appeal the decision of the Board of Revision, that appeal must be filed with the State Board of Tax Appeals within 30 days after the decision of the County Board of Revision was mailed. A copy of the written appeal must also be filed with the Board of Revision.

Step 3   Alternatively, the decision of the Board of Revision may be appealed to the County Court of Common Pleas rather than the State Board of Appeals. Such an appeal must be filed with the County Court of Common Pleas and the Board of Revision within thirty days after the decision of the Board of Revision was mailed.

Step 4   The decision of the State Board of Appeals or the County Court of Common Pleas may be appealed to the Court of Appeals in the county where the property is located.

Step 5   A decision of the State Board of Tax Appeals can also be appealed directly to the Ohio Supreme Court. Again it is necessary to file the appeal 30 days after the decision of the Board of Tax Appeals or the Court of Common Pleas has been recorded.

You should exhaust all the administrative appeals before asking for a judicial review. You must pay the current property tax (under protest) the state alleges you owe or the courts will not hear your case.

Level of government responsible for assessment: *County*

Tax assessors:

* Elected for a four year term.

* No minimum educational requirement.

* No special education or certification is required.

State issued assessor's manuals: No, Ohio does not publish a state issued manual.

Equalization: *Yes*

Property tax maps mandatory: *No*

Allow real property to be assessed at financially better use rather than current use: *Yes, highest and best use*

Frequency of state ratio studies: *Yearly*

Are state ratio studies accessible to the public: *Yes*

State agency information and contact person:

Ohio Department of Taxation
Division of Tax Equalization
P. O. Box 530
Columbus, Ohio 43266-0030
Mr. Ronald Hohman
Tel: (614) 466-5744 • Fax: (614) 466-8654

OKLAHOMA

Name of real property tax: *Ad Valorem Tax*

Official valuation standard: *Fair cash value,*

> *"estimated at the price the property would bring at a fair, voluntary sale for (1) the highest and best use for which the property was actually used during the preceding calendar year; or (2) the highest and best use for which the property was last classified for use if not actually used during the preceding calendar year."*

Annual assessment of real property: *Yes*

Reassessment cycle: *Yes, every 4 years*

Assessment date: *January 1*

Classification of property:

Class I   Real Property, (residential, agricultural, commercial, industrial): 11% - 14% of assessed value

Class II   Personal Property: 35% of assessed value

Class III   Public Service: 35% of assessed value

Assessment rate:

Residential: 11%-14% of fair cash value = taxable value

Tax relief available to homeowners:

Homestead Exemption:

1. Homestead exemption in the amount of $1,000 of assessed value is available to homeowners.

2. An additional $1,000 of assessed value is available to persons with income less than $10,000 annually who are over the age of 65 or who are totally disabled.

3. Veterans may receive a $200 exemption on personal property.

4. Homeowners may receive a $100 exemption on personal property.

Circuit Breaker
Income tax based payment rebate for persons older than 65 years old
and have less than $10,000 combined income.

Exemptions:

- Government property

- Religious property

- Charitable property

- Educational property

- Hospitals

- Cemeteries

Appeal procedure:

Step 1   After receiving the notice of assessment, have an in-
               formal meeting with the local tax assessor and try to
               resolve the problem. If after the meeting you are dis-
               satisfied with the decision, go to step 2.

Step 2   After an unsuccessful informal meeting with the tax
               assessor, file an appeal with the County Board of
               Equalization.

Step 3   If after presenting all of your evidence before the
               County Board of Equalization you are still not satis-
               fied, you may appeal to the District Court.

Step 4   If after presenting all of your evidence before the
               District Court you are unhappy with the decision, you
               may appeal to the Court of Appeals.

Step 5   Lastly you may appeal to the State Supreme Court.

---

*You must exhaust all of the administrative appeals be-
fore asking for a judicial review. You must pay the current property tax (under protest) the state alleges you
owe or the courts will not hear your case.*

Appeal calendar:

1.   January 1: Assessment day.

2. January to March: Notice of valuation sent to taxpayers.

3. Within 20 days of notice of valuation, make an informal inquiry to the county assessor.

4. Within 10 days of assessor's unfavorable response, make formal written appeal to County Board of Equalization.

5. April 1 to May 31: County Board of Equalization listens to complaints and conducts hearings.

6. Within 60 days of County Board of Equalization's unsatisfactory response, make a formal appeal to District Court.

Level of government responsible for assessment: County, State

Tax assessors:

- Elected for a four year term.

- No minimum education is required.

- Special education and certificate are required.

State issued assessor's manual: *Oklahoma State Appraisal Manual*

Equalization: *Yes*

Property tax maps mandatory: *Yes*

Allow real property to be assessed at financially better use rather than current use: *No, current use.*

Frequency of state ratio studies: *Yearly*

Are state ratio studies accessible to the public: *Yes*

State agency information and contact person:

State of Oklahoma
Oklahoma Tax Commission
Ad Valorem Tax Division
2501 Lincoln Blvd.
Oklahoma City, Oklahoma 73194
Ms. Cathy Gibson
Tel: (405) 521-3178• Fax: (405) 521-3991

NOTES

OREGON

Name of real property tax: *Property Tax*

Official valuation standard: *Real market value*

> *"is the minimum amount of cash the property would reasonably sell for if offered for sale in the open market during the tax year. It also assumes that the buyer and the seller are well informed and under no undue compulsion to sell or buy."*

Annual assessment of real property: *Yes*

Reassessment cycle: *Yes, every six years*

Assessment date: *July 1*

Classification of property:

Class I	Residential
Class II	Rural
Class III	Farm
Class IV	Commercial
Class V	Industrial
Class VI	Exempt
Class VII	Forest
Class VIII	Miscellaneous
Class IX	Utilities
Class X	Personal Property

Assessment rate:

Residential property assessed at 100% of real market value.

Tax relief available to homeowners:

Senior Citizen's Property Tax Deferral:
Oregon homeowners age 62 or over may delay paying property taxes on their residences. The taxes must be paid, with interest, when the owner dies or sells the property, moves, or changes ownership.

Program requirements are:

1. 62 years of age or older

2. applies only to owners homestead

3. total household income less than $19,500

Veteran's Property Tax Exemption:
If you are a veteran, disabled veteran or surviving spouse of a veteran you may be entitled to exempt $7,500 or $10,000 of your homestead property's real market value from property taxation. The exemption is first applied to your home and then to your taxable personal property.

Exemptions:

*   Government property
*   Religious property
*   Charitable property
*   Educational property
*   Historical property
*   Some hospitals
*   Cemeteries
*   Literary & scientific institutions

Appeal procedure:

Step 1   Schedule an informal conference with local assessor after receiving the property tax statement.

Step 2   File a written petition with the County Board of Equalization.

Step 3   File with either the small claims division of Oregon Tax Court (non-appealable) or the Department of Revenue. The small claims division of the Oregon Tax Court will only hear appeals where:
*   the value of the land is $250,000 or less
*   the value of the building is $250,000 or less
*   the combined land and building value is $250,000 or less
*   the personal property value is $250,000 or less

Step 4   Appealing Department of Revenue Decision - regular division of Oregon Tax Court.

Step 5   Oregon Supreme Court

Appeal calendar:

1. Assessment date: July 1.

2. Property tax statement mailed to taxpayer in October.

3. Informal conference with local assessor: October.

4. Appeal to the County Board of Equalization between October 25 and December 31.

5. When appealing to either the Small Claims Division of the Oregon Tax Court or the Department of Revenue the taxpayer must file an appeal within 30 days after County Board of Equalization's decision is mailed.

6. Appeal the decision of the Department of Revenue of the regular division of the Oregon Tax Court within 60 days after the date of the Department's decision.

Level of government responsible for assessment:
County, State

Tax assessors:

*   Elected for a four year term or appointed for terms of varying length.

*   High school minimum education is required.

*   Special education and certificate are required.

State issued assessor's manual: *Oregon Appraisal Methods for Real Property*

Equalization: *Yes*

Property tax maps mandatory: *Yes*

Allow real property to be assessed at financially better use rather than current use: *Yes, highest and best use*

Frequency of state ratio studies: *Yearly*

Are state ratio studies accessible to the public: *Yes*

State agency information and contact person:

Oregon Department of Revenue
Property Tax Division
955 Center Street N.E.
Salem, Oregon 97310
Ms. Cathie Woods
Tel: (503) 945-8292 • Fax: (503) 945-8737

PENNSYLVANIA

In Pennsylvania, the assessment process is under the jurisdiction of county governments. There are 67 counties and therefore 67 different assessment organizations. No state agency oversees the county assessment offices. The assessments done by the counties are used by the counties, municipalities, and school districts to levy property taxes.

Name of real property tax: *Property Tax*

Official valuation standard: *Assessors are required to value property–*

> *"according to the actual value thereof and at such rates and prices for which the same would separately bona fide sell." Actual value has been interpreted by the courts to mean market value. Market value has been defined as the price which a purchaser is willing but not obligated to pay an owner who is willing but not obligated to sell, taking into consideration all uses to which the property is adapted.*

Annual assessment of real property: *Varies from county to county*

Reassessment cycle: *Varies from county to county*

Assessment date: *Varies from county to county*

Classification of property: *Varies from county to county*

Assessment rate:

Statutory rate limitations on real estate taxes have been established for all classes of taxing jurisdiction in Pennsylvania, except the cities of Philadelphia, Pittsburgh, Scranton, and the Philadelphia school district.

Tax relief available to homeowners:

The specifics of tax relief programs vary from county to county. The Pennsylvania Constitution (article VIII, section 2) mandates that residential real estate owned and occupied by paraplegic, amputee, blind, or totally disabled veterans or their surviving unmarried spouses certified as needy by the state Veterans Commission be given tax relief.

The senior citizens rebate and assistance act provides for rebates on local property taxes and that portion of rent representing the tenant's share of property taxes. Rebates are granted to senior citizens, widows, widowers and permanently disabled persons with incomes less than $15,000 per year on a sliding scale basis.

PENNSYLVANIA TAXING JURISDICTION RATE LIMIT

TAXING JURISDICTION	Rate Limit
Counties, second class(Allegheny)	25 mills
Counties, second class A(Bucks, Delaware and Montgomery)	30 mills
Counties, third through eighth class	25 mills
Institution districts	10 mills
Cities, third class	25 mills
Boroughs	30 mills
Townships, first class	30 mills
Townships, second class	14 mills
School districts, first class A(Pittsburgh)	32.25 Mills
School districts, second, third & fourth class	25 mills

* For third through eighth class counties, cities, boroughs and townships, an additional 5 mills maybe imposed with court approval.

Exemptions:

- Government property
- Religious property
- Charitable property
- Educational property
- Hospitals
- Cemeteries

Appeal procedure:

Step 1   After receiving notice of assessment, make an informal administrative appeal to the local county assessor and try to resolve the problem. If after the meeting you are not satisfied with the decision, go to step 2.

Step 2   After an unsuccessful informal meeting with the local county assessor, file a written appeal to the County Board of Assessment Appeals.

Step 3   If after presenting all of your evidence before the County Board of Assessment Appeals you are dissatisfied, you may appeal to the County Court of Common Pleas.

Step 4   If after presenting all of your relevant evidence before the County Court of Common Pleas you are still displeased, you may appeal to the Commonwealth Court.

Step 5   If you are unhappy with the decision of the Commonwealth Court, you may appeal to the State Supreme Court.

> *You must exhaust all of the administrative appeals before asking for a judicial review. You must pay the current property tax (under protest) the state alleges you owe or the courts will not hear your case.*

Appeal calendar:

COUNTY BOARD OF ASSESSMENT APPEALS CALENDAR

County	Filing Date Deadline	Hearing Date Deadline
First Class	First Monday in October	as determined by board
Second Class	Last day of February	as determined by board
Second Class A & Third	Sept.1 or within 40 days of assessment notice	October 31
Fourth to Eight Class	Sept. 1 or within 40 days of assessment notice	October 31
Cities Third Class	Within 30 days after delivery of notice to taxpayer	as determined by board

Level of government responsible for assessment:
County

Tax assessors:

- Varies by county, elected or appointed.

- Minimum high school education is required.

- All assessors must be certified by the State Board of Real Estate Appraisers and must complete a 90 hour basic appraisal course.

State issued assessor's manuals: *No*

Equalization: *Yes*

Property tax maps mandatory: *Yes*

Allow real property to be assessed at financially better use rather than current use: *Varies from county to county*

Frequency of state ratio studies: *Triennial*

Are state ratio studies accessible to the public: *No*

State agency information and contact person:

In Pennsylvania there is no state agency.
Contact your local county assessor.

RHODE ISLAND

Name of real property tax: *Property Tax*

Official valuation standard: *Full and fair cash value or a locally determined uniform percentage of full and fair cash value (not defined by statute).*

Annual assessment of real property: *No*

Reassessment cycle: *Yes, at least every 10 years*

Assessment date: *December 1*

Classification of property:

Class I	Real Property: 100%
Class II	Personal Property
Class III	Motor Vehicles

Assessment rate:

Residential property assessed at 100% of full and fair cash value.

Tax relief available to homeowners:

Veterans Exemption:
Each of Rhode Island's thirty-nine cities and towns independently determines the type and value of the veterans exemptions that it grants. A breakdown of specific benefits granted may be obtained from the city or town assessor or from a booklet published by the office of municipal affairs entitled "Veterans' Exemptions of R.I. Cities and Towns 1993."

Veterans' exemptions as authorized by Title 44, Chapters 3, 4 and 5 of the General Laws of Rhode Island include the following categories:

1. Veterans regular exemption

2. Unmarried widow/widower of qualified veteran

3. Veterans exemption for totally disabled through service connected disability

4. Veterans exemption for partially disabled through service connected disability

5.   Gold Star parents exemption: prisoner of war exemption

6.   Specially adapted housing exemption

Old Age and Disabled Exemption
(Title 44, chapter 33 R.I. General Laws):
Rhode Island residents 65 years of age or older or who are disabled (receiving Social Security disability payments) and who meet certain eligibility requirements may be entitled to property tax relief credit. This relief is provided in the form of tax credits against the state personal income tax by filing the appropriate form (RI-1040h). If a claimant is not required to file a Rhode Island personal income tax return, the RI-1040h form may be filed by itself as a return. The maximum credit allowed is $200 per year.

To qualify for the property tax relief credit you must meet all of the following conditions:

1.   You must have been 65 years of age or over on December 31 or a disabled person who has received Social Security disability payments during the year.

2.   You must have been a legal resident of Rhode Island for the entire calendar year.

3.   Your household income must have been $12,500 or less.

4.   You must have lived in a household or rented a dwelling that was subject to property tax.

5.   You must be current on property tax due on your homestead for all prior years and be current on all installments due during the year.

Exemptions:

•   Government property

•   Religious property

•   Charitable property

•   Educational property

•   Hospitals

•   Cemeteries

Appeal procedure:

Step 1   After receiving notice of assessment, make an informal appeal to the local tax assessor and try to resolve the problem. If after the meeting you are not satisfied with the decision, go to step 2.

Step 2   After an unsuccessful informal meeting with the local tax assessor, file a formal written appeal to the Local Board of Assessment Review.

Step 3   If after presenting all of your evidence before the Local Board of Assessment review you are dissatisfied with their decision, you may appeal to the Superior Court of Rhode Island.

You must exhaust all administrative appeals before asking for a judicial review. You must pay the current property tax (under protest) the state alleges you owe or the courts will not hear your case.

Appeal calendar:

Dates of notice to taxpayer and hearing filing deadlines vary between the 39 different towns and municipalities.

Level of government responsible for assessment:
Municipality, Town

Tax assessors:

- Elected or appointed - local option.

- High school minimum education is required.

- Special education and certificate are required.

State issued assessor's manuals: No assessor's manual issued

Equalization: *Yes*

Property tax maps mandatory: *No*

Allow real property to be assessed at financially better use rather than current use: *Local option*

Frequency of state ratio studies: *Yearly*

Are state ratio studies accessible to the public: *Yes*

State agency information and contact person:

State of Rhode Island
Department of Administration
Office of Municipal Affairs
One Capitol Hill
Providence, RI 02908-5873
Mr. James S. Savage, Supervisor-Tax Equalization
Telephone: (401) 277-2885 • Fax: (401) 277-3809

SOUTH CAROLINA

Name of real property tax: *Property Tax*

Official valuation standard: *Act 208, as passed by the General Assembly in 1975, provides that all real property will be valued at its current fair market value, the price your property would sell for on today's real estate market.*

Annual assessment of real property: *No specified period; based on sales ratio studies.*

Reassessment cycle: *No specified period; based on sales ratio studies.*

Assessment date: *December 1*

Classification of property:

Class I   Residential (legal residence): 4% of fair market value

Class II   Residential (non-owner occupied): 6% of fair market value

Class III   Private Agriculture (use): 4% of fair market value

Class IV   Corporate Agriculture: 6% of fair market value

Class V   Transportation, Railroads, Airlines, Pipelines (Real and Personal Property): 9.5% of fair market value

Class VI   Utilities (Real & Personal Property): 10.5% of fair market value

Class VII   Manufacturers (Real & Personal property): 10.5% of fair market value

Class VIII   Personal Property: automobiles, boats, campers: 10.5% of fair market value

Class IX   All Other Real Property (commercial & industrial, etc.): 6% of fair market value

Assessment rate:

Residential (legal residence) property assessed at 4% of fair market value.

Tax relief available to homeowners:

Homestead Exemption:

The elderly (age 65 and over), the blind, the disabled, and a surviving spouse may be eligible for a $20,000 deduction from the assessor's fair market value appraisal of their legal residence.

Veteran Exemption:

1. The legal residence of any veteran who is one hundred percent permanently and totally disabled from a service-connected disability shall be exempt from ad valorem taxation. This exemption is also granted to the surviving spouse of a disabled veteran as long as he/she does not remarry.

2. The legal residence of a surviving spouse of a serviceman killed in action in the line of duty shall be exempt from ad valorem taxation as long as he/she does not remarry.

Disabled Exemption:

The legal residence of a paraplegic or hemiplegic person, is exempt from all property taxation provided the person furnishes satisfactory proof of his/her disability to the state tax commission. The exemption is allowed to the surviving spouse of the person so long as the spouse does not remarry.

Exemptions:

- Government property
- Religious property & parsonages
- Charitable property
- Educational property
- Public libraries
- Cemeteries
- Household personal property
- Inventories of manufacturers (except retail)
- Fuel held by public utility
- All new manufacturing establishments located in this state after July 1, 1977 for five years from time of establishment
- All facilities or equipment used for prevention of pollution

Appeal procedure:

Under the provision of state law (South Carolina Tax Commission regulation 117-3), the property owner may challenge his assessment.

Step 1   Within 30 days after dated notice of assessment is received by the property owner, a written objection must be filed with the assessor by the property owner or his/her agent.

Step 2   Within 20 days of receipt of the property owner's written objection, the assessor must schedule a conference to discuss the objection.

Step 3   At the conference, the property owner may request that the assessor conduct an on-site field review of the property.

The assessor may request that the property owner provide within 30 days all additional written data and evidence to substantiate the property owner's valuation.

Step 4   After the on-site field review has been completed, the assessor will notify the property owner of his decision in writing.

Step 5   If the property owner disagrees with the findings of the assessor, he/she may make a written appeal to the County Board of Assessment Appeals.

Step 6   If the property owner disagrees with the decision of the County Board of Assessment Appeals, he/she may make a written appeal to the South Carolina Tax Commission.

Step 7   If the property owners disagrees with the findings of the Tax Commission, he/she may hire an attorney and seek judicial relief (Circuit Court, Supreme Court), having exhausted all administrative remedies.

> You must exhaust all of the administrative appeals be-
> fore asking for a judicial review. You must pay the cur-
> rent property tax (under protest) the state alleges you
> owe or the courts will not hear your case.

Level of government responsible for assessment:
County, State

Tax assessors:

- Appointed for varying terms.

- College degree is required.

- Special education and certificate are required.

State issued assessor's manuals: No state assessor's manual

Equalization: *No*

Property tax maps mandatory: *Yes*

Allow real property to be assessed at financially better use rather than
current use: *Yes, highest and best use*

Frequency of state ratio studies: *Yearly*

Are state ratio studies accessible to the public: *Yes*

State agency information and contact person:

State of South Carolina
Department of Revenue and Taxation
301 Gervais Street
P. O. Box 125
Columbia, South Carolina 29214
Mr. Ronald L. Cassels, Tax Supervisor
Telephone: (803) 737-4463 • Fax: (803) 737-4685

SOUTH DAKOTA

Name of real property tax: *Property Tax*

Official valuation standard: *True and full value in money. "The director shall value each article or description by itself and at an amount or price as he believes the property to be fairly worth in money." SDCL 10-6-33.*

Annual assessment of real property: *Yes*

Reassessment cycle: *No*

Assessment date: *November 1*

Classification of property:

Class I	Agricultural: 100% of assessed value
Class II	Non-agricultural: 100% of assessed value
Class III	Utilities: 100% of assessed value
Class IV	Mobile Home: 100% of assessed value

Assessment rate:

Residential property assessed at 100% of true and full value in money.

Tax relief available to homeowners:

Freeze on assessment of single-family dwellings. Conditions determining entitlement. SDCL 10-6a-2

1. Has a household income of less than $12,000 if the household is a single-member household; or

2. Has a household income of less than $15,000 if the household is a multiple-member household; and

3. Has owned a single-family dwelling, in fee or by contract to purchase, for at least three years, or has been a resident of South Dakota for at least five years; and

4. Has resided for at least eight months of the previous calendar year in the single family dwelling; and

5. Has established a base year.

Tax exemption of dwelling of paraplegic or amputee veteran. SDCL 10-4-24.9 And SDCL 10-4-24.1

All dwellings or parts of multiple family dwellings which are specifically designed for use by paraplegics as wheelchair homes, and are owned and occupied for the full calendar year in which a tax is to be levied, or the unremarried widow or widower of such a veteran, shall be exempt from property taxation.

REDUCTION OF TAX ON DWELLING
OWNED BY PARAPLEGIC (Non-veteran)

Single Member Household		
If household income is more than:	But not more than:	Tax reduction on current levy is:
$0	$5,000	100%
5,000	6,000	75%
6,000	7,000	50%
7,000	8,000	25%
more than $8,000		0%
Multiple Member Household		
$0	$ 9,000	100%
9,000	10,000	75%
10,000	11,000	50%
11,000	12,000	25%

Exemptions:

- Personalty
- Government property
- Religious property
- Charitable property
- Educational property
- Historical property (depending on ownership)
- Hospitals
- Cemeteries

Appeal procedure:

Step 1   Upon receipt of the notice of assessment schedule an informal meeting with the Director of Equalization to try and work out any differences. If the parties fail to agree:

Step 2   A notice of a complaint or grievance shall be filed in writing with the clerk of the Local Board of Equalization no later than the Thursday preceding the third Monday in March.

Step 3   Any person feeling aggrieved may appeal the decision of a Local Board of Equalization to the County Board of Equalization by filing a written notice of appeal with the county auditor on or before the third Tuesday in April.

Step 4   An appeal to the State Board of Equalization from a County Board of Equalization shall be perfected by filing a notice of appeal with the Secretary of Revenue, Pierre, South Dakota, no later than the third Friday in May.

Step 5   If the taxpayer is dissatisfied with the decision of the State Board of Equalization, he/she may appeal to the Circuit Court by filing a written appeal within twenty days after receipt of the decision of the State Board of Equalization.

> *You must exhaust all of the administrative appeals before asking for a judicial review. You must pay the current property tax (under protest) the state alleges you owe or the courts will not hear your case.*

Appeal calendar:

1.   November 1: Legal assessment date.

2.   March 1: Notice of assessment must be mailed out to taxpayers by this date.

3.   Third Monday in March: Local Boards of Equalization start sessions last 5 days in March.

4. Second Tuesday in May: County Boards of Equalization start in session for two weeks.

5. Third Monday in June: State Board of Equalization starts in session until work is done.

Level of government responsible for assessment:
County

Tax assessors:

*   Appointed for a five year term.

*   No minimum education is required.

*   Special education and certificate are required.

State issued assessor's manuals: *The 1993 Residential Cost Handbook*, Marshall and Swift Publication Co., *The 1993 Marshall Valuation Service*, Marshall and Swift Publication Co.

Equalization: *No*

Property tax maps mandatory: *Yes*

Allow real property to be assessed at financially better use rather than current use: *No, current value*

Frequency of state ratio studies: *Yearly*

Are state ratio studies accessible to the public: *Yes*

State agency information and contact person:

South Dakota Department of Revenue
700 Governors Drive
Pierre, South Dakota 57501-2291
Mr. Jim Schade
Telephone: (605) 773-3311 • Fax: (605) 773-6729

TENNESSEE

Name of real property tax: *Property Tax*

Official valuation standard: *"The value of all property shall be ascertained from the evidence of its sound intrinsic and immediate value, for purposes of sale between a willing seller and a willing buyer without consideration of speculative values." (Tennessee Code Annotated 67-5-601).*

Annual assessment of real property: *Yes*

Reassessment cycle: *Yes, 6 years*

Assessment date: *January 1*

Classification of property:

Class I	Residential: 25%
Class II	Commercial/Industrial: 40%
Class III	Public Service: 55%
Class IV	Farm: 25%
Class V	Personal Property: 30%

Assessment rate:

Residential property assessed at 25% of market value.

Tax relief available to homeowners:

Senior Citizen Tax Exemption

To qualify for a partial tax exemption, a taxpayer must have been age 65 or older on December 31 of the tax year and owned and lived in his/her own home in Tennessee, which was the taxpayer's legal residence during the tax year. The senior citizen exemption also limits the total combined income to no more than $10,000. The amount of this exemption will vary depending on the taxpayer's property assessment and the tax rate in his/her jurisdiction.

Disabled Exemption

If a taxpayer is disabled, the disability must be total and permanent as rated by the Social Security Administration, Railroad Retirement Board,

Civil Service, Veterans Administration, or another qualified agency on or before December 31 of the tax year.

Furthermore the combined gross income may not exceed $10,000. The amount of this exemption will vary depending on the taxpayer's property assessment and the tax rate in his/her jurisdiction.

Disabled Veteran Exemption
100 percent total and permanent disability rating from:

1. A service-connected disability which resulted in paraplegia or paralysis of both legs and lower body from traumatic injury or disease to the spinal cord or brain; or loss, or loss of use, of two or more limbs, or blindness (including industrial blindness).

2. A combat related disability.

3. Being a prisoner of war for at least five months.

4. Widow or widower of a disabled veteran - must have been married to the veteran who met one of these conditions and not remarried.

The amount of this exemption will vary depending on the taxpayer's property assessment and the tax rate of his/her jurisdictions. For those who qualify as a disabled veteran or widow or widower of a disabled veteran, there is no income limit.

Exemptions:

- Government property
- Religious property
- Charitable property
- Educational property
- Cemeteries
- Historic properties

Appeal procedure:

Step 1   After receiving notice of assessment, have an informal conference with the assessor and try to resolve the problem. If after the meeting you are not satisfied with the decision, go to step 2.

Step 2   After an unsuccessful informal meeting with the tax assessor, file a written notice with the County Board of Equalization.

Step 3   If after presenting all of your evidence before the County Board of Equalization you are still dissatisfied, you may appeal to the Administrative Law Judge.

Step 4   If after presenting all of your evidence before the Administrative Law Judge you are still unhappy, you may appeal to the Assessment Appeals Commission.

Step 5   If you are still dissatisfied, you may appeal to the State Board of Equalization.

Step 6   Lastly, if still unhappy you may appeal to the courts.

You must exhaust all of the administrative remedies available to you prior to asking for a judicial review. You must pay the current property tax (under protest) the state contends you owe or the courts will not hear your case.

Appeal calendar:

1. Assessment date: January 1

2. Notices of assessment are mailed to property owners no later than May 20.

3. Informal conferences with local assessor held for 10 days after notices are mailed.

4. Local Equalization Board commences hearings 10 days after assessment notices are mailed to property owners.

5. County Board of Equalization hearings and Metropolitan Boards of Equalization commence sessions on June 1 of each year.

6. Appeals to the State Board of Equalization from an action of a local Board of Equalization must be filed before August 1 of the tax year or within forty-five (45) days of the date that the notices of the local Board were sent, whichever is later.

7.   Property taxes are due the first Monday of October in the tax year.

Level of government responsible for assessment:
County, State, Municipality

Tax assessors:

- Elected for a four year term.

- High school education is required.

- Special education or certificate is not required.

State issued assessor's manual: *Tennessee Residential Listing Procedures Manual.*

Equalization: *No*

Property tax maps mandatory: *Yes*

Allow real property to be assessed at financially better use rather than current use: *No, current use (Tenn. Code Ann. 67-5-1001 Et seq.)*

Frequency of state ratio studies: *Every 2 years*

Are state ratio studies accessible to the public: *Yes*

State agency information and contact person:

State of Tennessee
Division of Property Assessment
James K. Polk State Office Building
Suite #1400
505 Deaderick Street,
Nashville, Tennessee 37243-0277
Mr. Tom Fleming, Director
Telephone: (615) 741-2837 • Fax: (615) 532-2224

TEXAS

Name of real property tax: *Property Tax*

Official valuation standard: *Market value is the cash price for which a property would sell when both buyer and seller want the best price and neither one is under pressure to buy or sell.*

Annual assessment of real property: *Yes*

Reassessment cycle: *Yes - at least once every 3 years*

Assessment date: *January 1*

Classification of property:

Class I	Utilities: 100%	
Class II	Commercial Personal: 100%	
Class III	Industrial Personal: 100%	
Class IV	Other Personal: 100%	
Class V	Residential Inventory: 100%	
Class VI	Intangible Personal and Uncertified: 100%	
Class VII	Oil, Gas, and Mineral: 100%	

Assessment rate:

Residential property assessed at 100% of market value.

Tax relief available to homeowners:

Homestead Exemption - All Homeowners
To qualify for homestead exemption a taxpayer must own a home on January 1, and use that home as his/her principal residence.

School Taxes
All homeowners qualify for $5,000 exemption on the value of their home.

County Taxes
All homeowners qualify for $3,000 exemption if their county collects a special tax for farm to market roads or flood control tax.

Optional Exemption

Any taxing unit, including a school district, city, county, etc., may offer an exemption for up to 20 percent of the market value of the home. This means that the school taxes on the home cannot increase as long as the senior taxpayer owns and lives in the home. When the senior taxpayer dies, the ceiling transfers to the surviving spouse if the survivor is 55 or older.

Disabled Veterans or Survivors

A Texas resident may qualify for a property tax exemption if:

1.   He/she is a veteran who was disabled while serving with U.S. Armed Forces; or

2.   He/she is the surviving spouse or child of a disabled veteran or of a member of the armed forces who was killed while on active duty.

This exemption ranges from $1,500 to $3,000 depending on the extent of the disability.

Exemptions:

- Government property
- Religious property
- Charitable property
- Educational property
- Historical
- Hospitals
- Cemeteries
- Non-income producing personality
- Residential homestead

Appeal procedure:

Step 1   Have an informal meeting with the local tax appraiser and try to resolve the problem. If after the meeting you are not satisfied with the decision, go to step 2.

Step 2   After an unsuccessful informal meeting with the tax appraiser, file a written protest to the Appraisal Review Board.

Step 3   If after presenting all of your evidence before the Appraisal Review Board you are still not satisfied, you may make a formal appeal to the State District Court.

Step 4   If after presenting all of your evidence before the State District Court you are still dissatisfied, you may appeal to the Court of Appeals.

Step 5   Lastly, if still dissatisfied you may make a formal appeal to the State Supreme Court.

You must exhaust all of the administrative appeals before asking for a judicial review. You must also pay the current property tax (under protest) the state alleges you owe or the courts will not hear your case.

Appeal calendar:

January 1: Valuation date.

January 1 - April 30: Informal appeal to local appraiser.

March 31: Deadline to file rendition with appraisal district.

May 15: Notice of appraised value sent to property owners.

May 31: Deadline to file rendition with appraisal district.

May 15 - July 20: Sessions held by Appraisal Review Board.

September 1: Deadline for filing appeal with State District Court.

Level of government responsible for assessment:
County Appraisal District

Tax assessors:

• Elected for a four year term.

• No minimum education is required.

• Special education and certification are required.

State issued assessor's manual: *International Association of Assessing Officers Assessment Textbook*

Equalization: *Yes*

Property tax maps mandatory: *Yes*

Allow real property to be assessed at financially better use rather than current use: *Yes, highest and best use.*

Frequency of state ratio studies: *Yearly*

Are state ratio studies accessible to the public: *Yes*

State agency information and contact person:

Comptroller of Public Accounts
Property Tax Division
4301 Westbank Drive Building B
Austin, TX 78746
Mr. Isaac L. Jackson, Director, Research
Telephone: (800) 252-9121 • Fax: (512) 305-9801

UTAH

Name of real property tax: *Property Tax*

Official valuation standard: *Market value is what a property would sell for if offered for a reasonable amount of time. This assumes that both the buyer and seller are unrelated, well informed, and under no pressure to buy or sell the property.*

Annual assessment of real property: *Yes*

Reassessment cycle: *Every 5 years*

Assessment date: *January 1*

Classification of property:

Class I	Vacant Land: 100%	
Class II	Primary Residential: 60%	
Class III	Other Residential: 100%	
Class IV	Local Commercial: 80%	
Class V	F.A.A.: 100%	
Class VI	Personal Property: 100%	
Class VII	Centrally Assessed: 100%	

Assessment rate:

Residential property assessed at 100% of market value.

Tax relief available to homeowners:

Veterans Exemption:
An exemption of up to $30,000 is available to eligible disabled veterans, their unremarried surviving spouses, or their minor orphaned children. To be eligible, the veteran must be at least 25% disabled, and, in the case of veterans who served in the military after 1920, the disability must be service related. Additionally, the applicant's total annual income must be $30,000 or less.

A veteran who is 100% disabled is entitled to the full exemption. If the percentage of disability is less than 100%, the exemption allowed is that percentage of $30,000. Surviving unremarried spouses or orphaned children are entitled to the same exemption as the veteran unless the veteran served prior to 1921. In that case the surviving spouse or orphaned minor children are entitled to 100% of the exemption for any disability over 25%.

Indigent Tax Relief:
An indigent person is entitled to a tax abatement of $300 or 50% of the total tax assessed, whichever is less. To be eligible, a person must be 65 years of age or older. However, a person under 65 years of age may qualify on the basis of disability or extreme hardship. Eligibility also depends on yearly household income as defined by statute. That amount varies from year to year due to cost of living adjustments. The applicant must reside in the residence for which tax relief is requested at least 10 months of the year.

A person qualifying under this section may also apply for a tax deferral. Taxes deferred accumulate with interest and represent a lien on the property.

Circuit Breaker Tax Relief:
A tax credit is available to a person who is 65 years of age or older, or who is a widow or widower, and whose household income falls within the guidelines prescribed by statute. That amount varies from year to year due to cost of living adjustments. The value of the tax credit varies from 50% to $475 in relation to income.

Blind Exemption:
The first $11,500 of taxable value of real and tangible personal property owned by blind persons, their unremarried surviving spouses, or orphaned minor children is exempt from taxation. Eligibility depends upon specific vision impairment as attested by a registered opthalmologist.

Exemptions:
1. Property exempt under the laws of the United States;
2. Property owned by the state, school districts, and public libraries;
3. Property owned by counties, cities, towns, special districts or other political subdivisions;
4. Property owned by a nonprofit entity which is exclusively used for religious, charitable, or educational purposes;
5. Places of burial not held or used for private or corporate benefit;

6. Certain property used for irrigation;

7. Farm equipment or machinery;

8. Livestock;

9. Personal household furnishings;

10. Inventory; and

11. Intangible property

Appeal procedure:

To appeal valuation or equalization of real property, the taxpayer applies to the County Board of Equalization within 30 days of the mailing of disclosure notice or valuation notice. The application must include the owner's estimate of market value and supporting evidence. The appellant may appeal the board's decision by filing an appeal with the State Tax Commission. The appellant may seek judicial review after exhausting all administrative remedies. The appellant must have paid the current property tax the state alleges is owed (under protest) or the courts will not hear the case.

Appeal calendar:

1. January 1: Lien date - a property (real and personal) is appraised based on this date for the tax year.

2. By July 22: The county auditors mail notices of valuation and tax changes to all property owners.

3. Within 30 days of mailing of notices, applications for appeal of locally assessed real property must be filed with the County Boards of Equalization.

4. By October 1: The County Boards of Equalization render decisions on real property appeals and notify taxpayers.

5. Within 30 days after final action by the County Boards, appeals to State Tax Commission of real property valuations must be filed with county auditors.

6. By March 1: The State Tax Commission decides real property appeals of County Board of Equalization decisions and reports to county auditors. County auditors must comply with the decisions.

Level of government responsible for assessment:
County

Tax assessors:

- Elected for a four year term.

- Minimum high school education is required.

- Special education and certificate are required.

State issued assessor's manual: *Board of Equalization Standards of Practice*

Equalization: *Yes*

Property tax maps mandatory: *Yes*

Allow real property to be assessed at financially better use rather than current use: *Yes, highest & best use*

Frequency of state ratio studies: *Yearly*

Are state ratio studies accessible to the public: *Yes*

State agency information and contact person:

Utah State Tax Commission
Herbert M. Wells Building
160 East 300 South
Salt Lake City, Utah 84134
Ms. Irene Rees
Telephone: (801) 530-6177 • Fax: (801) 530-6422

VERMONT

Name of real property tax: *Property Tax*

Official valuation standard: *Appraisal value*

> *"the price which the property will bring in the market when offered for sale and purchased by another, taking into consideration all the elements of the availability of the property, its use both potential and prospective, any functional deficiencies, and all other elements such as age and condition which combine to give property a market value."*

Annual assessment of real property: *No*

Reassessment cycle: *Not required by Vermont*

Assessment date: *April 1*

Classification of property:

Class I   Mobile Homes: 100%

Class II   Miscellaneous Land: 100%

Class III Other: 100%

Class IV   Personal Property: 100%

Assessment rate:

Residential property assessed at 100% of appraisal value.

Tax relief available to homeowners:

Veterans Exemption:
Under the provisions of 32 Vermont Statutes Annotated, Section 3802(11), a qualified veteran of any war, or unremarried widow or widower of such a veteran, is eligible to receive a $10,000 exemption (may be increased to up to $20,000 upon vote of town or city) on the listed value of his/her established residence. Only one exemption is allowed on a property.

To qualify, the residence must be owned by a veteran, his or her spouse, widow(er), child, or jointly by a combination of them. One or more of the above-mentioned persons must be receiving either:

1. Disability compensation for at least 50% disability; or

2. Death compensation; or

3. Dependence and indemnity compensation; or

4. A pension for disability paid through any military department,

5. Or the Veterans Administration.

Property Tax Rebate Program:

If a taxpayer owns or rents a house (or apartment) in Vermont as his/her principal residence, the taxpayer may be entitled to a rebate from the state if the property tax (or, if you rent, then 20% of the rent) exceeds 3 1/2 to 5 percent of the household income.

Landlords are required to provide each tenant with a rent certificate on or before January 31 of each year, unless the tenant has voluntarily signed a revocable waiver (separate from any written lease) of the right to receive the certificate. Renter certificate forms may be obtained by calling 828-2515.

The following table will give you a rough idea of whether or not you are entitled to a rebate from the state. Please refer to the instructions on the claim form for additional conditions. Only taxes on the principal residence and not more than two acres of land may be counted in the calculation. Renters may claim 20% of their rent for occupancy (excluding utilities) as property taxes.

QUICK REBATE QUALIFICATION TABLE

If your household income is:	You may file a rebate claim if your property taxes are in excess of this percentage of your household income:
0 - $ 3,999	3.5%
4,000 - 7,999	4.0%
8,000 - 11,999	4.5%
12,000 - 45,00	5.0%

Note: *No claims may be filed if your household income exceeds $45,000. Maximum credit may be limited by law. For assistance call (802) 828-2865.*

Use Value Appraisal Program: If you own agricultural or forestland, you may be eligible for one of the Use Value Appraisal programs. Applications must be submitted by September 1, 1994 for enrollment for calendar year 1995. Forms and information are available at your town clerk's office, or from Property Valuation and Review, 43 Randall Street, Waterbury VT 05676-1512 Tel.(802) 241-3505.

Exemptions:

- Government property
- Religious property
- Charitable property
- Educational property
- Hospitals
- Cemeteries
- Non-business
- Personalty

Appeal procedure:

Step 1   Listers' grievances: "On or before May 20, the listers shall meet at the place so designated by them and on that day and from day to day thereafter shall hear persons aggrieved by their appraisals or by any of their acts until all questions and objections are heard and decided."

Step 2   The Board of Civil Authority hears appeals from tax-payers who have found no relief at listers' grievances hearings.

Step 3   The taxpayer who is dissatisfied with the decision of the Board of Civil Authority may appeal either to the State Board of Appraisers or the Superior Court.

Step 4   Whether the taxpayer has chosen to proceed using the Superior Court or the State Board of Appraisers, a further appeal on legal questions is available from the Vermont Supreme Court.

> *You must pay the current property tax (under protest) the state alleges you owe or the courts will not hear your case.*

Appeal calendar:

The dates for various appeals vary because of the size and ability of each town to administer the volume of appeals. The dates listed below are the dates prescribed by statute and should be used only as a guide. Contact your local lister's office or town clerk for exact dates.

April 1: Assessment date.

May 5th: Lodge the grand list book (tax-roll).

May 6th: Notice of change of assessment mailed to taxpayers.

May 20th: Listers' grievance hearings begin.

June 2: Listers' grievance hearings end.

June 19: Deadline for filing an appeal to Board of Civil Authority.

June 22: Board of Civil Authority hearings begin.

After the mailing of the decision by the Board of Civil Authority, a dissatisfied taxpayer has 21 days to appeal to either the State Board of Appraisers or the Superior Court.

After the mailing of the decision by either the State Board of Appraisers or the Superior Court, a dissatisfied taxpayer has 30 days to file an appeal with the Vermont Supreme Court.

See figure on following page.

Level of government responsible for assessment:
Municipality, Town

Tax assessors:

- Elected for a three year term.

- College education is required.

- Special education or certificate is not required.

State issued assessor's manuals: No state publication mandated

Equalization: *Yes*

Property tax maps mandatory: *No*

VERMONT STATE ASSESSMENT DATE APRIL 1

Time table shows the time when certain acts must be instituted or completed. Times vary depending on the population of the town or city. All acts may be performed before the dates indicated if the required notice is given. General notice is required. These dates may be extended under the provisions of 32 VSA, section 4342.

section	Population	0 to 1999	2000 to 2999	3000 to 3999	4000 to 74999	7500 to 9999	10,000 and over
		ALL DATES SHOWN BELOW ARE AS EXTENDED BY SECTION				4341	
4111(d)	Abstracts of individual lists lodged in town clerk's office	May 15	May 25	June 4	June 9	June 19	June 24
4111(g)	Objections in writing to listers	On or before day of grievance hearings					
4111(c)	Grievance hearings start	May 30	June 9	June 19	June 24	June 4	July 9
4007	Inventories lodged with town clerk (retained for 3 years)	June 11	June 21	July 1	July 6	July 16	July 21
4221	Greivance meetings closed	June 12	June 22	July 2	July 7	July 17	July 22
4224	Taxpayers notified of results of grievance hearings	June 16	June 26	July 6	July 11	July 21	July 26
4404(a) 4407	Appeal in writing to BCA by— or within 14 days of 4224 notice	June 29	July 9	July 19	July 24	Aug 3	Aug 8
4404(b) 4407	Appeal in writing to BCA by— or within 10 days after appeal rec'd.	July 2	July 12	July 22	July 27	Aug 6	Aug 11
4404(c)	BCA notice of decision with reasons filed	within 40 days of hearing appeal					
4461	BCA decision appealable to court or director	within 21 days after mailing of decision					
4151	Grand list completed and lodged with town clerk	July 5	July 15	July 25	July 30	Aug 9	Aug 14
4185	Grand list, 411, 427 due At P.V. & R.	Aug 15	Aug 15	Aug 15	Aug 15	Aug 15	Aug 15

Allow real property to be assessed at financially better use rather than current use: *Yes, highest and best use.*

Frequency of state ratio studies: *Biennial*

Are state ratio studies accessible to the public: *Yes*

State agency information and contact person:

State of Vermont
Department of Taxes
Division of Property Valuation and Review
43 Randall Street
Waterbury, Vermont 05676-1512
Ms. Mary Jane Grace
Telephone: (802) 241-3500 • Fax: (802) 241-3510

VIRGINIA

Name of real property tax: *Property Tax*

Official valuation standard: *Fair market value*

> *undefined by state constitution or statute, courts recognize traditional definition. The amount in cash, or terms reasonably equivalent to cash, a well informed buyer is justified in paying for a property and a well informed seller is justified in accepting, assuming neither party to the transaction is acting under undue compulsion, and assuming the property has been offered in the open market for a reasonable time.*

Annual assessment of real property: *No*

Reassessment cycle: *The time between reappraisals should not be more than 6 years.*

Assessment date: January 1

Classification of property:

Class I	Real Estate: 100%
Class II	Tangible Personalty: 100%
Class III	Machinery and Tools: 100%
Class IV	Merchant's Capital: 100%
Class V	Public Service: 100%

Assessment rate:

Residential property is assessed at 100% of market value.

Tax relief available to homeowners:

Exemptions For Elderly and Handicapped

Such real estate shall be owned by, and be occupied as the sole dwelling of anyone at least sixty-five years of age or if provided in the ordinance, anyone found to be permanently and totally disabled as defined in S58.1-3217. Such ordinance may provide for the exemption from or deferral of that portion of the tax which represents the increase in tax liability since the year such taxpayer reached the age of sixty-five or became disabled, or the year such ordinance became effective, whichever is later. A dwelling jointly held by a husband and wife may qualify if either spouse is sixty-five or over who is permanently and totally disabled.(Article 2 statute 58.1-3210)

Restrictions and Exemptions

1. The total combined income received from all sources during the preceding calendar year by (1) owners of the dwelling who use it as their principal residence and (2) owners' relatives who live in the dwelling, shall not exceed the greater of $30,000, or the income limits based upon family size for the respective metropolitan statistical area, annually published by the Department of Housing and Urban Development for qualifying for federal housing assistance pursuant to s235 of the National Housing Act (12usc s1715z). The local government may also exclude up to $7,500 of income for an owner who is permanently disabled.

   If a person has already qualified for an exemption or deferral under this article, and if the person can prove by clear and convincing evidence that after so qualifying the person's physical or mental health has deteriorated to the point that the only alternative to permanently residing in a hospital, nursing home, convalescent home or other facility for physical or mental care is to have a relative move in and provide care for the person, and if a relative does then move in for that purpose, then none of the relative's income shall be counted towards the income limit.

2. The net combined financial worth, including the present value of all equitable interests, as of December 31 of the immediate preceding calendar year, of the owners, and of the spouse of any owner, excluding the value of the dwelling and the land, shall not exceed $75,000. The local government may also exclude furnishings. Such furnishings shall include furniture, household appliances and other items typically used in a home.

3. The Board of Supervisors or Council may, by ordinance, raise the income and financial worth limitations for any exemption or deferral program to a maximum of $40,000 for the total combined income amount, and $150,000 for the maximum net combined financial worth amount which shall exclude the value of the dwelling and the land not exceeding one acre, upon which it is situated. Any amount up to $6,500 of income of each

relative who is not the spouse of an owner living in the dwelling may be excluded under this subdivision. (Virginia Statute 58.1-3211)

Exemptions:

- Government property

- Religious property

- Charitable property

- Educational property

- Hospitals

- Cemeteries

Appeal procedure:

Step 1 After receiving the change of assessment notice make an informal appeal to the local tax assessor and try to resolve the problem. If after the meeting you are not satisfied with the decision, go to step 2.

Step 2 After an unsuccessful informal meeting with the tax assessor, file a written appeal with the Local Board of Equalization.

Step 3 If after presenting all of your evidence before the Local Board of Equalization you are dissatisfied with the decision, you may appeal to the Circuit Court.

Step 4 If after presenting all of your evidence before the Circuit Court you are unhappy with the decision, you may appeal to the Supreme Court.

The taxpayer does not have to follow any administrative appeal sequence; he may go directly to court if he so chooses. All current property taxes must be paid (under protest) in full before the court will hear the case.

Appeal calendar:

Calendar Year Assessment Cycle

1. Finish field work by December 1.

2. Month of December is used to input information on the computer and print the assessment notices.

3. On January 1 assessment notices are mailed out to the property owners.

4. The month of January is used to hold local assessor hearings for any taxpayers who appealed their assessments.

5. In February the Local Boards of Equalization hold hearings for those taxpayers who were dissatisfied with the assessors' decisions.

6. Hearings of Local Boards of Equalization are finished by March 1.

7. Permanent assessment rolls are printed in March.

Level of government responsible for assessment: *County, Municipality*

Tax assessors:

- 95 elected for a four year term; 40 appointed for indefinite term.

- No minimum education is required.

- No special education or certificate is required.

State issued assessor's manuals: No state manual published; each assessor is free to choose his own reference.

Equalization: *No*

Property tax maps mandatory: *No*

Allow real property to be assessed at financially better use rather than current use: *Yes, highest and best use*

Frequency of state ratio studies: *Yearly*

Are state ratio studies accessible to the public: *Yes*

State agency information and contact person:

Commonwealth of Virginia
Department of Taxation
Property Tax Division
2220 West Broad Street
P.O. Box 1-K
Richmond, Virginia 23201
Mr. Thomas E. Morelli
Telephone: (804) 367-8020 • Fax: (804) 367-2788

NOTES

WASHINGTON

Name of real property tax: *Property Tax*

Official valuation standard: *True and fair market value - the amount of money that a willing and unobligated buyer is willing to pay a willing and unobligated seller.*

Annual assessment of real property: *Yes*

Reassessment cycle: *At least once every four years*

Assessment date: January 1

Classification of property:

Class I   Real Property: 100%

Class II   Personal Property: 100%

Assessment rate:

100% of true and fair market value.

Tax relief available to homeowners:

Senior Citizen or Disabled Person Property Tax Exemption Program

1. To qualify a taxpayer must be 61 years old or older on December 31 of the filing year (no age requirement for disabled persons.)

2. Must be the owner and occupant of a single family dwelling, mobile home, or one unit in multi-unit or cooperative.

3. Have a combined disposable income of $26,000 or less for the prior year (including income of spouse and co-tenant).

Deferred Tax Plan for Senior Citizen or Disabled Person
A senior citizen or disabled person whose income is below $30,000 may defer property taxes and special assessments up to 80 percent of the equity of the home. The amount of the deferment becomes a lien on the property which becomes payable with interest upon sale, transfer, or inheritance of the property.

Taxpayer's Home Improvement Exemption
If a taxpayer improves his single family residence by remodeling, adding new rooms, decks, patios, or other improvements, the taxpayer may apply for a three-year exemption from property taxes on the value of the physical improvements.

Damaged or Destroyed Property Exemption
If taxpayer's residential property is damaged or destroyed, the taxpayer may be eligible for reduced assessed value for taxes payable in the following year.

Exemptions:

- Government property
- Religious property
- Charitable property
- Educational property
- Hospitals
- Cemeteries

Appeal procedure:

Step 1 Immediately after receiving the notice of assessment have an informal meeting with the local tax assessor's office and try to resolve the problem. If after the meeting you are not satisfied with the decision, go to step 2.

Step 2 After an unsuccessful informal meeting with the local tax assessor, file a written notice with the County Board of Equalization.

Step 3 If after presenting all of your evidence before the County Board of Equalization you are still not satisfied, you may appeal to the State Board of Tax Appeals.

Step 4 If after presenting all of your evidence before the State Board of Tax Appeals you are still not satisfied, you may appeal to the Superior Court.

Step 5 If you are still not satisfied with the decision of the Superior Court, you may appeal to the Court of Appeals.

Step 6　　Lastly, if you are dissatisfied with the ruling of the Superior Court you may appeal to the State Supreme Court.

> *You must exhaust all of the administrative appeals before asking for a judicial review. You must also pay the current property tax (under protest) the state alleges you owe or the courts will not hear your case.*

Appeal calendar:

1. January 1: Assessment Date

2. In the spring of the tax year, taxpayer receives by mail "change of value notice."

3. By July 1 or within 30 days of receiving "notice of value," appeal to the County Board of Equalization.

4. July 15: County Board of Equalization meets in open session.

5. August 15: Scheduled end of open meetings of County Board of Equalization.

6. Decisions of the County Board of Equalization are sent within 30 to 60 days of the hearing.

7. Within 30 calendar days of receiving the decision of the County Board of Equalization, a dissatisfied taxpayer may file a petition to the State Board of Tax Appeals.

8. Within 30 days of the decision mailed by the State Board of Tax Appeals, a dissatisfied taxpayer may file an appeal with the State Superior Court (under chapter 84.68 RCW).

Level of government responsible for assessment:
County, State

Tax assessors:

• Elected for a four year term.

• No minimum education is required.

• No special education or certificate is required.

State issued assessor's manuals: *Levy Manual, Board of Equalization Manual; Washington Administrative Code*

Equalization: *Yes*

Property tax maps mandatory: *Yes*

Allow real property to be assessed at financially better use rather than current use: *Yes, highest and best use.*

Frequency of state ratio studies: *Yearly*

Are state ratio studies accessible to the public: *Yes*

State agency information and contact person:

State of Washington
Department of Revenue
Property Tax Division
P. O. Box 47471
Olympia, Washington 98504-7471
Ms. Nancy Rackleff
Telephone: (206) 586-2902 • Fax: (206) 586-7602

WEST VIRGINIA

Name of real property tax: *Property Tax*

Official valuation standard: *Market value,*

> *"the price for which such property would sell if voluntarily offered for sale by the owner upon such terms as such property, the value of which is sought to be ascertained, is usually sold, and not the price which might be realized if such property were sold at a forced sale."*

Annual assessment of real property: *Yes*

Reassessment cycle: *Yes, 3 years*

Assessment date: *July 1*

Classification of property:

Class I	Agricultural, Personal Property, and Public Utilities: 60%
Class II	Owner Occupied Real Property and Farms: 60%
Class III	All Real & Personal Property Situated Outside Municipalities: 60%
Class IV	All Real & Personal Property Situated Inside Municipalities: 60%

Assessment rate:

Residential property is assessed at 60% of true and actual value.

Tax relief available to homeowners:

Homestead Exemption

1. Single family, owner occupied homes where the owner is 65 or older receive a homestead exemption of $20,000 from the assessed value.

2. Totally disabled property owners receive a homestead exemption of $20,000 from the assessed value.

Exemptions:

- Government property
- Religious property
- Charitable property
- Educational property
- Hospitals
- Cemeteries

Appeal procedure:

Step 1   After receiving the notice of assessment, have an informal discussion with the county assessor and try to resolve the problem. If after the meeting you are not satisfied with the decision, go to step 2.

Step 2   After an unsuccessful informal meeting with the county assessor, file a written appeal to the Board of Review and Equalization.

Step 3   If after presenting all of your evidence before the Board of Review and Equalization you are still not satisfied, you may appeal to the Circuit Court.

Step 4   If after presenting all of your evidence before the Circuit Court you are still dissatisfied, you may appeal to the Supreme Court of Appeal.

You must exhaust all the administrative appeals available before asking for a judicial review. You must pay the current property tax (under protest) the state alleges you owe or the courts will not hear your case.

Appeal calendar:

1. Notices of assessment are mailed January 1 through 15.
2. Informal conferences are held any time during the year.
3. The Board of Review and Equalization meets from February 1 through February 28.

4. Within 30 days after the Board of Review and Equalization renders its decision, appeal to the Circuit Court.

5. West Virginia Supreme Court of Appeals

Level of government responsible for assessment:
County

Tax assessors:

•   Elected for a four year term.

•   No minimum education is required.

•   Special courses and certification are required .

State issued assessor's manuals: No state manual published

Equalization: *No*

Property tax maps mandatory: *No*

Allow real property to be assessed at financially better use rather than current use: *Yes, highest and best use*

Frequency of state ratio studies: *Yearly*

Are state ratio studies accessible to the public: *Yes*

State agency information and contact person:

State of West Virginia
Department of Tax and Revenue
Tax Division
P.O. Box 2389
Charleston, West Virginia 25328-2389
Ms. Barbara Brunner
Telephone: (304) 558-3940 • Fax: (304) 558-2324

NOTES

WISCONSIN

Name of real property tax: *Property Tax*

Official valuation standard: *Market value - assessments should be uniform "...at the full value which could ordinarily be obtained therefore at private sale" (section 70.32 of the Wisconsin Statutes).*

Annual assessment of real property: *Yes*

Reassessment cycle: *Yes, once every four years.*

Assessment date: *January 1*

Classification of property:

Class I	Residential: 100%
Class II	Commercial: 100%
Class III	Manufacturing: 100%
Class IV	Agricultural: 100%
Class V	Swamp and Waste: 100%
Class VI	Forest: 100%
Class VII	Personal Property: 100%

Assessment rate:

Residential assessed at 100% of market value.

Tax relief available to homeowners:

Homestead Credit
Low to moderate-income individuals and families can get direct payment from the state by claiming homestead credit. To qualify:

1. Your household income was below $19,154 in 1993 (including social security, AFDC, unemployment compensation, wages and other income sources). A $250 subtraction is allowed for each dependent living at home for more than 6 months during 1993.

2. You were 18 years of age or older on December 31, 1993.

3. You were a full-year Wisconsin resident in 1993 who owned or rented a homestead in the state.

The amount depends on total household income and property tax liability. Renters count part of their rent as taxes. The maximum benefit for 1993 is $1,160. The average benefit for 1992 was $439.

You cannot claim benefits if you: were under age 62 and were claimed as a dependent on someone else's 1993 Federal Income Tax Return; claimed or will claim a farmland preservation credit for 1993; currently reside in a nursing home and receive Title XIX Medical Assistance; or received $400 or more general relief for all 12 months of 1993 and/or AFDC payments of any amount for all 12 months of 1993.

Property Tax Deferral Loan Program
This program allows individuals 65 or older with a limited income to convert equity from their home into cash to pay all or a portion of their property taxes. Approved borrowers make no required monthly payments on principal and interest until ownership of the property is transferred, or until the borrower no longer lives in the house. An applicant may borrow up to $2,500 each year if he qualifies for the program. The interest rate of 7 percent compounded annually is fixed for the life of the loan. A borrower may pay back all or a portion of the loan at any time.

Eligibility requirements:

1. A borrower must be 65 years of age or older on the date of application and if married, the spouse must be 60 years of age. All co-owners of the qualifying home must be at least 60 years of age on the date of the application. If the borrower or the borrower's spouse is/are permanently disabled, there is no minimum age requirement for the spouse.

2. The borrower must own a qualifying home in Wisconsin and reside there for all of 1993. A borrower is considered as living in his/her home even if he/she temporarily lives in a health care facility, such as a nursing home or hospital.

3. The amount of outstanding liens and judgements on the home, not including Property Tax Deferral Loan and/or Wisconsin Housing & Economic Development Authority Rehabilitation Loans, may not exceed 33 percent of the assessed value of the home (for property tax purposes). The amount of outstanding liens and judgements on the home, including the Property Tax

Deferral Loan and Wisconsin Housing & Economic Development Authority Rehabilitation Loans, may not exceed 50 percent of the assessed value of the home for property tax purposes.

4. The total household income for 1993 cannot exceed $20,000. This includes all income received by all persons residing in the house. This should include all income reportable for Wisconsin income tax purposes along with Social Security and other types of nontaxable income.

5. A participant must insure his home and Wisconsin Housing & Economic Development Authority must be named as a lienholder on the Fire and Extended Casualty/Flood Insurance Policies. All outstanding tax liens must be satisfied prior to participating in the program.

Exemptions:

- Government property
- Religious property
- Charitable property
- Educational property
- Historical
- Utility
- Transportation
- Communication
- Hospitals
- Cemeteries

Appeal procedure:

Step 1   After receiving the notice of assessment, have an informal conference with the local assessor and try to resolve the problem. If after the meeting you are not satisfied with the decision, go to step 2.

Step 2   After an unsuccessful informal meeting with the tax assessor, file a formal written appeal to the Local Board of Review. The Board of Review is the first step in the appeal process for an individual taxpayer who protests an assessment. The taxpayer cannot appeal to the Circuit Court under an action of certiorari or to the Department of Revenue under section 70.85 unless an appearance has first been made before the Board of Review.

Step 3   When appealing a Board of Review decision under section 70.85, a written complaint must be received by the Department of Revenue within 20 days after the taxpayer receives the Board of Review's determination, or within 30 days of the date specified in the affidavit under section 70.47(12), if the taxpayer does not receive the notice. Appeal of the Department of Revenue's decision can be made by an action for certiorari in the Circuit Court of the county in which the property is located.

Step 4   Section 70.47(13) provides for an appeal of a Board of Review determination to be by action of *certiorari* (a court order to review the written record of the hearing) to the Circuit Court. The court will not issue an order unless an appeal is made to the Circuit Court within 90 days after final adjournment of the Board of Review. No new evidence may be submitted. The court decides the case solely on the basis of the written record made at the Board of Review.

You must exhaust each of the administrative appeals before asking for a judicial review. You must also pay the current property tax (under protest) the state alleges you owe or the courts will not hear your case.

Appeal calendar:

1. January 1: Assessment Date.

2. 10 days prior to the Board of Review meeting, notices of assessment increases are mailed to affected taxpayers.

3. Prior to the Board of Review meeting, informal meetings with the tax assessor are held.

4. 2nd Monday in May: Board of Review meeting.

5. 20 days after the Board of Review issues its decisions, taxpayers appeal to the Department of Revenue or;

6. 90 days after the final adjournment of the Board of Review, appeal to the Circuit Court.

7. December: Tax Bills are mailed.

Level of government responsible for assessment:
County

Tax assessors:

- Elected for a four year term.

- No minimum education is required.

- Special courses and certificate are required.

State issued assessor's manual: *Wisconsin Property Assessment Manual Vol I & II*

Equalization: *Yes*

Property tax maps mandatory: *Yes*

Allow real property to be assessed at financially better use rather than current use: *Yes, highest and best use.*

Frequency of state ratio studies: *Yearly*

Are state ratio studies accessible to the public: *Yes*

State agency information and contact person:

State of Wisconsin
Department of Revenue
Division of State and Local Finance
Bureau of Property Tax
125 South Webster Street
P.O. Box 8933
Madison, Wisconsin 53708-8933
Mr. Steven G. Budnik
Tel: (608) 266-2317 • Fax: (608) 264-6897

NOTES

WYOMING

Name of real property tax: *Ad Valorem Tax*

Official valuation standard: *"Fair market value" the amount in cash, or terms reasonably equivalent to cash, a well informed buyer is justified in paying for a property and a well informed seller is justified in accepting, assuming neither party to the transaction is acting under undue compulsion, and assuming the property has been offered in the open market for a reasonable time.*

Annual assessment of real property: *Yes*

Reassessment cycle: *Yes, at least once every four years*

Assessment date: *February 1*

Classification of property:

Class I   Industrial Property: 11.5%

Class II   Mineral Property: 100%

Class III   All Other Property: 9.5%

Assessment rate:

Residential property is assessed at 9.5% of fair market value.

Tax relief available to homeowners:

Veterans Exemption

The exemption for honorably discharged veterans is limited to an annual exemption of two thousand dollars ($2,000.00) of assessed value and not to exceed a total tax benefit of eight hundred dollars ($800.00) except as hereafter provided. The eight hundred dollar ($800.00) limitation does not apply to qualified widows of veterans nor veterans of the Spanish American War. Veterans who have received the entire eight hundred dollar ($800.00) exemption and who have a service connected disability certified by the Veterans Administration or a branch of the armed forces of the United States are entitled to additional annual tax exemption not to exceed two thousand dollars ($2,000.00) of assessed value times the ratio which the percent of disability certified bears to one hundred percent (100%). Disability certified less than ten percent

(10%) shall be treated as a ten percent (10%) disability (Wyoming Statute 39-1-202).

Homeowners Tax Credit
A person who occupies a specified homestead as his home and principal residence is entitled to a property tax credit. The amount of the tax credit is one thousand four hundred sixty dollars ($1460.00) times the mill levy to be applied against the property if the dwelling and land, not to exceed two (2) acres on which the dwelling is located, have a combined assessed value of less than three thousand nine hundred dollars ($3,900.00), or five hundred and ninety dollars ($590.00) times the mill levy to be applied against the property if the dwelling and land, not to exceed two (2) acres on which the dwelling is located, have a combined assessed value of at least three thousand nine hundred dollars ($3,900.00) but less than five thousand eight hundred fifty dollars ($5,850.00) and if:

1. The dwelling and land on which the dwelling is located are owned by the same person or entity; and

2. The dwelling has been occupied since the beginning of the calendar year by the applicant.

(Wyoming Statute 39-1-204)

Tax Refund to Elderly and Disabled
Wyoming residents who are sixty-five (65) years of age and older and Wyoming residents who are eighteen (18) years of age and older and are totally disabled during the one (1) year period immediately preceding the date of application for a refund under this article and are not residents of any state funded institution, are qualified for an exemption and refund of state taxes as provided in this section. A qualified single person whose actual income is less than seven thousand five hundred dollars ($7,500.00) shall receive five hundred dollars (500.00) reduced by the percentage that his actual income exceeds six thousand dollars ($6,000) and qualified married persons, at least one (1) of whom is at least sixty-five (65) years of age or totally disabled, whose actual income is less than eleven thousand dollars ($11,000) shall receive six hundred ($600.00) reduced by the percentage that their actual income exceeds eight thousand dollars ($8,000.00) per year.

(Amended Wyoming Statute 39-6-701 and 39-6-702(a))

Exemptions:
•   Government property

- Religious property
- Educational property
- Cemeteries

Appeal procedure:

Step 1   After receiving the notice of assessment have an informal conference with the county assessor and try to resolve the problem. If after the meeting you are not satisfied with the decision, go to step 2.

Step 2   After an unsuccessful informal meeting with the county assessor, file a written appeal with the County Board of Equalization.

Step 3   If after presenting all of your evidence before the County Board of Equalization you are dissatisfied with the decision, you may appeal to the State Board of Equalization.

Step 4   If after presenting all of your evidence before the State Board of Equalization you are still not satisfied with the ruling, you may appeal to the District Court of the county where property is located.

You must exhaust all administrative appeals before asking for a judicial review. You must also pay the current property tax (under protest) the state alleges you owe or the courts will not hear your case.

Appeal calendar:

1. February 1: Assessment date

2. Fourth Monday in May: Assessor mails assessment schedules to taxpayers.

3. For 30 days after notices of assessment schedules are mailed, informal conferences are held with county assessors.

4. Within 30 days after the date on the assessment schedule or postmark date of the assessment schedule, file a written appeal with the County Board of Equalization.

5.   Fourth Tuesday in May: County Board of Equalization opens hearings on taxpayer's protests.

6.   First Monday in August: County Board of Equalization decides all current years protests by written decision.

7.   First Monday in August: County commissioners levy the necessary taxes for the year.

Level of government responsible for assessment:
County, State

Tax assessors:

•   Elected for a four year term.

•   College education is required.

•   Special education and certificate are required.

State issued assessor's manuals: None

Equalization: *Yes*

Property tax maps mandatory: *Yes*

Allow real property to be assessed at financially better use rather than current use: *Yes, highest and best use.*

Frequency of state ratio studies: *Yearly*

Are state ratio studies accessible to the public: *No*

State agency information and contact person:

State of Wyoming
Revenue Department
Ad Valorem Tax Division
Herschler Building
122 West 25th Street
Cheyenne, Wyoming 82002-0110
Mr. James Felton
Telephone: (307) 777-5235 • Fax: (307) 777-7722

CANADA

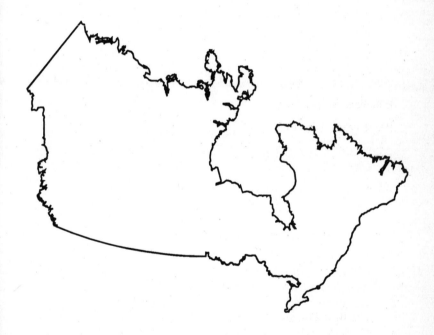

NOTES

ALBERTA

Name of real property tax: *Property Tax*

Official valuation standard: *"Actual value" means:*

i   *the most probable sale price of the property if a sale of the property was freely made with both parties having a reasonable knowledge of the actual and potential economic value of the property, or*

ii   *if there is no sales or economic data or if either is insufficient, the most probable sale price may be fixed solely in accordance with the depreciated physical value or the actual and potential economic value or in accordance with both.*

Annual assessment of real property: *Yes. The assessor shall reassess not later than December 31 in each year.*

Reassessment cycle: *Every eight years.*

Assessment date: *December 1*

Classification of property:

Class I	Commercial
Class II	Industrial
Class III	Residential
Class IV	Farm
Class V	Machinery

Assessment rate:

Class III   Residential - 100% of market value

Tax relief available to homeowners:

Property Tax Reduction Program

Almost every homeowner in Alberta receives assistance from the Property Tax Reduction Program. Homeowners automatically receive the basic tax reduction which always equals the Provincial Education Tax identified on their tax notice. There is no limit on the amount of

Provincial Education Tax the province will pay on the taxpayers behalf as a basic tax reduction through the property Tax Reduction Program.

Senior Citizen Homeowner Benefit
In addition to the basic tax reduction, if the taxpayer is are an "eligible senior citizen homeowner," the total tax reduction benefit could equal $1,000 or the total taxes due, whichever is less.

Requirements for eligibility for the Senior Citizen Homeowner Program Include:

1. Seniors 65 years of age or older:

2. Widows or widowers, age 60 to 64, whose spouses were 65 years of age or older at the time of death and eligible for the benefit;

3. Widows or widowers, age 55 to 64, receiving the widows pension or additional benefits under the Alberta Widows Pension Program;

4. Senior citizens who have not applied for a Senior Citizens Renter Assistance Grant in the tax year. Married couples may receive only one grant in any year;

5. Canadian citizens or landed immigrants who have lived in their own home in Alberta for at least 120 days of the year.

Exemptions:

*   Personalty
*   Government property
*   Religious property
*   Specific charitable property
*   Hospitals
*   Cemeteries
*   Mines or mineral

Appeal procedure:

Step 1   For 30 days after the mailing date of the Assessment Notices, property owners or their agents may review any file on the Property Assessment Roll for the purpose of comparing the assessment details for their properties with those of similar properties.

Step 2   If after a careful and detailed inspection of the facts the property owner believes the assessment is unfair or contains an error(s), the first step should be to arrange an informal meeting with the assessor in that municipality.

Step 3   If the taxpayer is unable to resolve the matter with the local assessor and wishes to take the complaint to the Court of Revision, he/she must file a written appeal within 30 days of the mailing of the assessment notice with the Municipal Secretary (or in a city, to the Assessor).

Step 4   The appellant will be advised in writing of the date, place and time of the scheduled appearance before the Court of Revision at least 10 days in advance.

Step 5   If after presenting the case before the Court of Revision, the taxpayer is dissatisfied with the ruling, he/she may take the case to the Alberta Assessment Appeal Board. The Board hears appeals from decisions of the Court of Revision. To file an appeal, the property owner must send a written notice to the Municipal Secretary (or, in a city, to the Assessor) within 21 days of the mailing of the Court of Revision's decision.

Appeal calendar:

1. December 31: All property is assessed.

2. February 28: Assessment notices are mailed to taxpayers.

3. February 28 to March 28: The assessment rolls are open to taxpayers or their agents for inspection.

4. March 28: Deadline for filing complaints with the Court of Revision.

5. Aggrieved parties are given 10 days notice prior to their hearings before the Court of Revision.

6. The session of the Court of Revision must be completed within 150 days.

7. Within 21 days after the mailing of the Court of Revision decisions, taxpayers, if dissatisfied, may appeal the decisions to the Alberta Assessment Appeal Board.

Level of government responsible for assessment:
Province, Municipality

Tax assessors:

- Appointed, for an indefinite term.

- High school education is required.

- Special courses are required to attain an Accredited Municipal Assessor of Alberta (A.M.A.A.).

Government issued assessor's manual: *1984 Alberta Assessment Manual*

Equalization: *Yes, Alberta equalizes for cost sharing programs between municipalities on different base years.*

Property tax maps mandatory: *No*

Allow real property to be assessed at financially better use rather than current use: *No, current value in its present use.*

Frequency of Provincial ratio studies: *Yearly*

Are Provincial ratio studies accessible to the public: *Yes*

Provincial agency information and contact person:

Alberta Municipal Affairs
Assessment Standards & Equalization
13th Floor, City Centre
10155 - 102 Street
Edmonton, Alberta
Canada T5J 4L4
Mr. Harold Williams, Director
Telephone: (403) 427-8969 • Fax: (403) 422-9105

BRITISH COLUMBIA

Name of real property tax: *Property Tax*

Official valuation standard: *Market value ("actual value") is the estimated sale price of a property - the price reasonably expected to be realized when sold by a willing vendor to a willing purchaser after adequate time and exposure to the market.*

Annual assessment of real property: *Yes*

Reassessment cycle: *Every two years.*

Assessment date: *July 1*

Classification of property:

Class I	Residential
Class II	Utilities
Class III	Unmanaged Forest Lands
Class IV	Major Industry
Class V	Light Industry
Class VI	Business and other
Class VII	Managed Forest Land
Class VIII	Recreational Property/Non-Profit Organizations
Class IX	Farms

Assessment rate:

Class I   Residential Property: 97% of market value.

Tax relief available to homeowners:

1. **Regular Homeowner Grant Program**
   The regular Homeowner Grant Program reduces property tax for all eligible property owners by as much as $470. To be eligible:

A. The property must be your principal place of residence; and

B. The taxpayer must complete, sign, and return the homeowner's grant application on the back of the property tax notice.

2. **The Additional Homeowner Grant Program**

The additional homeowner grant program reduces property tax for qualified applicants by as much as $745. To be eligible, the taxpayer must meet the criteria for the Regular Homeowner Grant Program and be:

A. Age 65 or older. If the home is jointly owned, only one of the owners need be 65 or older to qualify for the additional grant.

B. You may also be eligible if you are:

     i. A veteran, or spouse of a veteran receiving an allowance under the "War Veterans Allowance Act (Canada)" or the "Civilian War Pensions and Allowance Act (Canada)."

     ii. Disabled and receive handicapped income assistance under the "Guaranteed Available Income for Need (GAIN) Act."

Disabled people not receiving income assistance under GAIN, or those property owners with physically disabled spouses or relatives who reside permanently with them, may also qualify for the additional grant.

To be eligible, a signed doctor's certificate stating that the disabilities are permanent and require extensive physical assistance of costly modifications to the home in order for the person with the disability to remain there, must be attached to the homeowner grant application form.

You must pay a minimum amount of property tax before you can claim the basic homeowner grant. You must pay at least $350 in property tax before claiming a regular grant. You must pay at least $100 in property tax before claiming an additional grant.

3. **The Land Tax Deferment Program.**
   The Land Tax Deferment Program allows a homeowner to defer the payment of the annual property taxes on his home if he/she is:

   A. 60 years of age or older; or

   B. A widow or widower; or

   C. A handicapped person as defined in the "Guaranteed Available Income for Need Act (GAIN); and if he/she is

   D. A Canadian citizen or landed immigrant who has lived in British Columbia for at least one year before applying for tax benefits.

   Only taxes on your principal residence can be deferred. All the deferred taxes must be repaid, including simple interest:

   A. Before your home can be legally transferred to a new owner, other than your surviving spouse; or

   B. Upon the death of the agreement holder(s), repayment is made through the estate.

   Both conventional and manufactured homes qualify for tax deferment. The property owner must maintain a minimum equity in his/her home of 25% of the assessed value, as determined by the British Columbia Assessment Authority, in order to qualify for the program. All property taxes, fees, utility charges, penalty and interest charges from previous years must be paid before your tax deferment application can be considered.

4. **Assessment Relief - Section 26(4) of the Assessment Act**
   Property owners living in communities or neighborhoods where land use is changing and the demonstrated market value of the land is higher than its current residential value, would benefit from assessment relief. If eligible, the property owner's land will continue to be valued at its current "existing" use instead of its higher "potential" use.

   Residential property owners who have been living on property which is less than 2.03 hectares (approximately five acres) for more than 10 years, may be eligible for a lower property assessment.

To qualify for assessment relief:

A. The property must be the property owner's principal residence.

B. The property owner must have continuously occupied the property for 10 years, effective October 31 of each year.

C. The property's "potential" market value must be higher than the property's existing residential value.

Exemptions:

- Personalty
- Religious (Church building only)
- Educational (if under school system)
- Utility
- Communication
- Forest or orchards
- Hospitals
- Cemeteries

Appeal procedure:

Step1   If after receiving the notice of assessment the taxpayer has questions about the assessment, he/she should schedule an informal meeting with the local assessor.

Step 2   If the taxpayer is dissatisfied with the results of his informal meeting with the assessor, the taxpayer may appeal to the Court of Revision.

Step 3   If the taxpayer is dissatisfied with the decision of the Court of Revision, he/she may appeal to the Assessment Appeal Board.

Step 4   If the taxpayer is dissatisfied with the decision of the Assessment Appeal Board he/she may appeal to the

British Columbia Supreme Court on matters of law only.

Step 5   If the taxpayer is dissatisfied with the ruling of the B.C. Supreme Court, he/she may appeal to the British Columbia Court of Appeal on matters of law only.

Step 6   If the taxpayer is dissatisfied with the decision of the B.C. Court of Appeal, he/she may appeal to the Supreme Court of Canada on matters of law only.

Appeal calendar:

1. July 1: Reference date for value (market conditions)
2. October 31: Reference date for physical conditions and zoning
3. December 31: Assessment notices mailed
4. January 31: Deadline for filing appeals to the Court of Revision
5. February 1 to March 15: Court of Revision sits
6. March 31: Court of Revision's decisions rendered
7. April 30: Deadline for filing appeal of Court of Revision decision to Assessment Appeal Board
8. April: Tax Rates struck
9. June: Tax bills mailed
10. June 30: Tax payment deadline

Level of government responsible for assessment: Province

Tax assessors:

- Appointed, permanent appointment.
- High school education is required.
- Special education and certificate are required.

Government issued assessor's manuals: *Residential Improvements, Major Industrial, Marshall & Swift*

Equalization: *No*

Property tax maps mandatory: *No*

Allow real property to be assessed at financially better use rather than current use: *Yes, highest and best use (with exceptions). See Assessment Relief Section 26(4) of the Assessment Act.*

Frequency of Provincial ratio studies: *Yearly*

Are Provincial ratio studies accessible to the public: *No*

Provincial agency information and contact person:

British Columbia Assessment Authority
1537 Hillside Avenue
Victoria, British Columbia V8T 4Y2
Ms. Connie Hughes, Director
Policy, Audit & Legal Services
Telephone: (604) 595-6211 • Fax: (604) 595-6222

MANITOBA

Name of real property tax: *Property Tax*

Official valuation standard: *Based on market value in reference year. Market value is the "most probable selling price from a willing seller to a willing buyer."*

Annual assessment of real property: *No*

Reassessment cycle: *Manitoba is on a triennial (3 year) reassessment cycle. The reference year is the year following the last reassessment. Example: 1994 is the reassessment year and 1995 is the reference year until the 1997 reassessment.*

Assessment date: There is no valuation date. The value is based on the reference year.

Classification of property:

Class I	Residential
Class II	Commercial
Class III	Farm
Class IV	Pipeline Property
Class V	Railway Property
Class VI	Institutional Property
Class VII	Golf Course Property
Class VIII	Other Property

Assessment rate:

Class I	Single family residence: 45% of market value in reference year.
Class II	Commercial: 65% of market value in reference year.
Class III	Farm: 30% of market value in reference year.

Tax relief available to homeowners:

A. **$250 Minimum Property Tax Threshold**
   A $250 minimum property tax threshold applies to homeown-

ers (with a corresponding threshold for tenants). Only property taxes in excess of $250 will qualify for property tax credit programs.

B. **Residential Homeowner Tax Assistance**
This credit of up to $250 is available on property taxes over the minimum property tax threshold as an advance of Manitoba Tax credit to owner occupants of single-family dwellings.

C. **Income-Related Tax Credit Assistance**
For Manitobans over age 65, the maximum additional benefit is $100 greater than the maximum benefit available for people under 65. Eligible owners who did not receive the reduction from their property tax statements may claim full tax credits in respect of their principal residence on their income tax forms. Eligible tenants must also claim their credits through the income tax forms.

D. **Pensioner's School Tax Assistance (implemented via income tax credits)**
The Manitoba government offers assistance of up to $175 toward school taxes greater than $160 on the principal residence of eligible persons 55 or more years old.

If you are a homeowner over the age of 55, and your Family Net Income is less than $15,000, you may qualify for full School Tax Assistance; if Family Net Income is more than $15,000 and less than $23,800, assistance is reduced on a graduated scale; no assistance is payable at income levels greater than $23,800.

E. **The Home Renovation Program**
Homes built before January 1, 1981 and valued at under $100,000 (1994 assessed value for land and buildings) may qualify. The program provides a $1,000 grant after completion of a renovation project which incurs applicable costs of $5,000 or more between April 20, 1994 and April 1, 1995. The program is intended to assist families, enhance the value of Manitoba's housing, create jobs, and accelerate recovery in the home renovation sector of the economy.

F. **The Sale Tax Rebate Program**
This program, intended for first-time home buyers, will help

families acquire a home, and will create jobs by promoting the Manitoba home-building industry.

Exemptions:

- Government property
- Religious property
- Charitable property
- Educational property
- Historical property
- Cemeteries
- Communication
- Hospitals
- Day care centers

Appeal procedure:

Step 1   Assessment notices are mailed to property owners in the fall of the year prior to when the taxes are due.

Step 2   A property owner can submit an appeal to the Board of Revision. The Board can hear applications on four grounds:

1. Liability to taxation - Is the property owner responsible for the tax?

2. Amount of assessed value.

3. Classification of property.

4. Refusal by an assessor to amend an assessment roll.

The Board has the authority to dismiss the application or allow the appellant's appeal.

Step 3   An appellant can apply to the Municipal Board, in writing, not later than 21 days after receipt of the Board of Revision's decision. This board can hear cases where the appellant is questioning the assessed value or classification of property.

Step 4   "Liability of the property to taxation" cases are heard by the Court of Queen's Bench.

Step 5   Decisions of the Municipal Board or Court of Queen's Bench can be appealed to the Court of Appeal.

Appeal calendar:

1.   Appeals to the Board of Revision must be filed within 15 days prior to the commencement of the Board's Session.

2.   Appeals to either the Municipal Board or the Court of Queen's Bench must be filed, in writing, no later than 21 days after receipt of the Board of Revision's decision.

Level of government responsible for assessment: Province, Municipalities

Tax assessors:

* Appointed as an indefinite appointment.

* High school diploma is required.

* Four year accredited program leading to a certificate.

Government issued assessor's manuals: *Province of Manitoba Residential Assessment Manual, Province of Manitoba Farm Building Assessment Manual, Province of Manitoba Commercial Assessment Manual*

Equalization: *No*

Property tax maps mandatory: *No*

Allow real property to be assessed at financially better use rather than current use: *No, current value in its present use.*

Frequency of Provincial ratio studies: *Continual basis with focus on reassessment cycle.*

Are Provincial ratio studies accessible to the public: *No*

Provincial agency information and contact person:

Manitoba Rural Development
Assessment Branch
500-800 Portage Avenue
Winnipeg, Manitoba
Canada, R3G 0N4
Mr. Ken Graham, Provincial Municipal Assessor
Telephone: (204) 945-2605 • Fax: (204) 945-1994

NOTES

NEW BRUNSWICK

Name of real property tax: *Real Property Tax*

Official valuation standard:

> *All real property is to be assessed at its "Real and True Value" as of January 1 of each year. "Real and True Value" has been defined as "Market Value" with the courts. There is no definition of "Market Value" or "Real and True Value" in the act. However, the courts have ruled that the word "value" means exchangeable value - the price which the subject will bring when exposed to the test of competition. The value is not value to the particular owner but to any owner - the exchange value or the value to the prudent purchaser (the willing seller and willing buyer principle).*

Annual assessment of real property: *Yes, Section 23(1) Chapter A-14 Assessment Act.*

Reassessment cycle: *Yes, every 5 years. Section 24 Chapter A-14 Assessment Act.*

Assessment date: *January 1*

Classification of property:

Class I   Residential

Class II   Commercial

Class III   Resource

Assessment rate:

Class I   Residential: 100% of market value

Tax relief available to homeowners:

Residential Property Tax Credit

If on January 1 you are the assessed owner (or beneficiary) of a residential property (single family home, duplex, apartment building or a complex property) maintained as your principal place of residence, you are eligible for a tax credit on the owner-occupied portion and up to 0.5 hectares of land.

If you purchased residential property after January 1, 1983 and subsequently take up residency on the property, you are eligible for a tax credit for the number of days the property is owner-occupied.

If you own a completed or uncompleted single family residence vacant on January 1 and never previously occupied, you are eligible for a tax credit.

Property Tax Allowance Program
If you are the registered owner (or beneficiary) of a residential property on January 1 in which you maintain as your principal place of residence, and if neither your total income nor the total income of the joint owner(s) exceeded $12,000 and the combined total income of you and the joint owner(s) did not exceed $20,000 during the previous year, you are eligible on application for an allowance to a maximum of $200 toward the tax levy for the current year. Incomes from veterans allowances and disabilities (veteran disability only) are excluded from the total income.

The residential tax credits and the property tax allowances are determined in accordance with the legislation and policies in effect at the time.

Exemptions:

- Government property
- Religious property
- Charitable property
- Agricultural societies
- Not-for-profit cemeteries
- Literary & historic societies
- Rural voluntary fire departments

Appeal procedure:

Step 1   Assessment and tax notices are issued on March 1 of each year by the director of the New Brunswick Geographic Information Corporation to the property owner.

Step 2   The property owner, if dissatisfied with the assessment value placed on his/her property, may file a Notice of Referral with the Director of the New Brunswick Geographic Information Corporation. The Notice of Referral must be filed within 60 days of the mailing of the Tax Notice.

Step 3   The Director of the New Brunswick Geographic Information Corporation has 90 days to answer the Notice of Referral. After a referral review, a referral register is issued outlining the Director's conclusion as to the value of the property in question.

Step 4   If the property owner is still dissatisfied with the findings of the Director, he/she has 21 days to file a formal written appeal with the Regional Assessment Review Board.

Step 5   At the hearing of an appeal at the Regional Assessment Review Board, the Director shall file with the Board a copy of the assessment and tax notice, the notice of reference of assessment and the Referral Register pertaining to the real property in respect of which the appeal is taken and when so filed are proof that the information contained therein pertains to the real property in respect of which the appeal is taken.

At the hearing of an appeal, the party appealing shall state his reasons for objecting to the assessment under appeal and the onus of proving that the assessment exceeds the real and true value of the real property shall be upon the party appealing.

Step 6   If the property owner is dissatisfied with the ruling of the Regional Assessment Review Board, he/she may appeal to a judge of the Court of Queen's Bench of New Brunswick any order, ruling or decision of a Board on any question of law.

Step 7   If the property owner is unhappy with the ruling of the Court of Queen's Bench of New Brunswick, he/she may appeal to the Court of Appeals.

Appeal calendar:

1. Assessment Date: January 1.

2. Assessment and Tax Notices are issued by March 1 of each year.

3. A Notice of Referral must be filed with the Director of New Brunswick Geographic Information Corporation within 60 days of mailing of Assessment and Tax Notice.

4. The Director has 90 days to answer the Notice of Referral.

5. After receiving the decision of the Director (Referral Register), the property owner has 21 days in which to file a written appeal with the Regional Assessment Review Board.

Level of government responsible for assessment:
Provincial

Tax assessors:

*   Appointed, indefinite appointment.

*   Prefer university graduate.

*   No special courses or certificate is required.

Government issued assessor's manuals: *New Brunswick Assessment Manual & Boeckh Commercial Manual*

Equalization: *No*

Property tax maps mandatory: *No*

Allow real property to be assessed at financially better use rather than current use: *No, current use.*

Frequency of Provincial ratio studies: *Twice a year.*

Are Provincial ratio studies accessible to the public: *No*

Provincial agency information and contact person:

New Brunswick Geographic Information Corporation
P. O. Box 6000
Fredericton, New Brunswick
Canada E3B 5H1
Mr. Gèrard Losier, Chief Assessor
Telephone: (506) 453-2658 • Fax: (506) 453-3043

NEWFOUNDLAND & LABRADOR

Name of real property tax: *Real Property Tax*

Official valuation standard: *Real property shall be assessed at its fair market value, that being the amount which in the opinion of the assessor it would realize if sold in the open market by a willing seller to a willing buyer.*

Annual assessment of real property: *No, not required by statute.*

Reassessment cycle: *Yes, every 6 years.*

Assessment date: *Varied due to multi-jurisdictional responsibilities.*

Classification of property:

All classes valued at same level (100%).

Assessment rate:

Residential: 100% of market value.

Tax relief available to homeowners:

Section 135, Subsection M of the Municipalities Act: "The council, on a vote of 2/3 of the councilors in office, may grant an exemption, remission or deferment of taxes and interest on taxes, either in whole or in part for those periods of time that the council decides."

Exemptions:

- Personalty
- Government property
- Religious property
- Charitable property
- Educational property
- Cemeteries
- Productive farm lands

- Forests or orchards

- Hospitals

Appeal procedure:

The assessment roll must be completed prior to the issuing of notices of assessment. Normally the roll is completed by October 2nd.

Step 1   The Assessment Roll is to be completed before October 2 (Section 53).

Step 2   Notices are sent after the roll is filed and homeowners have 21 days to respond.

Step 3   Appeals are registered with the Clerk of the Court and given to the Assessor.

Step 4   The Assessor will review the appeal and discuss the assessment with the appellant.

Step 5   If an adjustment to the Assessment is necessary, the assessor will bring it to the Court for confirmation.

Step 6   If the matter is unresolved, the appeal will proceed to the Assessment Appeal Court level.

Step 7   If the appellant is still not satisfied with the decision of the Appeal Court, he/she can then have 10 days in which to appeal to the Supreme Court of Newfoundland.

Appeal calendar:

1. January 1: Assessment date.

2. February 1: Tax bills are sent out.

3. October 2: Completion of Assessment Roll to be filed with the City Clerk.

4. Notices of Appeal are sent after completion of the Tax Roll. Taxpayers have 21 days in which to appeal to the Assessor.

5. Appeal to the Supreme Court may be made 21 days from the date the Assessment Review Commission renders its decision.

Level of government responsible for assessment:
Province, City of St. John's

Tax assessors:

- Appointed for an indefinite appointment.

- High school education is required.

- Special education and certificate are required.

Government issued assessor's manuals: *Boekch Valuation Manuals*

Equalization: *Yes*

Property tax maps mandatory: *No*

Allow real property to be assessed at financially better use rather than current use: *Yes, highest and best use.*

Frequency of Provincial ratio studies: *Every 5 years.*

Are Provincial ratio studies accessible to the public: *No*

Provincial agency information and contact person:

Government of Newfoundland and Labrador
Department of Municipal and provincial Affairs
P. O. Box 8700
Confederation Building (West)
St. John's, Newfoundland
Canada A1B 4J6
Mr. Stephen White, Director of Assessments
Telephone: (709) 729-3701 • Fax: (709) 637-2331
or
City of St. John's
P. O. Box 908
St. John's, Newfoundland
Canada A1C 5M2
Mr. Lloyd B. Winsor, Chief Assessor
Telephone: (709) 576-8233 • Fax: (709) 576-8603

NOTES

NORTHWEST TERRITORIES

Name of real property tax: *Property Tax*

Official valuation standard:

> *Where the regulations do not provide for the manner in which, or the method by which, an assessed value is to be given to:*

a. *a parcel, the assessor shall assess the parcel in a manner that to the assessor appears fair, having regard to any similar parcels in the same vicinity;*

b. *an improvement, the assessor shall assess the improvement in a manner that to the assessor appears fair, having regard to any similar improvements in the same vicinity; and*

c. *a mobile unit, the assessor shall assess the mobile unit in a manner that to the assessor appears fair, having regard to any similar mobile units in the same vicinity.*

Annual assessment of real property: *Yes*

Reassessment cycle: *Yes, at least once in every 9 years.*

Assessment date: *October 31*

Classification of property:

Class I	Commercial
Class II	Industrial
Class III	Property principally used for the extraction of hydro-carbons
Class IV	Property principally used for the extraction of minerals
Class V	Property principally used for a pipeline
Class VI	Property for production, transmission, or delivery of electricity
Class VII	Residential, single unit
Class VIII	Mobile home

Class IX   Multiple residential units, but less than 40 units per hectare

Class X   Multiple residential units greater than 40 but less than 150 units per hectare

Class XI   Multiple residential units greater than 150 units per hectare

Assessment rate:

Land - 100% of Fair Actual Value

Improvements - 66.7% of Fair Actual Value

Tax relief available to homeowners:

Homeowners Property Tax Rebate Act

An owner of a dwelling who has occupied that unit for a minimum of 184 days during the current tax year and who has paid property tax on that unit in full is eligible for a rebate of:

a.   General Taxation Area - up to 50% of taxes paid, up to a maximum of $75.00.

b.   Municipal Taxation Areas - up to 50% of taxes paid, up to a maximum of $300.00.

Senior Citizens and Disabled Persons Property Tax Relief Act:

Any disabled person or any person 65 years of age or older who is the owner or part owner of land and ordinarily lives in a single-family dwelling or mobile unit on that land may be eligible for total exemption from property tax. In the General Tax Area qualified individuals receive a 100% exemption from property tax. However, the amount of relief varies from one Municipal Taxation Area to another because they provide relief on an optional basis, through their individual municipal by-laws.

Exemptions:

- Personalty
- Government property
- Educational property
- Forest or orchards
- Indian Reserves

Appeal procedure:

Step 1   Assessment Notices are sent out by the respective taxing authority.

Step 2   If after receiving the Assessment Notice the taxpayer disagrees with the value placed on his/her property, or the owner feels that the property has been erroneously assessed, he/she may schedule an informal conference with the assessor.

Step 3   After an unsuccessful informal conference, the assessed owner or anyone else can complain to the taxing authority's Board of Revision. He must file a written appeal within 45 days from the date of the mailing of the Assessment Notice with the Board of Revision.

Step 4   If a party to the complaint, or anyone affected by the Board of Revision's decision is not satisfied with the Board of Revision's decision, he may appeal the decision to the Northwest Territories Assessment Appeal Tribunal. A written appeal must be filed with the Tribunal within 45 days from the mailing date of the decision from the Board of Revision.

Step 5   The Assessment Appeal Tribunal hears all appeals from across the Northwest Territories regardless of the taxation area from which the appeal arose. A party to the appeal, or any party affected by the Tribunal's decision, may appeal the decision to the Supreme Court of the Northwest Territories (but only on a point of law) within 45 days of the mailing of the decision of the Assessment Appeal Tribunal.

Appeal calendar:

1. Delivery of the Certified Assessment Rolls to each of the taxing authorities, on or before October 31.

2. The taxing authority must return the assessment roll, with any errors and omissions identified, within 21 days of the date the Certified Assessment Roll was delivered.

3. The Director of Assessment must make any revisions he agrees with within 21 days of the date the Certified Roll was returned.

4. This returned Roll is called the Certified Assessment Roll - 1st Revision. The First Revision Roll is used to generate Assessment Notices to the property owners.

5. Property owners may appeal to the Board of Revision within 45 days from the date of mailing of the Assessment Notice.

6. Property owners may appeal decisions of the Board of Revision to the Assessment Appeal Tribunal within 45 days from the mailing date of the Board's decision.

7. Property owners may appeal a point of law to the Supreme Court of Northwest Territories from the decision of the Assessment Appeal Tribunal. This appeal must be filed within 45 days of the mailing of the Tribunal's decision.

8. The tax year runs from January 1 to December 31.

Level of government responsible for assessment:
Territorial Government

Tax assessors:

*   Appointed, indefinite appointment.

*   High school education is required.

*   Special courses and a certificate are required.

Government issued assessor's manuals: *Alberta Assessment Manual; Boeckh Manual; Marshal & Swift Manual*

Equalization: *Yes, for distribution grants.*

Property tax maps mandatory: *No*

Allow real property to be assessed at financially better use rather than current use: *Yes, highest and best use.*

Frequency of Provincial ratio studies: *Yearly*

Are Provincial ratio studies accessible to the public: *No*

Provincial agency information and contact person:

Government of the Northwest Territories
Municipal & Community Affairs
Municipal Operations and Assessment Division
P. O. Box 21, Northwest Tower 600
5201 - 50th Avenue
Yellowknife, Northwest Territories
Canada X1A 3S9
Mr. Gerry Towns, Assistant Director of Assessment
Telephone: (403) 873-7997 • Fax: (403) 920-6156

NOTES

NOVA SCOTIA

Name of real property tax: *Property Tax*

Official valuation standard:

> *All property shall be assessed at its market value, such value being the amount which in the opinion of the assessor would be paid if it were sold on a date prescribed by the Director in the open market by a willing seller to a willing buyer, but in forming his opinion the assessor shall have regard to the assessment of other properties in the municipality so as to ensure that taxation falls in a uniform manner upon all residential and resource property and in a uniform manner upon all commercial property in the municipality. (Section 42(1) of Assessment Act R.S., C.23)*

Annual assessment of real property: *No*

Reassessment cycle: *Every 3 years.*

Assessment date: *January 1*

Classification of property:

Class I	Residential Property
Class II	Commercial Property
Class III	Resource Property

Assessment rate:

100% at Base Date

Tax relief available to homeowners:

The Assessment Act, (Section 123)
Upon the petition of a taxpayer supported by affidavit, the council may:

a. Relieve, from the payment of all or any portion of the rates and taxes for the current taxation year, a taxpayer who declares that from sickness or extreme poverty he is unable to pay his rates or taxes and may also order the treasurer to refund rates or taxes for the current taxation year already paid by that person;

b. Relieve, from the payment of all or any portion of the rates and taxes for the current or the previous taxation year, a taxpayer who by reason of any gross and manifest error in the assessment roll has been wrongly charged; or

c.   By resolution order, for a stated period or until the death of the ratepayer or until other contingency specified in the resolution, the postponement of the taking of proceedings to enforce the collection of the rates and taxes for the current taxation year or for the preceding taxation year upon the real property of a ratepayer occupied by him as his home, if his income for the year preceding the passing of the resolution, together with that of his spouse and four hundred eighty dollars for each other person living in the house whose income is at a rate exceeding that amount, is less than one thousand dollars or such smaller amount as the council may determine by resolution.

Property Tax Rebate Program

A Property Tax Rebate program offers senior citizen homeowners who are in receipt of the Guaranteed Income Supplement or Spouse's Allowance in January of the year of application, a fifty percent rebate on their residential property taxes up to a maximum of $400.

The eligibility criteria are as follows:

a.   The senior must be a recipient of the Guaranteed Income Supplement or Spouse's Allowance in *January of the year of application.*

b.   The senior must own and reside on the property.

c.   The property must be in Nova Scotia.

d.   The taxes must have been paid for the rebate year.

e.   An application form must be completed, signed by the senior and returned to the Department of Community Services, together with the tax bill and receipt for taxes paid for the rebate year.

Rental Assistance

Singles and couples who rent in the private market and are in receipt of the Guaranteed Income Supplement or Spouse's Allowance, and single persons, 65 and over, whose income does not exceed $17,475 per year are eligible for Rental Assistance.

The maximum monthly rent on which the supplement is paid is $437 for single pensioners and $553 for married seniors.

The amount of Rental Assistance ranges from 50% to 75% of the rent in excess of 30% of the senior citizen's income.

The percentage varies depending on the amount of income.

Exemptions:
- Government property
- Religious property
- Charitable property
- Educational property
- Non-profit cemeteries
- Railroad property
- Boy Scouts, Girl Guides
- Non-profit community organizations
- Hospitals

Appeal procedure:

Step 1   If you disagree with your assessment, you may appeal, but you must appeal within 21 days of the mailing of the assessment notice.

Step 2   As soon as your appeal is filed, it is sent to the Director of Assessment for review. If the Director of Assessment upholds the original assessment, or amends the notice to your dissatisfaction, you may make a further appeal to the Regional Assessment Appeal Court.

Step 3   This means signing the Notice of Dissatisfaction on the back of the Amended Notice and returning it to the assessment office within seven days of the date the Amended Notice was received.

Step 4   If the Regional Appeal Court hands down a decision on your assessment with which you still disagree, you are entitled to appeal your assessment to the Nova Scotia Municipal Board.

Step 5   Appeals to the Municipal Board must be made within 30 days of the date the Regional Court decision is received.

Appeal calendar:

1. Assessment notices are mailed from January 1 to March 31.

2.   The taxpayer has 21 days after receipt of the assessment notice to file an appeal with the Director of Assessment.

3.   To file an appeal with the Regional Assessment Appeal Court, return the Notice of Dissatisfaction within 7 days of the date the Amended Notice was received.

4.   Appeals to the Nova Scotia Municipal Board must be made within 30 days of the date the Regional Court decision is received.

Level of government responsible for assessment: Provincial

Tax assessors:

- Appointed, indefinite appointment.

- High school diploma is required.

- Special courses and certificate are required within a four year period.

Government issued assessor's manual: *Nova Scotia Assessment Manual*

Equalization: *Not applicable*

Property tax maps mandatory: *No*

Allow real property to be assessed at financially better use rather than current use: *No, current value.*

Frequency of Provincial ratio studies: *Every 3 years (re-assessment)*

Are Provincial ratio studies accessible to the public: *No*

Provincial agency information and contact person:

Nova Scotia
Department of Municipal Affairs
Assessment Division
P. O. Box 216
Halifax, Nova Scotia
Canada B3J 2M4
Mr. John C. MacKay, Provincial Director of Assessment
Telephone: (902) 424-5671 • Fax: (902) 424-0531

ONTARIO

Name of real property tax: *Real Property Tax*

Official valuation standard: *Market value is defined in Chapter A.31 Section 19(1) of the Ontario Assessment Act as "the amount that the land might be expected to realize if sold in the open market by a willing seller to a willing buyer."*

Annual assessment of real property: *Yes*

Reassessment cycle:

> *"In every fourth year, commencing in 1993, the Ministry shall examine the amounts of the assessments of rateable property in each municipality and locality on the last returned assessment roll of each municipality and locality and determine as nearly as may be what the total of the amounts of the assessment of the rateable property should be so that costs may be apportioned and grants provided on a basis which is just and equitable as between municipalities and localities." R.S.O. 1990 C.A.31, S.51(1); 1991 C.11, S3(1).*

Assessment date:

> *"In every municipality the assessment shall be made annually commencing in the year 1974 and at any time between the 1st day of January and the third Tuesday following the 1st day of December, and the assessment roll of the municipality shall be returned to the clerk not later than the third Tuesday following the 1st day of December in the year in which the assessment is made." Chapter A.31 Section 36(1) Ontario Assessment Act.*

Classification of property:

> *Classification of property is not mandated by statute. Classification of property, like assessment levels, is determined at the discretion of each municipality and locality. Classifications are generally divided into residential, commercial, and industrial.*

Assessment rate:

> *Assessment levels are not mandated by statute. Assessment rates are determined at the discretion of each locality and municipality. They vary from 5% to 100%.*

Tax relief available to homeowners:

Seniors and Disabled in the Community Program
C.A. 31, S.3(22) of Ontario Assessment Act.

"All alterations, improvements and additions commenced after the 15th day of May, 1984 and made to a parcel of land containing an existing residential unit for the purpose of providing accommodation for, or improved facilities for the accommodation of, a person who would, but for the accommodation or improved facilities provided, require care in an institution and who has attained sixty-five years of age or is a handicapped person, where the owner of the property applies to the Minister for the exemption and the exemption is approved by the Minister, provided that,

    a. a person who would otherwise require care in an institution and who has attained sixty-five years of age or is a handicapped person resides in the premises as his or her principal residence, and

    b. the land is assessed as residential and comprises not more than three residential units;

but the alteration, improvement or addition is not exempt where the person occupying the property in which the person who has attained sixty-five years of age or the handicapped person resides is in the business of offering care to such persons."

Elderly Tax Relief
Municipalities may provide through Bylaws relief to Senior Citizens of varying amounts of money. Depending on the terms agreed upon in the Bylaw, the amount may be registered as liens against the property and must be repaid upon transfer of the property.

Exemptions:

- Government property
- Religious property
- Charitable property
- Educational property
- Historic property
- Non-profit cemeteries
- Public hospitals

- Machinery used in manufacturing
- Personalty
- Indian lands
- Mineral land and minerals
- Certain property of telephone and telegraph companies

Appeal procedure:

Step 1 If after receiving your Notice of Assessment you feel your property has been unfairly or erroneously assessed, you should have an informal meeting with your assessor. This may be accomplished by a scheduled appointment or at Open Houses which are conducted by your Regional Assessment Office shortly after your Notice of Assessment is mailed out.

Step 2 If after an informal conference with your assessor you are still dissatisfied, you may appeal to the Assessment Review Board. The steps you must take to lodge an appeal with the Regional Registrar of the Assessment Review Board are listed on the back of your Notice of Assessment. The address of the Board is also shown on the notice.

Step 3 Assuming that the Assessment Review Board has ruled against you and you remain dissatisfied, you may appeal to the Ontario Municipal Board. Appeals to the Board must be made within 21 days of the mailing of the written notice of the Assessment Review Board's decision.

The Board hearing is a whole new trial of the issue (de novo action), so you can introduce any fresh evidence you have as well as restating the arguments you made before the Assessment Review Board. The government assessor has the same right and privilege.

Step 4 An Ontario Municipal Board decision can be appealed to the Ontario Court (General Division) on questions of law only.

Step 5   A decision from the Ontario Court (General Division) may be made to the Appeal Court of Ontario.

Step 6   A decision from the Appeal Court of Ontario may be made to the Supreme Court of Canada.

Appeal calendar:

1. Roll return: Third Tuesday following the first day of December.

2. Appeal to the Assessment Review Board: 21 days after roll is returned or date notice of assessment is mailed.

3. The regional registrar shall give notice of any hearing by the Assessment Review Board to the parties at least 14 days before the date fixed for the hearing.

4. An Appeal to the Ontario Municipal Board must be made within 21 days of the mailing of the written notice of the Assessment Review Board's decision.

Level of government responsible for assessment: Province, Municipality

Tax assessors:

- Appointed, indefinite appointment.

- High school diploma is required.

- Accreditation from IMA or AIC is required.

Government issued assessor's manuals: *Ontario Valuation Manual - 1980 for Residential & Farm; 1969 for Industrial, Commercial and Exempt*

Equalization: *Yes*

Property tax maps mandatory: *No*

Allow real property to be assessed at financially better use rather than current use: *No, current value.*

Frequency of Provincial ratio studies: *Ratio studies are not generally done except for use in Court and in inserting new properties on the assessment roll.*

Are Provincial ratio studies accessible to the public: *Yes, when impact studies are done for reassessment.*

Provincial agency information and contact person:

Province of Ontario
Ministry of Finance
Appraisal Services Branch
33 King Street West
Oshawa, Ontario
Canada L1H 8H5
Mr. Nizam Ali, Senior Valuation Analyst
Telephone: (905) 433-5727 • Fax: (905) 433-6020

NOTES

PRINCE EDWARD ISLAND

Name of real property tax: *Real Property Tax*

Official valuation standard: *Market value means the most probable sale price indicated by consideration of the cost of reproduction, the sale price of comparable properties and the value indicated by rentals or anticipated net income.*

Annual assessment of real property: *Yes*

Reassessment cycle: *Every five years.*

Assessment date: *January 1*

Classification of property:

Class I   Residential

Class II   Commercial

Class III   Non-Commercial

Class IV   Farm

Assessment rate:

Class I   Residential: 100% of market value

Tax relief available to homeowners:

Tax Deferral Program For Senior Citizens

When a senior citizen is accepted into the Tax Deferral Program, he/she stops paying property taxes. Instead, the government keeps a record of taxes owing each year, and the taxes will be paid out of the senior citizen's estate. There is no interest charged while under this program. If the property owner's estate cannot cover the amount of the taxes, the provincial government will forgive any shortages. If the senior citizen decides to sell the property, all the accumulated taxes to date will have to be paid.

To be eligible, a senior citizen must own a residence on Prince Edward Island and the total combined annual household income must not exceed $15,000. The senior citizen must have lived in the home at least six months before applying to the program. Taxes may be deferred on only one property.

Provincial Tax Credit
Real Property Tax Act (R.S.P.E.I. Chapter R-4 Section 5)
Resident property owners receive a tax credit of 50, 60, or 70 cents per $100 of assessment depending upon the area of the province in which the property is located.

    a.   Property located in the City of Charlottetown or the Town of Summerside is eligible to receive a tax credit at the rate of 70 cents per $100 assessment;

    b.   Property located in a municipality other than Charlottetown or Summerside that provides its own police protection, is eligible to receive a tax credit at the rate of 60 cents per $100 assessment;

    c.   Property to whom or to which clauses (a) or (b) do not apply is eligible to receive a tax credit at the rate of 50 cents per $100 of assessment.

Farm Assessment (R.A.P.E.I. 1988 Chapter R-4 Sections 4-8)
Bona fide farmers receive a farm assessment on their land only, which ranges from 10% to 20% of the market value.

Exemptions:

- Personalty
- Government property
- Religious property
- Educational property
- Forest or orchards
- Mines and minerals
- Non-profit cemeteries
- Buildings of purification systems
- Designated public squares

Appeal procedure:

Step 1   Upon receiving an assessment notice and tax bill, a taxpayer has 45 days to "refer" his assessed value to the Minister.

Step 2   After review by the Minister, the decision is mailed to the taxpayer, who has 21 days to appeal to the Island Regulatory & Appeals Commission.

Step 3   The decision of the Island Regulatory & Appeals Commission may be appealed to the Supreme Court of the Province within 45 days.

Appeal calendar:

1. Assessment date: January 1

2. Upon receipt of assessment notice and tax bill a taxpayer has 45 days to refer his assessed value to the Minister.

3. The Minister has a maximum 45 days from the receipt of reference to forward his decision and his reasons therefore back to the taxpayer.

4. Upon receipt of the Minister's decision, the taxpayer has 21 days to appeal to the Island Regulatory & Appeals Commission.

5. The decision of the Island Regulatory & Appeals Commission may be appealed by the taxpayer to the Supreme Court of the Province within 45 days.

Level of government responsible for assessment: Province

Tax assessors:

- Appointed, indefinite appointment.
- High school diploma is required.
- CRA designation through the Appraisal Institute of Canada is required.

Government issued assessor's manuals: *Prince Edward Island Real Property Assessment Manual; Marshall & Swift Valuation Manual*

Equalization: *No*

Property tax maps mandatory: *No*

Allow real property to be assessed at financially better use rather than current use: *No, current use.*

Frequency of Provincial ratio studies: *Yearly*

Are Provincial ratio studies accessible to the public: *No*

Provincial agency information and contact person:

Prince Edward Island
Department of Provincial Treasury
P. O. Box 2000
Charlottetown, Prince Edward Island
Canada C1A 7N8
Mr. Kevin Dingwell, AACI
Chief Assessor Residential & Farm Properties
Telephone: (902) 368-4070 • Fax: (902) 368-5544

QUEBEC

Name of real property tax: *Taxe foncière*

Official valuation standard: *The actual value of a unit of assessment is its exchange value in the free and open market, that is, the price most likely to be paid at a sale by agreement made under the following conditions:*

1. *The vendor and the purchaser are willing, respectively, to sell and to purchase the unit of assessment, and they are not compelled to do so: and*

2. *the vendor and the purchaser are reasonably informed of the condition of the unit of assessment, of the use that can most likely be made of it and of conditions in the real estate market.*

Annual assessment of real property: *No*

Reassessment cycle: *Every three years.*

Assessment date: *July 1*

Classification of property:

Class I	Residential
Class II	Transport
Class III	Farms & Natural Resources
Class IV	Service
Class V	Industrial
Class VI	Commerce
Class VII	Cultural/Recreational

Assessment rate:

Class I   Residential: 100% of actual value

Tax relief available to homeowners:

There is no specific provision for real estate or school tax exemptions for homeowners in the Municipal Taxation Act. There are however, tax credits available for municipal, real estate, service, or school taxes for homeowners in the Provincial Income Tax Act. The tax credits are available to homeowners based on net income, or number of dependents or age (65 years of age or older). The credits should be claimed on the yearly provincial income tax report.

Exemptions:

- Government property
- Religious property
- Charitable property
- Educational property
- Historical
- Agricultural
- Utility
- Non-profit hospitals & cemeteries

Appeal procedure:

Step 1   A taxpayer may file an appeal with the Quebec Board of Revision within 60 days after receiving a tax notice of assessment and taxation.

Step 2   If the taxpayer is dissatisfied after receiving the decision of the Board of Revision, he/she may appeal to the Court of Quebec.

Step 3   If after presenting all the pertinent evidence, the taxpayer is dissatisfied with the decision of the Court of Quebec, he/she may appeal to the Court of Appeal.

Step 4   If after receiving a decision from the Court of Appeal, the taxpayer is still dissatisfied, he/she may appeal to the Superior Court.

Step 5   The last appeal a taxpayer may make is to the Quebec Supreme Court.

Appeal calendar:

1. Assessment date: July 4th
2. Notice of Assessment sent to taxpayer: sometime after the last day of February.

3. The taxpayer has 60 days to appeal to the Quebec Board of Revision.

4. After the Board of Revision renders a decision, the taxpayer has 60 days to appeal to the Court of Quebec.

Level of government responsible for assessment:
City or Municipality

Tax assessors:

- Appointed, variable appointment.

- 17 years of formal education including 3 years of university.

- Certificate from the Professional Corps of Assessors and special courses are required.

Government issued assessor's manuals: *Manuel d'evaluation foncière du Quebec (13 volumes).*

Equalization: *No*

Property tax maps mandatory: *No*

Allow real property to be assessed at financially better use rather than current use: *No, current value in its present use.*

Frequency of Provincial ratio studies: *Yearly*

Are Provincial ratio studies accessible to the public: *Yes*

Provincial agency information and contact person:

Gouvernement du Quebec
Ministère des Affaires Municipales
Direction generale des politiques et de la fiscalite
20 Rue Chauveau
Quebec G1R 4J3
Mr. Gaston Vachon
Telephone: (418) 691-2039 • Fax: (418) 643-3204

NOTES

SASKATCHEWAN

Name of real property tax: *Property Tax*

Official valuation standard:

1. *Land is to be assessed at its fair value exclusive of the value of any improvements.*

2. *The dominant and controlling factor in the assessment of land is equity.*

3. *The value at which land is assessed is to bear a fair and just proportion to the value at which other lands in the municipality are assessed.*

Annual assessment of real property: *Yes*

Reassessment cycle: *Every 7 years.*

Assessment date: *The base date for assessments for all property in Saskatchewan is 1965. The cost manual reflects 1965 costs. Land is valued using a schedule that reflects the 1965 market values.*

Classification of property:

Class I	Building: 50%	
Class II	Agricultural Land: 60%	
Class III	Non-agricultural Land: 100%	
Class IV	Industrial: 100%	
Class V	Business: 100%	

Assessment rate:

Land: 100% of fair value

Improvements: 50% of fair value

Tax relief available to homeowners:

No tax relief for homeowners of any type is provided by statute.

Exemptions:

- Personalty
- Government property
- Religious property
- Charitable property
- Educational property
- Publicly-owned utility
- Transportation & communication
- Forests & orchards
- Hospitals
- Cemeteries
- Farm buildings

Appeal procedure:

Step 1   Within 20 days after the day on which the notice of assessment is mailed, a taxpayer may formally appeal in writing to the Board of Revision.

Step 2   If after a hearing before the Board of Revision the property owner continues to disagree with the decision of the Board of Revision, he/she may appeal to the Saskatchewan Municipal Board.

Step 3   If after a hearing before the Saskatchewan Municipal Board the taxpayer is dissatisfied with the ruling, he/she may appeal to the Provincial Court of Appeal. The Court of Appeal is not a new hearing. Assessment issues are dealt with by using stated cases. If a case is of national importance it could be appealed to the Supreme Court of Canada.

Appeal calendar:

1. Assessment date: The date the roll is prepared in each municipality.

2. May 31: Assessor shall prepare an assessment roll.

3. June 1: Assessor shall mail assessment notices except for changes.

4. 20 days after notices of assessment are mailed is the deadline for filing appeals with the Board of Revision.

5. Notices are mailed out 15 days prior to the sitting of the Board of Revision, giving the dates and places of the hearings.

6. 14 days after receipt of the decisions by the Board of Revision is the deadline for filing an appeal with the Saskatchewan Municipal Board.

Level of government responsible for assessment:
Province, City

Tax assessors:

*   Appointed, indefinite term.

*   Education requirements: Urban Grade-12; Rural degree in Agriculture.

Government issued assessor's manuals:
Saskatchewan Urban Assessment Manual 1982
Saskatchewan Rural Assessment Manual 1982
Saskatchewan Industrial Assessment Manual 1982

Equalization: *No*

Property tax maps mandatory: *No*

Allow real property to be assessed at financially better use rather than current use: *No, current value.*

Frequency of Provincial ratio studies: *n/a*

Are Provincial ratio studies accessible to the public: *n/a*

Provincial agency information and contact person:

Saskatchewan Assessment Management Agency
1920 Brand Street, 16th Floor
Regina, Saskatchewan
Canada S4P 3N2
Mr. Bryan Webb, Chief Executive Officer
Telephone: (306) 924-8046 • Fax: (306) 924-8060

NOTES

YUKON

Name of real property tax: *Property Tax*

Official valuation standard: *Land shall be assessed at its fair value; improvements (to the land such as houses, garages, fences, etc.) shall be assessed at a value equivalent to their replacement cost.*

Annual assessment of real property: *Yes*

Reassessment cycle: *At least once every five years.*

Assessment date: *July 31 of tax year*

Classification of property:

Class I	1 & 2 family residences:	100%
Class II	Multi-family residences:	100%
Class III	Commercial:	100%
Class IV	Industrial:	100%
Class V	Agriculture:	100%
Class VI	Institutional:	100%
Class VII	Recreational:	100%

Assessment rate:

100% of total value

Tax relief available to homeowners:

Homeowners Grant

If the property being taxed is your principal residence and you lived there as of January 1 or for not less than 184 days in the taxation year, you may apply to the Yukon Government for a Homeowner's Grant. You must apply before February 15 of the year following the year taxes are levied. The grant is equal to 50 percent of your local taxes (75 per cent if you are 65 years of age or older) to a maximum regulated amount. The Homeowner's Grant is calculated on the general taxation levy. Local improvement taxes are excluded from the calculation.

Exemptions:

- Government property
- Religious property (churches only)
- Roads
- Mines & minerals
- Cemeteries

Appeal procedure:

Step 1   If after receiving your Notice of Assessment you disagree with the value of your property, or you feel that
your property has been erroneously assessed, you may
schedule an informal conference with your assessor.

Step 2   If after the informal conference at the Property Assessment office you are still dissatisfied, you may appeal
to the Assessment Review Board. To do this, you must
provide written notice to the Office of the Chief Assessor within 30 days after the mailing of your assessment
notice.

Step 3   If after hearing your case, the Assessment Review
Board's decision is not favorable and you are still
dissatisfied, you may appeal to the Assessment Appeal
Board. This is accomplished by sending a written
appeal to the Assessment Appeal Board within 30 days
of receipt of the ruling of the Assessment Review
Board.

Step 4   If the appeal is based on a point of law, and the ruling
of Assessment Appeal Board is unfavorable, you may
appeal to the Supreme Court.

Appeal calendar:

1. November 15: Chief Assessor delivers Assessment Roll to Tax
   Authority.

2. November 30: Tax Authority returns roll to Chief Assessor.
   Chief Assessor immediately mails Assessment Notices to all
   assessed properties.

3. Appeal to Assessment Review Board: Final day for taxpayer to appeal to the Board is 30 days after receipt of Assessment Notices.

4. Assessment Review Board must start hearings by February 15.

5. Assessment Review Board must finish hearings by March 15.

6. Appeals to Assessment Appeal Board must be made within 30 days of mailing of decision of the Assessment Review Board.

7. April 15: Taxing Authority establishes tax rates.

8. May 15: Tax notices are issued.

9. July 2: Taxes are due.

Level of government responsible for assessment:
Territorial government

Tax assessors:

- Appointed, indefinite term.

- High school diploma is required.

- Special education and certificate are required.

Government issued assessor's manual: *1994 Alberta Assessment Manual*

Equalization: *No*

Property tax maps mandatory: *No*

Allow real property to be assessed at financially better use rather than current use: *No, current value*

Frequency of Provincial ratio studies: *Yearly*

Are Provincial ratio studies accessible to the public: *No*

Provincial agency information and contact person:

Yukon Community and Transportation Services
Property Assessment and Taxation
P.O.BOX 2793
Whitehorse, Yukon
Canada, Y1A 2C6
Mr. D.B.(Dave) Dowie, Assistant Manager and Chief Assessor
Telephone: (403) 667-5234 • Fax: (403) 667-6109

NOTES

APPENDIX A

As an avid reader of "how to" books I am always skeptical of an author who makes claims that are not substantiated. The purpose of Appendix A is to verify the author's claims that the techniques described in this book work.

The first year I attempted to reduce the assessment on my home was for the tax year 1991. I successfully reduced the official valuation from $268,718 to $234,973, a reduction of $33,745. This translated into a tax savings of $837.23. Refer to the Special Master's Finding of Facts sheet on page 376 and the county check and refund stub on page 377.

The second year I was able to reduce the assessed value on my home from $260,556 to $235,597. This reduction in assessed value of $24,959 saved me $638.91 (refer to pages 378 and 379).

In 1993 I undertook to appeal four separate properties. First, I again challenged the assessment on my home and was able to reduce the assessed value from $260,545 to $231,145. This reduction of $29,400 in assessed value translated into a tax savings of $756.55 (see pages 380 and 381). That same year I also challenged the assessment on my father's home for the first time and was able to reduce his assessment from $111,781 to $94,000. This reduction in assessed value of $17,781 translated into a tax savings of $467.76 (see pages 382 & 383).

My father also owns a single family home which he rents out. I challenged the official assessed value on that property, which was $107,578. I was able to reduce the assessment to $86,000. This reduction in assessed value of $21,578 translated into a tax saving of $567.65 (see pages 384 & 385).

Lastly, I challenged the assessed value of a small commercial building that I own and occupy. I was able to reduce the assessed value from $42,604 to $38,343. This reduction in the assessed value of $4,261 translated into a tax reduction of $125.22 (see pages 386 & 387).

For the last three years I have been able to reduce the assessed value on six properties for a total of $131,724.00. I have saved a total of $3,393.32 without incurring any out-of-pocket expenses whatsoever.

FOLIO # 13-2227-001-6080-V
AGENDA # 13484
NAME FRANK J ADLER &W BELLA
ADDRESS
BAY HARBOR ISLANDS FL
33154
HEARING DATE 02/14/92   TIME   BD B
TYPE PROPERTY   ZONING 10:30

SPECIAL MASTER'S FINDINGS OF FACT
CONCLUSIONS OF LAW AND
RECOMMENDATIONS TO THE
VALUE ADJUSTMENT BOARD

V-A-L-U-A-T-I-O-N I-S-S-U-E-S

PROPERTY ADDRESS

SEQUENCE #
20

ZIP 33154-1901

TAX YEAR 1991	☐ REAL PROPERTY (INSERT TOTAL IN COLUMN 5)		☐ PERSONAL PROPERTY (INSERT TOTAL INTO COLUMN 5)		☐ REAL ☐ PERSONAL
	Col 1 LAND	Col 2 IMPROVEMENTS	Col 3 FF & E	Col 4 SUPPLIES	Col 5 TOTAL
Property Appraiser's Preliminary Tax Assessment	$ 176400	$ 92318	CALC $ ___ SITE $ ___	$	$ 268718
OTHER ACTION	$	$	CALC $ ___ SITE $ ___	$	$
Appraiser's Staff Recommendation to the VAB	$	$	CALC $ ___ SITE $ ___	$	$

FINDINGS OF FACT

1. ☒ TAXPAYER ☐ AGENT ☐ NO SHOW ☐ WITHDREW PETITION ☐ ACCEPTED P.A. RECOM.

2. PROPERTY APPRAISER'S DETERMINATION BASED ON:
   ☐ REPLACEMENT COST   ☒ COMPARABLE SALES   ☐ INCOME APPROACH

3. TAXPAYER CHALLENGES ASSESSMENT OF:
   ☐ LAND   ☐ IMPROVEMENTS   ☐ F.F. & E.   ☐ SUPPLIES   ☒ TOTAL

4. THE FOLLOWING DEMONSTRATIVE EVIDENCE WAS OFFERED:
   ☐ INDEPENDENT APPRAISAL   ☒ BLDG. CARD   ☐ BLDG. &/or AERIAL PHOTOS   ☐ MAPS
   ☐ FIELD REPORT   ☐ PHOTOGRAPH(S)   ☐ CLOSING STATEMENT   ☐ F.I.T. RETURN
   ☐ DEPRECIATION SCHEDULE (itemized)   ☐ FINANCIAL STATEMENT   ☐ AFFIDAVIT
   ☒ OTHER: _Comps_

5. SUMMARY OF EVIDENCE PRESENTED:
   A. BY PROPERTY APPRAISER: ☒ RECOMMENDED TAX ASSESSMENT   ☐ OTHER:
      Comps
   B. BY TAXPAYER: ☒ TESTIMONY   ☐ NONE OFFERED   ☒ OTHER: _____
      Comps

6. BASIC AND UNDERLYING FACTS:
   A.   RECOMMENDED TAX ASSESSMENT CORRECT, INSUFFICIENT OR NO EVIDENCE OFFERED
         TO THE CONTRARY: (Further explanation, if any) _____

   B. ☒ RECOMMENDED CHANGE: (Explanation) _Based on Comparable sales_

CONCLUSIONS OF LAW

7. FUNDAMENTAL ISSUE: WHETHER THE TAXPAYER PRESENTED EVIDENCE WHICH EXCLUDED
   EVERY REASONABLE HYPOTHESIS OF A LEGAL ASSESSMENT?   ☒ YES   ☐ NO

8. ULTIMATE FINDINGS:
   PRELIMINARY ASSESSMENT .... ☒ DOES .... ☐ DOES NOT ....
   EXCEED JUST VALUATION. IT IS RECOMMENDED THAT THE RELIEF APPLIED FOR IN THIS
   PETITION .... ☐ BE DENIED .... ☒ BE GRANTED .... AS INDICATED BELOW:

SPECIAL MASTER'S RECOMMENDATION TO THE VAB	Col 1 LAND	Col 2 IMPROVEMENTS	Col 3 FF & E	Col 4 SUPPLIES	Col 5 TOTAL
	$142,665	$ 92,318	CALC $ ___ SITE $ ___	$	$ 234,973

FILING FEE REFUND: If this "Findings of Fact" sheet reflects a recommended reduction to the VAB in the preliminary tax assessment of any particular parcel(s) of property, any filing fee previously paid with respect to any such parcel(s) will be refunded. Refund check(s) will be made payable to taxpayer or his agent, if any, and will be mailed to the address designated on the petition

2/14/92
DATE COMPLETED BY S.M.

Pauline Thompson
SPECIAL MASTER'S SIGNATURE

METRO-DADE

METROPOLITAN DADE COUNTY, FLORIDA

FINANCE DEPARTMENT
TAX COLLECTION DIVISION
140 W. FLAGLER STREET
MIAMI, FLORIDA 33130

1991 REAL ESTATE PROPERTY TAXES
13 2227 001 6080
FRANK J ADLER &W BELLA

000
LOAN #   263267261

1991 REFUND NOTICE

FRANK J ADLER &W BELLA
BAY HARBOR ISLANDS FL 33154-1901

DEAR TAXPAYER:

WE ARE ENCLOSING OUR CHECK BEARING
WARRANT NUMBER 012274l DATED 04/27/92
FOR $837.23 WHICH REPRESENTS
A REFUND OF TAX RECEIPT # 57/0000437A.

Form # 7171 Reordered 3/91   PRINTED IN U.S.A.

METRO-DADE

122741

METROPOLITAN DADE COUNTY, FLORIDA
SPECIAL SERVICES ACCOUNT

VOID AFTER SIX MONTHS
SOUTHEAST BANK, N.A.
MIAMI, FLORIDA

63-58
660

**EIGHT HUNDRED THIRTY SEVEN AND .23 DOLLARS
EXACTLY**
DOLLARS AND   CENTS

Date	Control Number	Amount of Check
04/27/92	570000437A	******837.23

TAX COLL. AD-VALOREM

To
The
Order
Of

FRANK J ADLER &W BELLA
MIAMI   FL

122741

BOARD OF COUNTY COMMISSIONERS
CLERK

⑈122741⑈ ⑆0660005B⑈ 0⑈8 66694⑈⑈

```
┌ ─ ─ ─ ─ ─ ─ ─ ─ ─ ─ ─ ─ ─ ─ ┐
  FOLIO #   13-2227-001-6080-V        SPECIAL MASTER'S FINDINGS OF FACT         ┌──────────┐
│ AGENDA #  17991                  │      CONCLUSIONS OF LAW AND                │ SEQUENCE │
  NAME  FRANK J ADLER &W BELLA            RECOMMENDATIONS TO THE                │ #        │
│ ADDRESS.                         │       VALUE ADJUSTMENT BOARD               │  37      │
  BAY HARBOR ISLANDS FL                                                         └──────────┘
│                         33154│       V-A-L-U-A-T-I-O-N  I-S-S-U-E-S
  HEARING DATE 01/29/93    TIME    BD B  PROPERTY ADDRESS
│ TYPE PROPERTY          ZONING 1:30│
                                                                   ZIP  33154-1901
└ ─ ─ ─ ─ ─ ─ ─ ─ ─ ─ ─ ─ ─ ─ ┘
```

TAX YEAR 1992	☐ REAL PROPERTY (INSERT TOTAL IN COLUMN 5)		☐ PERSONAL PROPERTY (INSERT TOTAL INTO COLUMN 5)		☐ REAL ☐ PERSONAL
	Col 1 LAND	Col 2 IMPROVEMENTS	Col 3 FF & E	Col 4 SUPPLIES	Col.5 TOTAL
Property Appraiser's Preliminary Tax Assessment	$ 176400	$ 84156	CALC $ SITE $	$	$ 260556
OTHER ACTION	$	$	CALC $ SITE $	$	$
Appraiser's Staff Recommendation to the VAB	$	$	CALC $ SITE $	$	$

FINDINGS OF FACT

1. ☒ TAXPAYER ☐ AGENT ☐ NO SHOW ☐ WITHDREW PETITION ☐ ACCEPTED P.A. RECOM.

2. PROPERTY APPRAISER'S DETERMINATION BASED ON:
   ☐ REPLACEMENT COST   ☒ COMPARABLE SALES   ☐ INCOME APPROACH

3. TAXPAYER CHALLENGES ASSESSMENT OF:
   ☐ LAND   ☐ IMPROVEMENTS   ☐ F.F. & E.   ☐ SUPPLIES   ☒ TOTAL

4. THE FOLLOWING DEMONSTRATIVE EVIDENCE WAS OFFERED:
   ☐ INDEPENDENT APPRAISAL   ☒ BLDG. CARD   ☐ BLDG. &/or AERIAL PHOTOS   ☐ MAPS
   ☐ FIELD REPORT   ☐ PHOTOGRAPH(S)   ☐ CLOSING STATEMENT   ☐ F.I.T. RETURN
   ☐ DEPRECIATION SCHEDULE (Itemized)   ☐ FINANCIAL STATEMENT   ☐ AFFIDAVIT
   ☒ OTHER: _Comparable Sales_

5. SUMMARY OF EVIDENCE PRESENTED:
   A. BY PROPERTY APPRAISER: ☒ RECOMMENDED TAX ASSESSMENT   ☒ OTHER:
      Comparable Sales
   B. BY TAXPAYER   ☐ TESTIMONY   ☐ NONE OFFERED   ☒ OTHER: _____
      Comparable Sales

6. BASIC AND UNDERLYING FACTS:
   A. ☐ RECOMMENDED TAX ASSESSMENT CORRECT, INSUFFICIENT OR NO EVIDENCE OFFERED
      TO THE CONTRARY: (Further explanation, if any) _____

   B. ☒ RECOMMENDED CHANGE: (Explanation) _Reduction based on Comparable
      Sales presented_

CONCLUSIONS OF LAW

7. FUNDAMENTAL ISSUE: WHETHER THE TAXPAYER PRESENTED EVIDENCE WHICH EXCLUDED
   EVERY REASONABLE HYPOTHESIS OF A LEGAL ASSESSMENT?   ☒ YES   ☐ NO

8. ULTIMATE FINDINGS:
   PRELIMINARY ASSESSMENT .... ☐ DOES .... ☐ DOES NOT ....
   EXCEED JUST VALUATION. IT IS RECOMMENDED THAT THE RELIEF APPLIED FOR IN THIS
   PETITION .... ☐ BE DENIED .... ☒ BE GRANTED .... AS INDICATED BELOW:

SPECIAL MASTER'S RECOM- MENDA- TION TO THE VAB	Col 1 LAND	Col 2 IMPROVEMENTS	Col 3 FF & E	Col 4 SUPPLIES	Col.5 TOTAL
	$ 160,206	$ 75,391	CALC $ SITE	$	$ 235,597

FILING FEE REFUND: If this "Findings of Fact" sheet reflects a recommended reduction to the VAB in the preliminary tax assessment of any particular parcel(s) of property, any filing fee previously paid with respect to any such parcel(s) will be refunded. Refund check(s) will be made payable to taxpayer or his agent, if any, and will be mailed to the address designated on the petition.

_1/29/93_
DATE COMPLETED BY S.M.

Pauline Thompson
SPECIAL MASTER'S SIGNATURE

CR/CT/VAB 6

METRO·DADE

METROPOLITAN DADE COUNTY, FLORIDA

FINANCE DEPARTMENT
TAX COLLECTION DIVISION
140 W. FLAGLER STREET
MIAMI, FLORIDA 33130

1992 REAL ESTATE PROPERTY TAXES

1992 REFUND NOTICE

FRANK J ADLER &W BELLA

000
LOAN #   4728

DEAR TAXPAYER:

WE ARE ENCLOSING OUR CHECK BEARING
WARRANT NUMBER 0192695 DATED 04/12/93
FOR $638.91 WHICH REPRESENTS
A REFUND OF TAX RECEIPT # 80/00003599A.

BELLA OR FRANK ADLER
BAY HARBOR ISLANDS FL 33154-1901

Form # 7171 Reorder 5/92 PRINTED IN U.S.A.

METRO·DADE

192695

METROPOLITAN DADE COUNTY, FLORIDA

SPECIAL SERVICES ACCOUNT

VOID AFTER SIX MONTHS
FIRST UNION NATIONAL BANK
OF FLORIDA
MIAMI, FLORIDA 33131

63-643
670

Date	Control Number	Amount of Check
04/12/93	800000399A	✽✽✽✽✽638.91✽
TAX COLL. AD-VALOREM		

✽✽✽SIX HUNDRED THIRTY EIGHT AND.91 DOLLARS✽
EXACTLY

DOLLARS AND   CENTS

192695

To
The
Order
Of

BELLA OR FRANK ADLER
MIAMI   FL

BOARD OF COUNTY CO'MMISSIO.

COUNTY COMMISSNRS
DADE
COUNTY
FLORID.

FOLIO # 13-2227-001-6080-V
AGENDA # 10579
NAME FRANK J ADLER &W BELLA
ADDRESS
BAY HARBOR ISLANDS FL
33154
HEARING DATE 12/16/93   TIME
TYPE PROPERTY   ZONING 2:30

BD C

SPECIAL MASTER'S FINDINGS OF FACT
CONCLUSIONS OF LAW AND
RECOMMENDATIONS TO THE
VALUE ADJUSTMENT BOARD

V-A-L-U-A-T-I-O-N   I-S-S-U-E-S

PROPERTY ADDRESS

SEQUENCE
44

ZIP 33154-190J

TAX YEAR 1993	☐ REAL PROPERTY (INSERT TOTAL IN COLUMN 5)		☐ PERSONAL PROPERTY (INSERT TOTAL INTO COLUMN 5)		☐ REAL ☐ PERSONAL
	Col 1 LAND	Col 2 IMPROVEMENTS	Col 3 FF & E	Col 4 SUPPLIES	Col 5 TOTAL
Property Appraiser's Preliminary Tax Assessment	$ 176400	$ 84145	CALC $ / SITE $	$	$ 260545
OTHER ACTION	$	$	CALC $ / SITE $	$	$
Appraiser's Staff Recommendation to the VAB	$	$	CALC $ / SITE $	$	$

FINDINGS OF FACT

1. ☒ TAXPAYER   ☐ AGENT   ☐ NO SHOW   ☐ WITHDREW PETITION   ☐ ACCEPTED P.A. RECOM.

2. PROPERTY APPRAISER'S DETERMINATION BASED ON:
   ☐ REPLACEMENT COST   ☐ COMPARABLE SALES   ☐ INCOME APPROACH

3. TAXPAYER CHALLENGES ASSESSMENT OF:
   ☐ LAND   ☐ IMPROVEMENTS   ☐ F.F. & E.   ☐ SUPPLIES   ☒ TOTAL

4. THE FOLLOWING DEMONSTRATIVE EVIDENCE WAS OFFERED:
   ☐ INDEPENDENT APPRAISAL   ☐ BLDG. CARD   ☐ BLDG. &/or AERIAL PHOTOS   ☐ MAPS
   ☐ FIELD REPORT   ☐ PHOTOGRAPH(S)   ☐ CLOSING STATEMENT   ☐ F.I.T. RETURN
   ☐ DEPRECIATION SCHEDULE (Itemized)   ☐ FINANCIAL STATEMENT   ☐ AFFIDAVIT
   ☐ OTHER: _Comp Sales_

5. SUMMARY OF EVIDENCE PRESENTED:
   A. BY PROPERTY APPRAISER: ☒ RECOMMENDED TAX ASSESSMENT   ☐ OTHER:
   Comp Sales
   B. BY TAXPAYER: ☒ TESTIMONY   ☐ NONE OFFERED   ☐ OTHER: _____
   Comp Sales

6. BASIC AND UNDERLYING FACTS:
   A. ☐ RECOMMENDED TAX ASSESSMENT CORRECT, INSUFFICIENT OR NO EVIDENCE OFFERED TO THE CONTRARY. (Further explanation, if any) _____

   B. ☒ RECOMMENDED CHANGE: (Explanation) _Discrepancy in land size (smaller size than actually assessed) and comp. sales supports the reduction_

   C. ☐ APPEAL BASED ON HURRICANE RELATED DAMAGE

CONCLUSIONS OF LAW

7. FUNDAMENTAL ISSUE: WHETHER THE TAXPAYER PRESENTED EVIDENCE WHICH EXCLUDED EVERY REASONABLE HYPOTHESIS OF A LEGAL ASSESSMENT?   ☒ YES   ☐ NO

8. ULTIMATE FINDINGS:
   PRELIMINARY ASSESSMENT .... ☒ DOES .... ☐ DOES NOT ....
   EXCEED JUST VALUATION. IT IS RECOMMENDED THAT THE RELIEF APPLIED FOR IN THIS PETITION .... ☐ BE DENIED .... ☒ BE GRANTED .... AS INDICATED BELOW:

SPECIAL MASTER'S RECOMMENDATION TO THE VAB	Col 1 LAND	Col 2 IMPROVEMENTS	Col 3 FF & E	Col 4 SUPPLIES	Col 5 TOTAL
	$ 147000	$ 84145	CALC $ / SITE $	$	$ 231145

FILING FEE REFUND: If this "Findings of Fact" sheet reflects a recommended reduction to the VAB in the preliminary tax assessment of any particular parcel(s) of property, any filing fee previously paid with respect to any such parcel(s) will be refunded. Refund check(s) will be made payable to taxpayer or his agent, if any, and will be mailed to the address designated on the petition.

12-16-93
DATE COMPLETED BY S.M.

Linda K Molman
SPECIAL MASTER'S SIGNATURE

METROPOLITAN DADE COUNTY, FLORIDA

FINANCE DEPARTMENT
TAX COLLECTION DIVISION
140 W. FLAGLER STREET
MIAMI, FLORIDA 33130

1993 REFUND NOTICE

DEAR TAXPAYER:

WE ARE ENCLOSING OUR CHECK BEARING
WARRANT NUMBER 0260501 DATED 03/14/94
FOR $756.55 WHICH REPRESENTS
A REFUND OF TAX RECEIPT # 59.000000I A.

IMPORTANT: THE INFORMATION CONTAINED HEREIN DOES NOT CONSTITUTE A TITLE SEARCH AND SHOULD NOT BE RELIED UPON AS SUCH.

1993 REAL ESTATE PROPERTY TAXES
13.2227 001 6080
FRANK J ADLER &W BELLA

100
LOAN # 010114130

BELLA OR FRANK ADLER
BAY HARBOR ISLANDS FL 33154-1901

METRO-DADE

260501

METROPOLITAN DADE COUNTY, FLORIDA
SPECIAL SERVICES ACCOUNT

VOID AFTER SIX MONTHS
FIRST UNION NATIONAL BANK
OF FLORIDA
MIAMI, FLORIDA 33131

3-22
463

*SEVEN HUNDRED FIFTY SIX AND.55 DOLLARS
EXACTLY   DOLLARS AND   CENTS

Date	Control Number	Amount of Check
03/14/94	590000G01A0000003756.55	

TAX COLL. AD-VALOREM

To
The
Order
Of

BELLA OR FRANK ADLER
MIAMI   FL

260501

BOARD OF COUNTY COMMISSIONS/LIENS

CHAIRPERSON
CLERK

⑈ 260501 ⑈ ⑈06 70064 3 2⑈: 2696 206694 ⑈98⑈

FOLIO # 14-2235-007-1710-V
AGENDA # 12678
NAME FELIX ADLER &W ERNA
ADDRESS
SURFSIDE FLA
33154
HEARING DATE 12/16/93   TIME
TYPE PROPERTY   ZONING   BD C   2:30

SPECIAL MASTER'S FINDINGS OF FACT
CONCLUSIONS OF LAW AND
RECOMMENDATIONS TO THE
VALUE ADJUSTMENT BOARD

V-A-L-U-A-T-I-O-N I-S-S-U-E-S

PROPERTY ADDRESS

SEQUENCE
47

ZIP   33154-2445

TAX YEAR 1993	☐ REAL PROPERTY (INSERT TOTAL IN COLUMN 5)		☐ PERSONAL PROPERTY (INSERT TOTAL INTO COLUMN 5)		☐ REAL ☐ PERSONAL
	Col 1 LAND	Col 2 IMPROVEMENTS	Col 3 FF & E	Col 4 SUPPLIES	Col.5 TOTAL
Property Appraiser's Preliminary Tax Assessment	$ 66334	$ 45447	CALC $ / SITE $	$	$ 111781
OTHER ACTION	$	$	CALC $ / SITE $	$	$
Appraiser's Staff Recommendation to the VAB	$	$	CALC $ / SITE $	$	$

FINDINGS OF FACT

1. ☐ TAXPAYER ☒ AGENT ☐ NO SHOW ☐ WITHDREW PETITION ☐ ACCEPTED P.A. RECOM.

2. PROPERTY APPRAISER'S DETERMINATION BASED ON:
☐ REPLACEMENT COST   ☒ COMPARABLE SALES   ☐ INCOME APPROACH

3. TAXPAYER CHALLENGES ASSESSMENT OF:
☐ LAND   ☐ IMPROVEMENTS   ☐ F.F. & E.   ☐ SUPPLIES   ☒ TOTAL

4. THE FOLLOWING DEMONSTRATIVE EVIDENCE WAS OFFERED:
☐ INDEPENDENT APPRAISAL ☒ BLDG. CARD ☐ BLDG. &/or AERIAL PHOTOS ☐ MAPS
☐ FIELD REPORT ☐ PHOTOGRAPH(S) ☐ CLOSING STATEMENT ☐ F.I.T. RETURN
☐ DEPRECIATION SCHEDULE (itemized) ☐ FINANCIAL STATEMENT ☐ AFFIDAVIT
☐ OTHER: _____ Comp Sales _____

5. SUMMARY OF EVIDENCE PRESENTED:
A. BY PROPERTY APPRAISER: ☒ RECOMMENDED TAX ASSESSMENT   ☐ OTHER:
_____ Comp Sales _____
B. BY TAXPAYER: ☒ TESTIMONY   ☐ NONE OFFERED   ☐ OTHER: _____
_____ Comp Sales _____

6. BASIC AND UNDERLYING FACTS:
A. ☐ RECOMMENDED TAX ASSESSMENT CORRECT, INSUFFICIENT OR NO EVIDENCE OFFERED
TO THE CONTRARY: (Further explanation, if any) _____

B. ☒ RECOMMENDED CHANGE: (Explanation) _____ Sales comparables _____
Support reduction

C. ☐ APPEAL BASED ON HURRICANE RELATED DAMAGE.

CONCLUSIONS OF LAW

7. FUNDAMENTAL ISSUE: WHETHER THE TAXPAYER PRESENTED EVIDENCE WHICH EXCLUDED EVERY REASONABLE HYPOTHESIS OF A LEGAL ASSESSMENT? ☒ YES   ☐ NO

8. ULTIMATE FINDINGS:
PRELIMINARY ASSESSMENT .... ☒ DOES .... ☐ DOES NOT ....
EXCEED JUST VALUATION. IT IS RECOMMENDED THAT THE RELIEF APPLIED FOR IN THIS
PETITION .... ☐ BE DENIED .... ☒ BE GRANTED .... AS INDICATED BELOW:

SPECIAL MASTER'S RECOMMENDATION TO THE VAB	Col 1 LAND	Col 2 IMPROVEMENTS	Col 3 FF & E	Col 4 SUPPLIES	Col.5 TOTAL
	$ 55800	$ 38200	CALC $ / SITE	$	$ 94000

FILING FEE REFUND: If this "Findings of Fact" sheet reflects a recommended reduction to the VAB in the preliminary tax assessment of any particular parcel(s) of property, any filing fee previously paid with respect to any such parcel(s) will be refunded. Refund check(s) will be made payable to taxpayer or his agent, if any, and will be mailed to the address designated on the petition.

12-16-93

METRO-DADE

262878

METROPOLITAN DADE COUNTY, FLORIDA

SPECIAL SERVICES ACCOUNT

VOID AFTER SIX MONTHS
FIRST UNION NATIONAL BANK
OF FLORIDA
MIAMI, FLORIDA 33131

3-32
493

To
The
Order
Of

☆PAY☆FOUR HUNDRED SIXTY SEVEN AND.76 DOLLARS

EXACTLY   DOLLARS AND   CENTS

FELIX ADLER &M ERNA
MIAMI   FL   262878

Date	Control Number	Amount of Check
03/24/94	630001A1A********467.76*	

TAX COLL. AD-VALOREM

BOARD OF COUNTY COMMISSIONERS

CHAIRPERSON

CLERK

⑆262878⑆ ⑈067006432⑈ 2696 20669419⑈

METRO-DADE

1993 REAL ESTATE PROPERTY TAXES   1993 REFUND NOTICE

000
LOAN #   001150181

FELIX ADLER &M ERNA

METROPOLITAN DADE COUNTY, FLORIDA

FINANCE DEPARTMENT
TAX COLLECTION DIVISION
140 W. FLAGLER STREET
MIAMI, FLORIDA 33130

DEAR TAXPAYER:

WE ARE ENCLOSING OUR CHECK BEARING
WARRANT NUMBER 0262878 DATED 03/24/94
FOR $467.76 WHICH REPRESENTS
A REFUND OF TAX RECEIPT # 63/0000141A.

FELIX ADLER &M ERNA

SURFSIDE FLA   33154-2445

Form # 7171 Reorder 8/93 PRINTED IN U.S.A.

FOLIO #   14-2235-001-1770-V
AGENDA # 12679
NAME FELIX ADLER &W ERNA
ADDRESS
  SURFSIDE FL
                              33154
HEARING DATE 12/16/93   TIME
TYPE PROPERTY   ZONING

SPECIAL MASTER'S FINDINGS OF FACT
CONCLUSIONS OF LAW AND
RECOMMENDATIONS TO THE
VALUE ADJUSTMENT BOARD

V-A-L-U-A-T-I-O-N   I-S-S-U-E-S

BD C
2:30   PROPERTY ADDRESS

SEQUENCE
' 4 '

ZIP 33154

TAX YEAR 1993	□ REAL PROPERTY (INSERT TOTAL IN COLUMN 5)		□ PERSONAL PROPERTY (INSERT TOTAL INTO COLUMN 5)		□ REAL □ PERSONAL
	Col 1 LAND	Col 2 IMPROVEMENTS	Col 3 FF & E	Col 4 SUPPLIES	Col.5 TOTAL
Property Appraiser's Preliminary Tax Assessment	$ 69319	$ 38259	CALC $ SITE $	$	$ 107578
OTHER ACTION	$	$	CALC $ SITE $	$	$
Appraiser's Staff Recommendation to the VAB	$	$	CALC $ SITE $	$	$

FINDINGS OF FACT

1. □ TAXPAYER ☒ AGENT □ NO SHOW □ WITHDREW PETITION □ ACCEPTED P.A. RECOM.

2. PROPERTY APPRAISER'S DETERMINATION BASED ON:
   □ REPLACEMENT COST   ☒ COMPARABLE SALES   □ INCOME APPROACH

3. TAXPAYER CHALLENGES ASSESSMENT OF:
   □ LAND   □ IMPROVEMENTS   □ F.F. & E.   □ SUPPLIES   ☒ TOTAL

4. THE FOLLOWING DEMONSTRATIVE EVIDENCE WAS OFFERED:
   □ INDEPENDENT APPRAISAL   ☒ BLDG. CARD   □ BLDG. &/or AERIAL PHOTOS   □ MAPS
   □ FIELD REPORT   □ PHOTOGRAPH(S)   □ CLOSING STATEMENT   □ F.I.T. RETURN
   □ DEPRECIATION SCHEDULE (Itemized)   ☒ FINANCIAL STATEMENT   □ AFFIDAVIT
   □ OTHER: _____ Comp Sales _____

5. SUMMARY OF EVIDENCE PRESENTED:
   A. BY PROPERTY APPRAISER: ☒ RECOMMENDED TAX ASSESSMENT   □ OTHER:
      _____ Comp Sales _____
   B. BY TAXPAYER: ☒ TESTIMONY   □ NONE OFFERED   □ OTHER: _____
      _____ Comp Sales _____

6. BASIC AND UNDERLYING FACTS:
   A. □ RECOMMENDED TAX ASSESSMENT CORRECT, INSUFFICIENT OR NO EVIDENCE OFFERED
      TO THE CONTRARY: (Further explanation, if any) _____
      _____
   B. ☒ RECOMMENDED CHANGE: (Explanation) _____ Comp Sales support
      _____ reduction and condition of improvemen
   C. □ APPEAL BASED ON HURRICANE RELATED DAMAGE.

CONCLUSIONS OF LAW

7. FUNDAMENTAL ISSUE: WHETHER THE TAXPAYER PRESENTED EVIDENCE WHICH EXCLUDED
   EVERY REASONABLE HYPOTHESIS OF A LEGAL ASSESSMENT? ☒ YES   □ NO

8. ULTIMATE FINDINGS:
   PRELIMINARY ASSESSMENT .... ☒ DOES .... □ DOES NOT ....
   EXCEED JUST VALUATION. IT IS RECOMMENDED THAT THE RELIEF APPLIED FOR IN THIS
   PETITION .... □ BE DENIED .... ☒ BE GRANTED .... AS INDICATED BELOW:

SPECIAL MASTER'S RECOMMENDATION TO THE VAB	Col 1 LAND	Col 2 IMPROVEMENTS	Col 3 FF & E	Col 4 SUPPLIES	Col.5 TOTAL
	$ 55400	$ 30600	CALC $ SITE	$	$ 86000

FILING FEE REFUND: If this "Findings of Fact" sheet reflects a recommended reduction to the VAB in the preliminary tax assessment of any particular parcel(s) of property, any filing fee previously paid with respect to any such parcel(s) will be refunded. Refund check(s) will be made payable to taxpayer or his agent, if any, and will be mailed to the address designated on the petition.

12-16-93
DATE COMPLETED BY S.M.

Linda Molina
SPECIAL MASTER'S SIGNATURE

METRO-DADE

METROPOLITAN DADE COUNTY, FLORIDA

SPECIAL SERVICES ACCOUNT

VOID AFTER SIX MONTHS
FIRST UNION NATIONAL BANK
OF FLORIDA
MIAMI, FLORIDA 33131

3-32
493

262877

Date	Control Number	Amount of Check
03/24/94	63000139A	****567.65*

FIVE HUNDRED SIXTY SEVEN AND.65 DOLLARS

EXACTLY   DOLLARS AND   CENTS

TAX CCLL. AD-VALOREM

To
The
Order
Of

FELIX ADLER &W ERNA
MIAMI   FL   262877

BO.RD OF COUNTY CO.MI.SCI: IERS

CLERK

⑆262877⑆ ⑉0670064 3⑉: 2696 206694 698⑈

METRO-DADE

262877

METROPOLITAN DADE COUNTY, FLORIDA

1993 REFUND NOTICE

FINANCE DEPARTMENT
TAX COLLECTION DIVISION
140 W. FLAGLER STREET
MIAMI, FLORIDA 33130

1993 REAL ESTATE PROPERTY TAXES
14 :2225 001 1770
FELIX ADLER &W ERNA

000
LOAN #   0011150181

DEAR TAXPAYER:

WE ARE ENCLOSING OUR CHECK BEARING
WARRANT NUMBER 262877 DATED 03/24/94
FOR $567.65 WHICH REPRESENTS
A REFUND OF TAX RECEIPT # 63/0000139A.

FELIX ADLER &W ERNA
SURFSIDE FL   33154-2445

Form # 7171 Reorder 8/93 PRINTED IN U.S.A

```
/‾ ‾ ‾ ‾ ‾ ‾ ‾ ‾ ‾ ‾ ‾ \           SPECIAL MASTER'S FINDINGS OF FACT          ┌─────────┐
|  FOLIO #   06-2230-007-0520-V |          CONCLUSIONS OF LAW AND             │ SEQUENCE│
|  AGENDA #  14194              |         RECOMMENDATIONS TO THE              │  #      │
|  NAME FRANELLA ENTERPRISES INC|           VALUE ADJUSTMENT BOARD            │  5 |    │
|  ADDRESS                      |                                            └─────────┘
|  NO MIAMI FL                  |         V·A·L·U·A·T·I·O·N  I·S·S·U·E·S
|                        33161| |
|  HEARING DATE 01/24/94   TIME   BD C   PROPERTY ADDRESS
|  TYPE PROPERTY          ZONING  2:30|
\_ _ _ _ _ _ _ _ _ _ _ /                                          ZIP   33161
```

TAX·YEAR 1993	□ REAL PROPERTY (INSERT TOTAL IN COLUMN 5)		□ PERSONAL PROPERTY (INSERT TOTAL INTO COLUMN 5)		□ REAL □ PERSONAL
	Col 1 LAND	Col 2 IMPROVEMENTS	Col 3 FF & E	Col 4 SUPPLIES	Col 5 TOTAL
Property Appraiser's Preliminary Tax Assessment	$ 13466	$ 29138	CALC $ ___ SITE $ ___	$	$ 42604
OTHER ACTION	$	$	CALC $ ___ SITE $ ___	$	$
Appraiser's Staff Recommendation to the VAB	$	$	CALC $ ___ SITE $ ___	$	$

FINDINGS OF FACT

1. ☒ TAXPAYER   □ AGENT   □ NO SHOW   □ WITHDREW PETITION   □ ACCEPTED P.A. RECOM.

2. PROPERTY APPRAISER'S DETERMINATION BASED ON:
   □ REPLACEMENT COST   ☑ COMPARABLE SALES   □ INCOME APPROACH

3. TAXPAYER CHALLENGES ASSESSMENT OF:
   □ LAND   □ IMPROVEMENTS   □ F.F. & E.   □ SUPPLIES   ☑ TOTAL

4. THE FOLLOWING DEMONSTRATIVE EVIDENCE WAS OFFERED:
   □ INDEPENDENT APPRAISAL   ☑ BLDG. CARD   □ BLDG. &/or AERIAL PHOTOS   □ MAPS
   □ FIELD REPORT   □ PHOTOGRAPH(S)   □ CLOSING STATEMENT   □ F.I.T. RETURN
   □ DEPRECIATION SCHEDULE (itemized)   □ FINANCIAL STATEMENT   □ AFFIDAVIT
   □ OTHER: _____

5. SUMMARY OF EVIDENCE PRESENTED:
   A. BY PROPERTY APPRAISER: ☑ RECOMMENDED TAX ASSESSMENT   □ OTHER:
      COMP SALES
   B. BY TAXPAYER: ☑ TESTIMONY   □ NONE OFFERED   □ OTHER: _____
      COMPARABLE

6. BASIC AND UNDERLYING FACTS:
   A. □ RECOMMENDED TAX ASSESSMENT CORRECT, INSUFFICIENT OR NO EVIDENCE OFFERED
      TO THE CONTRARY: (Further explanation, if any) _____

   B. ☒ RECOMMENDED CHANGE: (Explanation) *MARKET ANALYSIS*
      WARRANT A REDUCTION

   C. □ APPEAL BASED ON HURRICANE RELATED DAMAGE.

CONCLUSIONS OF LAW

7. FUNDAMENTAL ISSUE: WHETHER THE TAXPAYER PRESENTED EVIDENCE WHICH EXCLUDED
   EVERY REASONABLE HYPOTHESIS OF A LEGAL ASSESSMENT?   ☑ YES   □ NO

8. ULTIMATE FINDINGS:
   PRELIMINARY ASSESSMENT .... ☑ DOES .... □ DOES NOT ....
   EXCEED JUST VALUATION. IT IS RECOMMENDED THAT THE RELIEF APPLIED FOR IN THIS
   PETITION .... □ BE DENIED .... ☑ BE GRANTED .... AS INDICATED BELOW:

SPECIAL MASTER'S RECOMMENDATION TO THE VAB	Col 1 LAND	Col 2 IMPROVEMENTS	Col 3 FF & E	Col 4 SUPPLIES	Col 5 TOTAL
	$ 13466	$ 24,877	CALC $ ___ SITE $ ___	$	$ 38743

FILING FEE REFUND: If this "Findings of Fact" sheet reflects a recommended reduction to the VAB in the preliminary tax assessment of any particular parcel(s) of property, any filing fee previously paid with respect to any such parcel(s) will be refunded. Refund check(s) will be made payable to taxpayer or his agent, if any, and will be mailed to the address designated on the petition.

_1-24-94_
DATE COMPLETED BY S.M.   SPECIAL MASTER'S SIGNATURE

METRO-DADE

262861

METROPOLITAN DADE COUNTY, FLORIDA
SPECIAL SERVICES ACCOUNT

VOID AFTER SIX MONTHS
FIRST UNION NATIONAL BANK
OF FLORIDA
MIAMI, FLORIDA 33131

3-22
493

Date	Control Number	Amount of Check
03/24/94	630005537A******125.22*	TAX CCLL. AD-VALOREM

***ONE HUNDRED TWENTY FIVE AND.22 DOLLARS

EXACTLY

DOLLARS AND   CENTS

To
The
Order
Of

FRANELLA ENTERPRISES INC
MIAMI   FL   262861

BOARD OF COUNTY COMMISSIONERS

Signature CHAIRPERSON

Signature CLERK

⑈262861⑈ ⑆067006432⑆ ⑈696206694198⑈

METRO-DADE

METROPOLITAN DADE COUNTY, FLORIDA

1993 REAL ESTATE PROPERTY TAXES   1993 REFUND NOTICE

06 2230 007 0520
FRANELLA ENTERPRISES INC
000
LOAN #   0215806

DEAR TAXPAYER:

WE ARE ENCLOSING OUR CHECK BEARING
WARRANT NUMBER 0262861 DATED 03/24/94
FOR $125.22 WHICH REPRESENTS
A REFUND OF TAX RECEIPT # 63/0000557A.

FINANCE DEPARTMENT
TAX COLLECTION DIVISION
140 W. FLAGLER STREET
MIAMI, FLORIDA 33130

FRANELLA ENTERPRISES INC
NO MIAMI FL   33161-4821

Form # 7171 Reorder 9/93 PRINTED IN U.S.A.

NOTES

APPENDIX B

How to Compute Your Property Taxes

1. The fair market value of this home is $105,000, the current tax rate is $2.15 per hundred dollars (.0215), and the assessment rate is computed at 50% of fair market value. How much tax is due?

    Step 1   In this state the fair market value is multiplied by 50% (.50) to obtain the assessed value.

    $105,000 x .50 = $52,500 assessed value.

    Step 2   Divide the assessed value by one hundred dollars.

    $52,500 ÷ 100 = 525

    Step 3   Multiply 525 by the tax rate $2.15 which yields the amount of property tax owed.

    525 x $2.15 = $1128.7
    $1128.75 is the amount of property tax due.

    A shorter way to calculate this same problem is as follows:
    $105,000 (fair market value) x .50 = $52,500 (assessed value
    $52,500 x .0215 (tax rate) = $1,128.75 (amount of property tax due)

2. In Alabama the assessment rate for residential property is 10% of fair market value. For a home that has a fair market value of $200,000, and a tax rate of 19.20 per thousand dollars of assessment, what is the amount of property tax due?

    The long method:
    $200,000 x .10 = $20,000
    (fair market value) x (assessment rate) = (assessment value)
    $20,000 ÷ 1,000 = 20
    20 x $19.20 (tax rate) = $384 (property tax due)

    The short method:

The short method:
$200,000 x .10 x .0192 = $384
(fair market value) x (assessment rate) x (tax rate) = (property tax amount)

3. In Connecticut the assessment rate is 70% of fair market value. The tax rate is .03019 per thousand dollars of assessment. The home's fair market value is $175,000. How much property tax is due? How much is the tax rate in dollars per thousand?

    (fair market value) x (assessment rate) = (assessed value)
    $175,000 x .70 = $122,500
    (tax rate) = .03019 x $1,000 = $30.19
    $122,500 ÷ $1,000 = 122.50
    122.50 x $30.19 = $3,698.28 (property tax due)

    Short method:
    $175,000 x .70 x .03019 = $3,698.28
    (fair market value) x (assessment rate) x (tax rate) = (property tax due)

Tax Rate Conversion

1) .06217 per thousand dollars of assessed value = $62.17
    .06217 x 1000 = $62.17

2) .03821 per each hundred dollars of assessed value = $3.821
    .03821 x 100 = $3.821

3) .03821 per each thousand dollars of assessed value = $38.21
    .03821 x $1,000 = $38.21

4) $59.25 tax rate per thousand dollars of assessed value = .05925
    $59.25 ÷ 1,000 = .05925

5) $39.21 tax rate per hundred dollars of assessed value = .3921
    39.21 ÷ 100 = .3921

APPENDIX C

IN THE CIRCUIT COURT OF THE
11TH JUDICIAL CIRCUIT IN AND
FOR DADE COUNTY, FLORIDA
GENERAL JURISDICTION
CASE NO. 94-13340 CA13

FRANK JACK ADLER
a primary residence property owner
in Dade County
    Plaintiff,
vs.

JOEL W. ROBBINS, as Property
Appraiser of Dade County,
Florida; FRED GANZ, as Tax
Collector of Dade County,
Florida; and EXECUTIVE
DIRECTOR of the Department
of Revenue of the State of
Florida,

    Defendants.
————————————-/

COMPLAINT

FRANK JACK ADLER, a primary residence property
owner in Dade County, files this complaint
against Defendants, JOEL W. ROBBINS, as Property Appraiser of Dade County, Florida; FRED
GANZ, as Tax Collector of Dade County, Florida;
and the EXECUTIVE DIRECTOR of the Department of
Revenue of the State of Florida, and alleges:

1.   This is an action for equitable and statu-
    tory relief pursuant to Section 194.036,
    Fla. Stat. and Section 194.171, Fla.
    Stat., Section 26.012, Fla. Stat., and Ar-

ticle V, Section 20 (C) of the Florida Constitution.

2.   Plaintiff, FRANK JACK ADLER (hereafter "Plaintiff") is a private citizen, a primary residence property owner and the taxpayer of the subject Property, as described hereinafter, for the 1993 tax year.

3.   Plaintiff is contesting the assessment of ad valorem taxes for 1993 upon the land and improvements described under Folio No. 13-2227-001-6080 (hereinafter the "Property"). The Property is legally described as follows:

Lot 13 plus West 1/2 of Lot 14, Block 32, of Bay Harbor Island, according to the Plat thereof, as recorded in Plat Book 46, at Page 5, of the Public Records of Dade County, Florida.

4.   Defendant, JOEL W. ROBBINS (hereafter "ROBBINS or Tax Appraiser") lawfully holds the office of Property Appraiser of Dade County, Florida. He is charged with the burden of discharging the duties of said office.

5.   Defendant, FRED GANZ (hereafter "GANZ" or "Tax Collector"), is the duly appointed Tax Collector for Dade County, Florida. He is charged with the burden of discharging the duties of said office.

6.   Defendant, the EXECUTIVE DIRECTOR of the Department of Revenue for the State of Florida (hereafter EXECUTIVE DIRECTOR), is made a party defendant in compliance with and as mandated by Section 194.181 (5), Fla. Stat., since the tax assessment is also being contested on the grounds

that it is contrary to the laws and Constitution of the State of Florida.

7. Defendant ROBBINS made a preliminary assessment of the Property for the year 1993 in the amount of $260,545.00, which was in excess of the just value of the property.

8. A formal appeal for property tax reduction was filed with the Clerk of the Value Adjustment Board of Dade County (the "VAB") pursuant to Section 194.011, Florida Statutes, et seq., contesting the preliminary assessment of the Property for the year 1993.

9. Under Florida Law, the VAB meets, among other things, for the purpose of hearing petitions relating to assessments and remains in session until such time as all petitions and disputes are properly resolved.

10. Plaintiff protested the preliminary assessment of the Property at a hearing before a Special Master appointed by the VAB.

11. The Special Master found that the preliminary assessment was unlawful and not in compliance with Florida law and recommended a reduction in the preliminary assessment to a final value of $231,145.00. Despite this reduction, such assessment exceeds just value.

12. The decision of the Special Master was approved and adopted by the VAB and written notice of such decision was mailed to Plaintiff on December 16, 1993.

13. Plaintiff, under protest, has paid the taxes on the Property to the offices of Defendant Tax Collector GANZ. A true and correct copy of the receipt evidencing

said payment is attached hereto as Exhibit "A" and incorporated by reference as if fully set forth herein.

14. Plaintiff has exhausted its administrative remedies and has complied with all conditions precedent to the maintenance of this lawsuit. This action is brought within sixty (60) days from the date the assessment being contested is certified for collection under Section 193.122(2) Florida Statutes.

15. Plaintiff will be severely financially damaged if Defendants are permitted to impose and enforce the collection of the subject unlawful and excessive ad valorem taxes.

FIRST CLAIM FOR RELIEF

16. Plaintiff incorporates the allegations set forth in Paragraph 1 through 15 as if fully set forth herein.

17. The final assessed value of the Property, as of January 1, 1993, is in excess of just value, as defined under Florida law.

18. Defendant ROBBINS failed and refused to properly consider and/or correctly employ all of the factors set forth in Section 193.011, Fla. Stat., and the Rules and Regulations of the State of Florida, Department of Revenue, in the determination of the 1993 ad valorem assessment of Plaintiff's Property.

19. Defendant ROBBINS' failure to properly consider and/or correctly employ the factors set forth in Section 193.011, Fla. Stat., combined with the final assessment of the Property in excess of just value, renders the tax assessment excessive, illegal, and void.

20. The final assessed value of Plaintiff's Property is also in violation of Article VII, Section 4 of the Constitution of the State of Florida.

SECOND CLAIM FOR RELIEF

21. Plaintiff incorporates the allegations set forth in paragraphs 1 through 15 as if fully set forth herein.

22. When compared with the assessments of other similar properties in Dade County, Florida, the tax assessment of the Property is excessive.

23. Defendant ROBBINS has intentionally and systematically discriminated against Plaintiff by imposing additional taxes upon Plaintiff which were not imposed upon a substantial number of properties of the same class in Dade County, Florida.

24. Plaintiff has been denied equal protection under the law, contrary to rights guaranteed Plaintiff by the Constitution of the United States and the State of Florida, as a consequence of the arbitrary action of Defendant ROBBINS in so assessing Plaintiff's Property.

25. Defendant ROBBINS' disregard for the mandatory and essential requirements of law governing ad valorem assessments has resulted in an assessed value for the Property far in excess of its just value. The final assessment is so arbitrary and unjust that it has shifted a disproportionate and discriminatory share of the 1993 tax burden upon Plaintiff and renders such assessment in violation of Florida law.

WHEREFORE, as to each and every cause of action, Plaintiff requests this Court to:

(i)   take jurisdiction of this cause and the parties thereto;

(ii)   direct the Tax Collector to issue a refund of any excess taxes paid by Plaintiff;

(iii)   declare the subject tax assessment for the year 1993 to be unconstitutional and null and void;

(iv)   issue an order declaring the just value of the Property and directing such adjustments between parties as may be necessary in connection therewith or direct Defendant ROBBINS to reassess the Property in compliance with Florida law;

(v)   assess costs in favor of Plaintiff pursuant to Section 194.192, Fla. Stat.; and

(vi)   grant such other and further relief as this Court deems just and proper and retain jurisdiction for the enforcement of its Final Judgement.

Respectfully submitted,
Frank Jack Adler

BY:_____
Frank Jack Adler
Pro Se

IN THE CIRCUIT COURT OF THE
11TH JUDICIAL CIRCUIT IN AND
FOR DADE COUNTY, FLORIDA
GENERAL JURISDICTION
CASE NO. 94-13340 CA 13

FRANK JACK ADLER
a primary residence property owner
in Dade County
        Plaintiff,

vs.

JOEL W. ROBBINS, as Property
Appraiser of Dade County,
Florida; FRED GANZ, as Tax
Collector of Dade County,
Florida; and EXECUTIVE
DIRECTOR of the Department
of Revenue of the State of
Florida,
        Defendants.

————————————————————-/

ANSWER

Plaintiff's answer to the Defendants as follows:

1.   Paragraph 2 of the Defendants' answer is
      denied because it is not accurate and
      makes no sense. The Defendants does not
      claim to own this property, the Plaintiff
      does. Furthermore the property is regis-
      tered as Frank J. Adler & W Bella. The
      Plaintiff never claimed to be sole owner
      or taxpayer. The original paragraph is
      quoted below:

"2.   Plaintiff, FRANK JACK ADLER (hereafter
      "Plaintiff") is a private citizen, a pri-
      mary residence property owner and the tax-
      payer of the subject Property, as
      described hereinafter, for the 1993 tax
      year."

2.   Paragraph 3 of the Defendants' answer is denied because it is an opinion subject to evidence before the court.

3.   Paragraph 5 of the Defendants' answer is denied because Plaintiff did attach receipts of its good faith payment to the original complaint as required by Florida Statute (see exhibit A).

4.   Paragraph 6 of the Defendants' answer is denied because it is not necessary for more than one owner of a property to bring this action. For example the property tax refund check from the Dade County Tax Collector was made payable to Bella or Frank Adler (see exhibit B).

5.   Paragraph 7 of the Defendants' answer is denied because a cause of action is clearly stated. The cause of action requested from the court is:

   (i)   take jurisdiction of this cause and the parties thereto;

   (ii)   direct the Tax Collector to issue a refund of any excess taxes paid by Plaintiff;

   (iii)   declare the subject's tax assessment for the year 1993 to be unconstitutional and null and void:

   (iv)   issue an order declaring the just value of the Property and directing such adjustments between parties as may be necessary in connection therewith or direct Defendant ROBBINS to reassess the Property in compliance with Florida law;

ANSWER TO COUNTERCLAIM

Plaintiff's answer to the counterclaim as follows:

1. Plaintiff admits the allegations in paragraphs 1, 2, 3, 4, 5, 6, 7, 8, 9, 10 of the counterclaim.

2. Paragraph 11 is denied insofar as it states that the assessed value approved by the Value Adjustment Board is below just value.

3. Paragraph 12 is denied insofar as it states that the reduced assessed value is in violation of Florida Statutes, and the Florida Constitution.

Respectfully submitted,
Frank Jack Adler

BY:_____
Frank Jack Adler
Pro Se

CERTIFICATE OF SERVICE

I HEREBY CERTIFY that a true and correct copy of the foregoing was hand-delivered this 13 day of September 1994 to:

MITCHELL A. BIERMAN, ESQ., Assistant County Attorney, Metro-Dade Center, Suite 2810, 111 N.W. First Street, Miami, Fl. 33128-5151.

_____
Frank Jack Adler
Pro Se

```
                              IN THE CIRCUIT COURT OF THE
                              11TH JUDICIAL CIRCUIT IN AND
                              FOR DADE COUNTY, FLORIDA
                              GENERAL JURISDICTION DIVISION
                              CASE NO. 94-13340 CA 13
                              NOTICE FOR TRIAL
```

FRANK JACK ADLER
a primary residence property owner
in Dade County
     Plaintiff,

vs.

JOEL W. ROBBINS, as Property
Appraiser of Dade County,
Florida; FRED GANZ, as Tax
Collector of Dade County,
Florida; and EXECUTIVE
DIRECTOR of the Department
of Revenue of the State of Florida,
     Defendants.
_____-/

COMES NOW, the petitioner, and he represents to
the court that this action is at issue and ready
to be set for non-jury trial at the next ensuing
term of Court.

It is estimated that this action will require
one half (1/2) day for a non-jury trial.

```
                         BY:_____
                         Frank Jack Adler
                         Pro Se
```

I HEREBY CERTIFY that a true and correct copy of
the foregoing Notice of Trial was mailed this 14
day of September 1994 to: MITCHELL A. BIERMAN,
ESQ., Assistant County Attorney, Metro-Dade
Center, Suite 2810, 111 N.W. First Street, Miami, Fl. 33128-5151.

```
                         _____
                         Frank Jack Adler
                         Pro Se
```

GLOSSARY

Actual Age—The number of years elapsed since the original construction up to the effective valuation date.

Ad Valorem Taxation—Taxation of property based on the value of the property.

Appeal—The taxpayer's right to protest his assessment within a prescribed time frame and procedure.

Appellant—Taxpayer or representative who appeals to a higher tribunal.

Apportion—Once the amount of taxes to be levied by each taxing jurisdiction has been determined, the total tax levy must be divided, or apportioned, among all the taxation districts which contain territory in the jurisdiction.

Appraisal—An estimate, usually in written form, of the value of a specifically described property as of a specified date. It may be used synonymously with "valuation" or "appraised value." An opinion of value, supported by evidence.

Appraised Value—An opinion of the value of a property, based on data collected and analyzed by a real estate appraiser.

Appraiser—A person who estimates value or possesses the expertise to direct the execution of an appraisal.

Approaches To Value—The three generally accepted techniques used to calculate the value of a residential property for tax purposes are the market, cost or replacement, and equity approach.

Arm's Length Transaction— A transaction between unrelated parties, each seeking the best deal possible, and each being well informed or well-advised, and acting in his own best interest.

Assessed Value — An official approximation of the full current market value or a fraction thereof, of a property in the opinion of the tax assessor. The assessed value is used in conjunction with the tax rate to derive the amount of property tax due.

Assessment—The value of taxable property to which the tax rate is applied in order to compute the amount of taxes. It may be used synonymously with "assessed value," "taxable value," and "tax base."

Assessment Date—The specific day that the property is valued for tax purposes.

Assessment Level—The relationship between the assessed value and the market value of all taxable property within a district (town, village, or city). For example, if the assessed value of all the taxable property in Town "A" is $2,700,000 and the market value of all taxable property in Town "A" is $3,000,000 then the "assessment level" is said to be 90%.

Assessment/Sales Ratio—A percentage determined by dividing the assessed value by the actual sales price for that same property. If a parcel sold for $50,000 and is assessed for $46,000 it is said to have a "ratio" of 92%.

$$Assessment\ Ratio = \frac{Assessed\ Value}{Market\ Value} = \frac{\$46,000}{\$50,000} = 92\%$$

Assessor—The administrator charged with the assessment of property for ad valorem taxes.

Chattel—In law, any property other than a freehold or fee estate in land. Chattels are treated as personal property, although they are divisible into chattels real, and chattels personal.

Circuit Breaker—A program of tax relief which shuts off or short-circuits taxation when certain levels or conditions are reached.

Comparables—Properties that have recently been sold (verifiable arm's length transactions), that have similar features as to land size and building, and are used for comparison purposes in the assessment or appeal process.

Classification—The practice of classifying various types of property according to use and assigning different assessment levels to each class. Its purpose is to tax various kinds of property at different effective tax rates, though the nominal rate is the same.

Cost Approach—An approach to value used in the assessment or appeal process where the cost to replace or duplicate a building is determined using standard cost data supplied by a cost research firm and allowing for normal depreciation.

Current Use—Assessment of a property based on its present value and use as opposed to its highest and best potential use and value.

Deed—A written legal instrument which conveys an estate or interest in real property.

Depreciation—A loss in value caused by deterioration and/or obsolescence. Physical obsolescence (normal usage), functional obsolescence (impairment of functional capacity or efficient), or economic obsolescence (damage of desirability arising from economic forces unrelated to the property itself).

Effective Age—The age allocated to a building based upon its condition, utility, and remaining economic life expectancy as of the effective valuation date.

Equalization—A mass appraisal or reappraisal of all property within a given taxing jurisdiction with the goal of equalizing values in order to assure that each taxpayer is bearing only his fair share of the tax load.

Equalization Factor—The factor that must be applied to local assessments to bring the percentage increase or decrease that will result in an equalized assessed value in a taxing jurisdiction.

Equalized Assessed Value—An assessed value of a property after it has been multiplied by a statistically computed state or local balancing factor in order to achieve a greater degree of uniformity and fairness.

Equalized Value—An assessed value which has been adjusted by a state or local statistically computed balancing factor in order to achieve a greater degree of uniformity and fairness.

Equity—Means the tax load is distributed fairly or equitably. It is the opposite of "inequity," which refers to an unfair or unequitable distribution of the tax burden. "Inequity" is a natural product of changing economic conditions which can only be effectively cured by periodic equalization programs.

Escheat—The ownership of property reverts to the state when the owner dies without leaving a will or heirs.

Exemption—The removal of property from the tax base. An exemption may be partial, as a homestead exemption, or complete as, for example, for a church building used exclusively for religious purposes.

Exempt Property—Property owned by governmental, educational, charitable, religious and similar non-profit organizations that is granted total or partial freedom from taxation.

Full Market Value—The dollar amount obtainable through fair negotiations between a willing seller and a willing buyer for a property.

Grantee— The person(s) who buys the property.

Grantor— The person(s) who sells the property.

Gross Area—The total floor area of a building measured from the exterior of the walls.

Highest & Best Usage— The assessment of a property based on potential use which will generate the highest net return to the property.

Homestead—A parcel of land which husband and wife, or other head(s) of household, own and use as their primary residence.

Homogeneous— An area or neighborhood in which property types and uses possess the quality of similarity and compatibility.

Improvements—Any changes or additions to the land, or the things permanently attached to the land, which have the net effect of creating a betterment.

Legal Description—The characterization of a parcel of land which identifies and differentiates that parcel from another in a manner authorized by law.

Level Of Assessments—The percentage of full value which state statute prescribes that property must be assessed at.

Levy—The amount of money a taxing body certifies to be raised from the property tax.

Lister—A field inspector whose principal duty is to collect and record property data.

Lien—A charge against a property that can be collected either by distraint (personal property) or foreclosure (real property) and sale of that property. A lien placed by government for delinquent taxes takes precedence over any other lien.

Market Data Approach—Fair market value is determined using comparable sales, defined as properties which have sold recently and are similar to other properties which have not sold.

Market Price—The highest price in terms of money a property will bring in a competitive and open market.

Market Value—The amount of money which a willing, knowledgeable buyer would, in practical circumstances, pay to a willing seller to acquire the property, in a transaction free of duress for either party.

Mass Appraisal—Appraisal of property on a wholesale scale, such as an entire community, generally for ad valorem tax purposes, using standardized appraisal techniques and procedures to effect uniform equitable valuations within a minimum of detail, within a limited time period, and at a limited cost.

Mortgage—A conditional conveyance of property to a creditor as security, as for the repayment of money.

Multiplier Or Equalization Factor—A statistical tool derived from assessment/sales ratio studies, used to adjust average assessment levels in a taxing jurisdiction to the same percentage of full market value.

Neighborhood—A geographical area exhibiting a high degree of homogeneity in residential amenities, land use, economic and social trends, and housing characteristics.

Notice Of Revision—A letter mailed to a property owner after a property's assessment is changed by an assessing official.

Overassessed—A condition wherein a property is assessed proportionally higher than comparable properties.

Overlapping Taxing Districts—Those taxing districts located in more than one county.

Parcel—A piece of land with the same ownership.

Parcel Identification Number (Permanent Index Number)—A numeric or alphanumeric description of a parcel which identifies it uniquely.

Personal Property—Property that is not permanently affixed to and a part of the real estate, and further defined by state statute and rule.

Property Record Card—A document specially designated to record and process specified property data. It may serve as a source document, a processing form, or a permanent property record. This is a public record and the law requires that it be maintained.

Real Property—Land plus any anything permanently attached to the land.

Real Estate—The physical land and all things of a permanent and substantial nature affixed thereto.

Reassessment—Redoing the existing assessment roll because of substantial inequities. All the property in the district is viewed, valued, and placed on the new assessment roll, which is then substituted for the original roll.

Replacement Cost—The current cost of reproducing an improvement of equal utility to the subject property.

Residential Property—Vacant or improved land devoted to, or available for use primarily as, a place to live. Residential property is normally construed to mean a building where fewer than three families reside in a single structure.

Revaluation—Placing new values on all taxable property for the purpose of a new assessment. The previous year's assessment roll is not affected.

Rollback—Limitation on annual assessed value increase or a reduction in the amount of property tax paid.

Sales Ratio Study—compares bona fide sales prices to assessed values. For example, if a property's assessed value is $10,000 and it sells for $30,000 the ratio of its assessment to its sales price would be 10,000/30,000 or 33 1/3 percent.

Tax Assessor—The government official responsible for establishing the value for property for ad valorem tax purposes.

Tax Bill—An itemized statement showing the amount of taxes owed for certain property and forwardable to the party legally liable for payment.

Taxing Body—A governmental organization that levies a property tax.

Tax Collector—The government employee who is responsible for the distribution of tax bills and the collection of the tax from property owners.

Tax District—A geographic area within which property is taxed by the same taxing unit at the same total rate. A taxing unit is an entity that has the power to impose ad valorem property taxes.

Taxing Jurisdiction—Any entity authorized by law to levy taxes on general property which is located within its boundaries.

Tax Levy—The total revenue which is to be realized by the tax.

Tax Rate—The rate generally expressed in dollars per hundred or dollars per thousand which is to be applied against the tax base or assessed value to compute the amount of taxes. The tax rate is derived by dividing the total amount of the tax levy by the total assessed value of the taxing district.

Underassessed—A property is assessed proportionally lower than comparable properties.

Uniformity—As applied to assessing, means a condition where all properties are assessed by the same standard of value.

NOTES

Index

AJFT, 15
authority, 2

BDR, 15
Board of Review, 48
budget, 3-5
building value, 14

classified, 4, 19, 22
County Board, 51
cross-examine, 49

delinquent, 7, 11, 404
depreciation, 15, 18, 24, 26, 32, 34, 36, 37, 47, 49, 402, 403
discounts, 11, 54
discover, ix, 4

Equalization Board, 48
Equity approach, 39, 41, 43, 50, 401
exemptions, 7, 11, 12, 19, 23, 61

fiscal year, 3
folio number, 13
foreclosure, 11, 404

International Association of Assessing Officers, 17

judicial system, 51

land value, 14, 32
legal description, 7, 13, 15, 19, 20, 404
local appeal board, 46, 48

mapping system, 4, 13, 15

market approach, 4
mortgage, 2, 7, 10, 53, 54, 405

non-ad valorem assessments, 9

on-site inspection, 14, 15, 23

Permanent Index number, 405
physical depreciation, 26, 32, 34
PIN, 14
plot book, 15
property record card, 13, 18-20, 22, 25, 32, 33, 405

real property, xiii, 1, 3, 18, 26, 57, 59, 61, 62, 403, 404, 406
rebate, 11
regressive tax, 2

sales ratio approach, 43
sales ratio study, 42, 62, 406
sales tax, 1
State Board, 51

Tax Commission, 48
treacherous, 1

usage code, 42

valuation, 4, 17, 18, 23, 24, 33, 34, 39, 43, 44, 46-49, 57, 59, 61, 401, 403
value, ix, xi-xiii, 1, 2, 4, 5, 7, 15, 17, 18, 20, 22, 25, 26, 28, 30-32, 34, 39, 40, 42, 43, 45-51, 53, 54, 57, 59, 61, 62, 401-407
valuing, 3, 24, 31-32

NOTES

About The Author

Frank J. Adler, an average middle-class resident of Miami, Florida, watched his property tax bill leap 15% during a crippling recession. Since no books were available to help him understand his predicament, Adler launched his own investigation into the complex and highly subjective tax system. He mastered its many ins, outs, and loopholes, then exercised his right to challenge the government—and won. To date, he has beaten City Hall *eleven* times, receiving $6,000 in overpaid taxes and reducing assessments by $250,000— that's an average of $550 per refund and $22,700 in reductions per property. His method works, and it can work for you.

NOTES

NOTES

NOTES

NOTES

NOTES

NOTES

NOTES